REASSERTING THE CO-OPERATIVE MOVEMENT

(Published on the Occasion of Centennial Celebration of Indian Co-operative Movement)

REASSERTING THE CO-OPERATIVE MOVEMENT

(Published on the Occasion of Centennial Celebration of Indian Co-operative Movement)

Edited by

Dr. V. B. Jugale

Prof. & Head
Department of Economics
Shivaji University
Kolhapur

Dr. P. A. Koli

Reader
Department of Economics
Shivaji University
Kolhapur

SERIALS PUBLICATIONS
New Delhi

First Published - 2005

ISBN : 81-86771-83-2

Published by

Head Office : **SERIALS PUBLICATIONS**
4, B.S.S. Hall, Khyber Pass Market
Civil Lines, Delhi-110054 (India)
Phone : 23245225
Fax : 91-11-23272135
E-mail: serials@satyam.net.in

Branch Office : 4830/24, Prahlad Street, Ansari Road
Darya Ganj, New Delhi-110002 (India)

Foreward

One Hundred Years in the life of any institution is an occasion for joy, a sense of fulfillment and time for introspection on the trials and triumphs of the bygone years. But when it comes to the Centenary of a massive human endeavour of the size and dimension of the Indian Cooperative Movement, the sense of fulfilment can rightfully be supplemented by a sense of pride for achieving the almost impossible task of bringing about fusion of so diverse cultures, religions and ethnic identities under the cooperative fold. This was possible because, the cooperative ideology, unlike other isms and philosophies that dominated our planet, did not harm anyone nor did it come in conflict with any socio-economic and political system.

When the Indian Society for Studies in Cooperation, in its humble way, planned the Centenary Celebrations, Dr. Jugale, Head of the Department of Economics of Shivaji University in Kolhapur was the first to respond to our call and organize the Seminar on Reasserting the Cooperative Movement. The response was spontaneous and the quality of papers read at the Seminar speak volumes of the time and effort spent by participants in researching on almost all major areas in which the cooperatives have become a way of lie for the people associated with those activities.

Dr. P.R. Dubhashi's scathing criticism on the present trend towards increased Government controls on cooperative management in almost all major sectors of the cooperative movement; Dr. Vijay Kakade' reminder of the ICA Statement on Cooperative Identity; Prof. Biradar's emphasis on rediscovering the cooperatives; and Shri S.T. Bhide's caution about lost opportunities to reverse the trend of officiations are timely reminders for revising our strategy on cooperative development, while D. Joel Edwinraj urges relaxation of government controls for enabling cooperatives to improve their competitive ability.

Despite all the problems, challenges and constraints, there is a current of optimism running through the papers, and reiteration of faith in the inner strength and dynamism of the Cooperative Movement. Prof. R.S. Pandir and Vishwa Ballaph plead for liberalization while Prof. A.P. Kansal stresses the need for forward and backward integration to strengthen ability to face the market. A dual approach to remedy the present situation through deregulation and corporate governance is advocated by Dr. Sangram Chavan and Dr. P.A. Koli. Equal emphasis is given by Dr. G.V. Madiwal, Dr. V.V. Reddy and Dr. M.R. Patil, on corporate approach and removal of state boundaries for rational distribution of sugarcane for all sugar cooperatives in the country. Dr. S.K. Lopoyetum stresses the need for increasing fodder production and professionalization to sustain dairy development and quality improvement in view of the fact that milk consumption in the country has almost doubled in recent decades.

Specialized cooperatives have received considerable attention by researchers and the results of effort through empirical approach have brought out their successes and maladies. Dr. A.S. Joshi's performance analysis of housing cooperatives, Dr. M.R. Patil's empirical study of urban cooperative banks and Dr. Junare's study of urban cooperative banks in Gujrat plead for professionalization. Performance analysis of thirty PACS through 30 parameters is a noteworthy effort by Dr. V. Kulandaiswamy and Shri P. Murugesan. On the other hand, Messers M.P. Thorat and P. Das of the Reserve Bank of India have examined Performance Evaluation Model for primary non-agricultural credit societies and credited such societies in Maharashtra with better performance. The temporal status analysis of agro-processing by Dr. B.V. Pagire, Dr. H.R. Shinde and Dr. D.S. Navadkar and Shri D.V. Kasar plead for autonomy and major policy and business strategy orientation. The study of the status of women employees by Dr. P. Shivaprakasam and Smt. R. Suriakala is an eye opener on prevailing situation of gender bias in cooperative employment.

Lastly, the two interesting studies give us the contrast in the prevailing situation in the cooperative world of our times.

One is the outstanding performance of Warna's Multi-disciplined enterprise, analysed by Dr. P.K. Deshmukh and Shri P.N. Gavade and the other, a case study of a defunct society in Tamil Nadu by Dr. T. Tamilmani with constructive suggestions for its revival. All these studies add lustre to the mosaic of our cooperative world and strengthen our faith in this unique mode of socio-economic development the success and failure of which is in our own hands and within our own capability. Dr. V.B. Jugale and Dr. P.A. Koli deserve to be congratulated for their outstanding contribution to the enrichment our of cooperative dialogue. The Seminar has brought into sharp focus the Cooperative Movement in its myriad forms and reminded us of seven colours of the Rainbow; and we have every reason to believe in its internal strength and vitality and strengthen our will to reassert ourselves for the Twentyfirst Century and Beyond.

Madhav V. Madane

Acknowledgements

We would like to record our appreciation of the contributions of the following writers without whom this edited book would not have been made possible; Vishwa Ballabh, R. S. Pundir, V.B. Kakade, S.T. Bhide, R.D. Biradar, D.J. Edwinraj, Sangram Chavan, V. Kulandaiswamy, A.P. Murugesan, Y.S.P. Thorat, M. Pradeep, P. Das, K. Ravichandran, M.R. Bala, P. Kansal, G.V. Madiwal, Y.V. Reddy, P.K. Deshmukh, P.N. Gavade, Tamilmani, Samwel Lopoyetum, A.S. Joshi, M.R. Patil, R.B. Teli, S.O. Junare, Y.S. Patil, D.S. Navadkar, V.D. Kasar, B.V. Pagire, H.R. Shinde, M.M. Tapkir.

We are grateful to the authorities of the UGC who allowed us to conduct the National Seminar on Reasserting the Cooperatives under SAP/DRS. We are also thankful to the members of advisory committee (SAP, DRS) especially Dr. D. K. Marothia, Indira Gandhi Agricultural University, Raipur and Dr. R. S. Deshpande, Institute of Social Economic Change, Bangalore.

We thank immensely our former Vice-Chancellor Dr. M.G. Takwale and Pro. Vice Chancellor Dr. V.M. Chavan for their administrative support.

Thanks are also due to Mr. Madhav Madane, Chairman Indian Society for Studies in Cooperation, Pune for his forwarding remarks and Dr. P.R. Dubhashi IAS (Rtd.) for delivering the key-note address in the seminar.

We are also thankful to Mr. S.K. Jha, of Serials Publications, New Delhi for bringing out this handsome book.

Dr. V. B. Jugale

Dr. P. A. Koli

Contents

1

Century of Indian Co-operative Movement : A Review

P.R. Dubhashi

The co-operative movement was originated in India in British period. The foundation store of co-operative movement in the world was laid by the Rochdale Pioneers who were mill workers by forming consumers' co-operative in U.K. in 1844. Then after the co-operative movement was introduced in Germany in agricultural credit. The retired officer named Raiffeisen formed the agricultural credit co-operatives just to make the farmers free from the clutches of money lenders. The co-operative movement in UK and Germany was initiated as the people's movement but in India, the co-operative movement was started by the British Government. By the end of 19th Century there were agitations by the farmers against the money lenders due to high rate of interest and the exploitation of farmers by giving work without wages. With a view to provide the easy credit facilities, the then British Government deputed Sir Fredrik Nicholson of Madras to study the co-operative credit societies of Germany. Mr. Nicholson submitted his report by stating that the Indian farmers can get easy credit if Government forms the agricultural credit societies on the lines of Raiffeisen. Accordingly, the British Government in India passed the first Co-operative Societies Act in 1903 and the act was made applicable from 1904. From 1904, the Registrar of Co-operative Societies was appointed to look after the activities of co-operatives. The Second Co-operative Act was passed in 1912 with view to form the marketing, processing, housing and other types of co-operatives. But the Registrar of co-operative societies was the chief of co-operative Movement.

Role of Indian Co-operators

Though the co-operative movement was started in India, yet there was limited scope to the co-operators. The officers of Co-operative Department were more concerned with the administration of co-operatives rather than development. Even in this situation the renowned co-operators like G. K. Deodhar, Vaikunth Mehta, Raobahadur, Talmaki, etc. were associated with the co-operative movement. Of course the contribution of British civil servants like Mr. Malcom Darling in co-operative movement can never be forgotten

Co-operative Movement After Independance

The co-operative movement has developed in real scence after independence. The first Prime Minister of India late Jawaharlal Nehru thought that without co-operatives a village cannot progress and hence the RBI appointed the All India Rural Credit Survey Committee (1951) to review the rural credit structure and the co-operative movement. The valuable recommendations of this committee were implemented in the successive five year plans.

Some of the recommendations of this committee were as follows;

1. Credit should be given as per the need of the member.
2. Credit may be sufficient and it should be made available on time.
3. Liking of credit with marketing and processing.
4. Warehousing network may be made available at the national level.

During the period the concept of co-operative commonwealth was brought forwarded by Dr. D.R. Gadgil, and it was thought that the welfare of the common man should be the final goal of co-operative movement.This concept was taken in to consideration by the All India Rural Credit Review Committee

(1966) which was appointed again by the RBI. The rural credit and subsidy was given through the co-operative structure. Of course there were many lacunas in the working of co-operatives such as overdues of credit. But the big, achievement was made by co-operatives by supplying the credit need of farmers which helped the farmer for Green Revolution. Without the financial support of co-operatives no Green Revolution in India would have been succeeded.

Urban Co-operative Banks

The Development of urban co-operative co-operative banks in India is another help line to the urban citizens. These banks developed due to the concession given by RBI in interest rate on deposits as well as on loan. We can see the largest urban co-operative bank like Saraswant Co-operative Bank (Mumbai) and now banks are fcrmed even by the women. The Bhagini Nivedita Women's Bank has done remarkable work by providing loans to needy women especially lower and middle class.

Agricultural Marketing and Processing Co-operatives

In India, the marketing co-operatives could not succeeded in providing the marketing services to the farmers. It was possible for these co-operatives atleast in fruits and vegitable produce. But here also this sector has failed. The White Revolution has worked satisfactory in Gujarat. The milk products are being sold in Gujarat and Maharashtra through co-operatives. Co-operatives have helped the sugarcane farmers in Maharashtra. Professor Dr. D.R. Gadgil and Padmashree Vithalrao Vikhe Patil organised first sugar factory at Loni (Br) in Ahmednagar in 1950. The replication of this efforts were made elsewhere in Maharashtra. Such sugar factories not only offered remunerative prices to sugar cane growers but they also provided the educational facilities to the members around them. The irrigation, dairy, poultry, medical facilities, etc. were some of the additional benefits of co-operative sugar factories. This was the socio-economic evolution made by co-operatives.

Consumers Co-operatives

The jerks of China war (1962) and the Devalution of Indian Rupee (1966) were the main responsible factors for inflation in

India. This situation forced the Indian Government to open the consumers stores in cities and in rural areas. The Super Bazaar in Canought place in Delhi was opened. The Swidish experts were invited to run that store.

Co-operative Education and Training

The number of co-operatives were growing, but at the same time, there was no arrangement of co-operative training and management in the field of co-operation. There was need to train the personnel in co-operative management ; and hence Dr. D. R. Gadgil expressed the need of National level co-operative management Institution and subsequently the foundation stone of present Vaikunth Mehta National Institution of Co-operative Management was laid in Pune. This institute has taken the resposibility of training and research in co-operative sector. But since last few years there is no full time Director ; and without director no direction to the co-operative training.

Excessive Role of Government and Politics

It is true fact that the co-operative movement was developed in India due to Government help ; but still now there is excess government control. The co-operatives have become the part and parcel of Government activities atleast in few states. There are no elections in many co-operatives since last 20 years in Tamil Nadu. The same is true in other parts of the country. In this situation where is the principle of autonomy ? Co-operatives are run on democratic principles. Many co-operatives are in the hands of same person and in the same family. There is no room for new board of directors. Therefore, it is obvious, that co-operatives have gone away from the fundamental principles and values of co-operatives.

Co-operative Movement In New Economic Era

Since 1991, India adopted the New Economic Policy and the era of Leberalisation, Privatisaion and Globalisation began. In this policy, the government aid and assistance was removed and some business activities were entirely entrusted to the private sectors. This policy is harmful to the co-operative movement. Now co-operatives must stand on their own feet. Few states have also accepted the new parall co-operative act. The multistate act has been also revised. Ten years back, Dubhashi Committee had also favoured the self supported co-operative societies Act. But this act is still in cold box ! It is well known fact, that not only new acts will run the co-operative movement on right lines ; but it is the efficient and self responsible management that can bring the success in co-operative movement. In many societies, there is mismanagement. In Maharashtra, out of 177 co-operative sugar factories about 13 factories have been liquidated and 56 factories are on death bed. Lack of sufficient raw material and excessive politics are the main causes behind this sluggis growth. The price of imported sugar is less than the price of co-operative factories. In this situation there is big question mark before the sugar co-operatives.

So far it was felt that urban co-operative banks are viable, especially in Maharashtra, Gujarat, etc. but unfortunately, these banks are having scams and frauds. The Madhavpura Co-operative Bank in Gujarat has become now indebted. Some banks in Maharashtra have also purchased the shares through private agents and now they have came in to financial trouble. Excessive loans to directors and their relatives is another disease which is entered in urban banks. On such banks ; the RBI has appointed its administrators. Such incidents are the black spots to the co-operative movement. The RBI has now accepted the Basel Committee norms to Indian banks, as a result of this many banks are facing the problem of NPA. This situation has come in to co-operative movement only because the co-operatives have gone away from values, ethics and principles of co-operatives. Still there is no transparency in accounts and general meetings and they are holding without considering the members' feeling. This has resulted in to an ugly face of co-operative movement.

Co-operatives are democratic organisations. Hence, they must be run as per principles of co-operation. If this happens then the co-operatives will be clean one and the members role and loyalty will increase. We can face the adverse effects of globalisation if above norms are well taken into practice. But if we keep ourself away from rules, regulation, values and principles of co-operation one should remember, that the co-operators are digging the graves for co-operatives while we are celebrating the century of co-operative movement !

2

Governance of Co-operatives in the New Economic Era : Challenges and Issues

R.S. Pundir and Vishwa Ballabh[1]

Introduction

A co-operative is a form of organisation that is widely prevalent in developing countries including India and that has great potential as an instrument of economic development. They have played an important role in the economic development of India, particularly in the fields of credit, supply of production inputs, and processing and marketing of agricultural produces.

Co-operatives in India started with the enactment of the 1904 co-operative societies Act. Although they had shown their presence much earlier in the country, their significance had not been realized. During the pre-independence period in India, the basic purpose of co-operatives was to provide relief to the farmers from the money lenders who exploited them. After independence, particularly with the advent of planning, the objective of co-operatives have been changed from relief measure to that of becoming a powerful instrument of economic development.

The economic rationale of co-operative organization lies in its endeavour to secure for its members the advantage of modern technology, economies of scale, access to national and international markets and professional management. A co-operative organization that does not want or cannot secure these advantages is deemed to failure sooner or later. Theoretically speaking there is hardly any better organizational structure than the co-operatives for achieving the dual goal of social and economic development but final access depends on the level of operational efficiency achieved by the co-operative (Dulfer 1974).

Governance structure in co-operatives refers, essentially, to the board and the chairman. Its function in a co-operative is to aggregate member preferences and represent this aggregate in formulating goals, policies and decisions pertaining to the interests of its members' business (Shah 1995a: 62).

The present paper is an attempt to address the issues and challenges related to the co-operatives in the country with emphasis on governance.

Evolution of Co-operatives

There are many forms of organisations such as public (government) agencies, sole proprietorships, partnerships, companies, co-operatives and charitable trusts that can and are, in fact, serving the needs of rural people in India. Government intervention in the rural sector in India can be traced to the last quarter of the 19th century. Since then, the government has expended thousands of crores of rupees on agricultural and rural development programmes and is, by all accounts, the biggest agent of rural development. Co-operatives also have played an important role in promoting agricultural and rural development in India, particularly in the field of credit, processing, and marketing. The dairy co-operatives of Gujarat and sugar co-operatives of Maharashtra are good examples of co-operatives that can promote and sustain rural development. (Singh and Pundir 2000).

From the philosophical perspective, co-operation and its opposite, competition, are two basic tendencies of human behaviour and both co-exit in every individual. Co-operation can emerge under highly diverse situations and accordingly there are several theories/propositions that seek to explain why people do and do not co-operate (Singh 1996). The origin of formal co-operation in the form of a co-operative organisation is traced to Europe, particularly, England, France and Germany, in the mid-nineteenth century. Robert Owen of England, Charles Fourier of France, and Herr F.W. Raiffeisen and Herr Franz Schulze of Germany are considered as the founding fathers of the modern co-operation (Craig 1980:38, Madan 1994:25-27). In 1844, a group of people in Rochdale, England, formed the Rochdale Society of Equitable Pioneers to obtain higher wages from their employers and to set up a co-operative store. The Rochdale Society became the model for similar stores and related enterprises throughout the world. Around the same time, Fourier established "phalanxes" in France and Raiffeisen and Schulze pioneered and implemented the idea of co-operative banks in Germany. Subsequently, in other European countries also, co-operatives emerged primarily as people's response to their exploitation by moneylenders and traders. With the emergence of co-operative movement in Europe, the International Co-operative Alliance (ICA) was established in 1895. Its main responsibility was to co-ordinate the activities of affiliated co-operative federations in various parts of the world. Establishment of communism in USSR and subsequently in other countries was instrumental in promoting government-directed, or parastatal co-operatives. Some co-operatives failed and some others succeeded. Despite their failures and weaknesses, co-operatives have survived over time and now control significant shares of markets in many developed and developing countries including market-oriented economies. For example, in USA, co-operatives command 70 per cent of the fluid milk market, 80 per cent of the fresh fruits market, 35 per cent of agricultural credit of all types, and 30 per cent of the grains and oilseeds market (Dwivedi 1996:723).

In most developing countries including India, co-operatives were promoted by their governments as instruments of rural development. In India, thanks to the British legacy, the co-operative form of organisation was born in 1904 consequent upon the enactment of the Co-operative Credit Societies Act. Subsequently, a more comprehensive act, the Co-operative Societies Act, was enacted in 1912. This Act provided, *inter alia*, for the creation of the post of Registrar of Co-operative Societies, registration of co-operative societies for various purposes, and audit. Under the Montaque-Chelmsfort Reforms effected in 1919, co-operation became a Provincial Subject and the provinces were authorised to make their own co-operative laws. Under the

Government of India Act 1935, "co-operative societies" were treated as a State Subject. In order to facilitate the establishment of co-operatives having membership from more than one Province, the Government of India enacted the Multi-Unit Co-operative Societies Act, 1942. Later a more comprehensive Central legislation, the Multi-State Co-operative Societies Act, 1984, was enacted by Parliament with a view to consolidate different laws governing the same types of co-operative societies.

After India attained Independence in August 1947, co-operatives assumed greater significance as an instrument of socio-economic development and became an integral part of India's Five Year Plans. The All India Rural Credit Survey Committee Report, 1954 recommended an integrated approach to co-operative credit and emphasised the need for viable credit co-operative societies by enlarging their area of operation, encouraging rural savings, and diversifying their business. The Committee also recommended that the government should contribute to the share capital of the co-operatives. In 1958, the National Development Council (NDC) adopted a Resolution on National Policy on Co-operatives. Subsequently, in January 1959, the Working Group on Co-operative Policy set up by the Ministry of Food and Agriculture, Government of India, recommended a blueprint for implementing the NDC's Resolution. The Government of India has since provided massive financial, technical and administrative support to co-operatives both directly and indirectly through State governments (Dwivedi 1996:13-14).

Determinants and Performance of Co-operatives

So far as the determinants of performance of co-operatives are concerned, there are three distinct schools of thought. One, which may be called 'structuralist' believes that it is primarily the strategy, and the organisation structure/design of a co-operative that determine to a large extent its performance – success or failure. Shah (1996), who is an ardent proponent of this school, studied a large number of cases of successes and failures in the co-operative sector and identified three critical determinants of success of co-operatives, namely, swayambhu (creation by members themselves), complete autonomy, and member loyalty and allegiance. He asserts that these attributes are an outcome of "design" and not of exceptionally good leaders and managers (Shah 1996:285-86). The second school of thought, which may be called 'contextualist' emphasises the importance of the context—socio-economic, political, legal, and policy—as a major factor affecting the performance of co-operatives (Baviskar 1980 and Attwood and Baviskar 1987). The third school, which is management-oriented, argues that it is the quality of management and leadership which matters most in determining the success and failure of co-operatives (Singh 1996 and 2000). There are some other researchers like Singh and Pundir (2000) who believe that it is all the three sets of factors, i. e., structural, contextual, and management, that together determine the performance of a co-operative, or for that matter any other organisation and that, to some extent, they could be substituted for one another.

Shah (1995a: 62) while discussing about the governance structure in the co-operatives stressed that a governance structure, which feels powerless, is a major cause of under-performance and insalience. The location of the co-operative's locus of control is determined by birth conditions, macro policy environment, and the extent and quality of critical linkages offered by the federal agency. A federal system operating style, government policies, and design features that enhance the internality of locus of control help the governance structures to play their expected role in co-operatives.

Now we present brief profiles of some of the important types of co-operatives in India and examine their performance by mainly drawing upon some of the published research studies.

Credit Co-operatives

Credit co-operatives and co-operative banks are the oldest and most numerous of all the types of co-operatives in India. Quite a large number of micro level studies on the performance and impact of credit co-operatives are available. The performance of Primary Agricultural Co-operative Society (PACS) was found satisfactory and their impact positive in a number of studies (see, for example, Bandyopadhyay (1996), Jayalatha *et al*., (1996) and Kumar (1996). According to those studies, PACS played an important role in providing credit, seeds, fertilisers, gainful employment to local people, mobilising local resources through a wide variety of activities, and providing various welfare services to the poor.

In a nutshell, we could conclude that although the credit co-operatives have made considerable progress in providing credit to agriculture and allied activities, they suffer from the problem of low recovery which has been further exacerbated by populist measures such as loan waivers, disbursement of loans in loan melas and stay orders on legal processes of recovery. In view of this, there is need for all party consensus at the national level for doing away with all such populist measures to ensure that co-operatives are not misused by politicians and other vested interests for their self-aggrandisement.

Dairy Co-operatives

Dairy development in India, including all the three major aspects i.e., production, processing and marketing, entered the phase of high growth only after establishment of the national Dairy Development Board (NDDB). The NDDB was established in 1965 with its headquarters in Anand. NDDB designed a programme called Operation Flood (OF) to replicate the Anand Pattern co-operatives in the country. OF is perhaps the world's biggest dairy development programme. Launched on July 1, 1970 in 18 selected milksheds, OF now covers 175 milksheds in India and is now in its Phase IV.

One of the salient features of the Anand pattern dairy co-operatives is that they are controlled by their producer members in a democratic manner. At each level in the system i.e., milk producers' co-operative society at village level, milk union at district level and federation at state level, all activities are governed by the democratically elected representatives who are accountable to their producer members. This system of governance has achieved wide spread appreciation within the country as also out side the country. Although the system has not got the success on equal footings across the states in the country, it has achieved remarkable success in the state of Gujarat.

OF has contributed significantly to the modernisation and development of India's dairy industry. It has invested over Rs. 2000 crore in creating and strengthening the basic infrastructure for procurement, processing, transport, storage, and marketing of milk and milk products, for compounding of cattle feed, for provision of animal health care and breeding services, for manufacturing of dairy machinery, equipment and other materials, and for education and training of rural managers, farmers, and members of Boards of Directors of co-operative dairy unions and federations (Singh and Singh 1998).

All in all, the Anand Pattern milk co-operatives are considered to have been most successful in serving their members as well as society at large. They have been most intensively studied by research scholars and have been both applauded and criticised. At the national level OF has enabled India to attain self –sufficiency in milk and milk products and created a strong foundation for future growth and development of India's dairy industry (Singh and Pundir 2001).

Sugar Co-operatives

Like the Anand –pattern dairy co-operatives of Gujarat, sugar co-operatives of Maharashtra are also considered successful as instrument of rural development. While reviewing the growth and performance of sugar co-operatives in Maharashtra, Gadgil (1975:280-293) identified several determinants of their success. They included a producer oriented pricing policy that ensured remunerative and stable price of sugarcane; producer owned and controlled co-operative sugar factories; provision for a proper depreciation reserve and compulsory deposits by members; provision of technical guidance and inputs to sugarcane growers by the agriculture departments created within each factory; equitable distribution of benefits from sugar factories among the members; and provision of welfare services. He also lists some undesirable, albeit unintended, effects of sugar co-operatives such as keen competition among their members and bitter and expensive elections to gain control over the co-operatives, lack of focus on improving the internal management and efficiency, and indiscriminate extension of sugarcane cultivation to areas which were water-stressed.

Baviskar (1980:4-5) identified a number of social, political, economic, and institutional factors that affect the performance of co-operatives. In his opinion, those co-operatives which are imposed from above by the Government or any other authority are likely to fail. On the other hand, if and when co-operatives are organised by the people themselves in response to their felt needs or to fight against some sort of exploitation, they are likely to succeed.

Apte (1996) examined the causes of success and failure of sugar co-operatives in the state. He identified several factors like installation of plants in shortest possible time, provision of irrigation facilities, bringing large areas under sugarcane cultivation, democratic functioning, provision of remunerative prices to the farmers, business-like approach, and diversification as the key to the success of sugar co-operatives. He also lists several factors including corruption and malpractices, which are responsible for the ruin of some of the sugar co-operatives in the state.

To sum up, sugar co-operatives of Maharashtra present an example of how a single commodity co-operative could initiate a process of transformation of the entire rural economy through backward, forward and lateral linkages. The model needs to be studied more intensively and rigorously and lessons of experience of sugar co-operatives distilled carefully for their possible use in future policies.

Natural Resource Management Co-operatives

Natural resources management (NRM) co-operatives are of relatively recent origin in India but they are playing an important role in promoting participatory management of renewable natural resources such as wastelands, fisheries, water, and minor forest produce. Many micro level studies have been conducted recently in India to assess the impact of NRM co-operatives on rural development (Singh and Ballabh 1996).

Marothia and Gauraha (1996) examined the role of co-operative management of *tendu* leaf collection and marketing in Madhya Pradesh with special reference to the performance of five primary minor forest produce co-operative societies in Raipur district. The authors conclude that the management of societies is largely dominated by the government nominees and that the elected members of the management committees do not have any control over financial, administrative and technical affairs. The authors identified quite a few weaknesses in the structure and functioning of the co-operatives such as poor functional vertical linkages, lack of interaction among members, harassment of members by phadmunshis (depot incharges) and checkers and low stakes of members in the co-operatives. However, the authors found that the members of the co-operatives were getting proper (minimum) wages for collection of *tendu* leaves.

Drawing upon the findings of 14 case studies of NRM co-operatives, Singh and Ballabh (1996:35-38) conclude that most of the co-operatives were parastatal organisations and not member-owned and controlled autonomous co-operative societies. Most of them were not financially viable and were heavily dependent on government grants and support for their survival. Restoration, conservation, and sustainable use of natural resources received very little, if any, attention of the co-operatives studied; they were engaged in exploiting the resources that they owned. However, the authors believe that, in view of discouraging results of nationalisation and privatisation of natural resources, especially the common pool resources (CPRs), NRM co-operatives hold high potential as an institution for promoting judicious and sustainable use of CPRs. What is needed to realise their potential is the transformation of existing parastatal co-operatives into genuine co-operatives owned by their members, governed by their elected representatives and managed professionally.

The Future of Co-operative Legislation

It is a common knowledge as to how reluctantly and slowly both the Central and State Governments have moved in addressing the Co-operative law – a law that was and is an artifact of the colonial regime. However, Today, there is glimmer of a new dawn over the horizon. In 1995, Andhra Pradesh enacted a law that allows self-reliant co-operatives to manage their own affairs. The Andhra example has been followed by Bihar, Jammu and Kashmir and by Madhya Pradesh. At the same time, however other states have claimed to enact such legislation, but with such flaws that these laws can only be describes as wolves in the sheep-s clothing. The co-operative laws of most of our states prescribe virtually that is in the by-laws, most states have "model by-laws" which are not a "model" but a requirement. Many co-operative Registrars issue amendments to the by-laws from the state capital with no consideration of the nature of the co-operative or the interest of the members. We must leave to the members the responsibility of establishing their own by-laws and should show the greatest restraint in prescribing any limits (Kurien 2000).

Regarding challenges before co-operatives in the 21st Century, Mohan Dharia (2000) a leading co-operator in the country is of the view that de-centralisation of economy and power could alone ensure stability of Democracy and co-operative movement is based on the principle of de-centralisation, democracy and production by masses. Directive principles in our Constitution insist on this direction. In this regard, it is the responsibility of the Government to amend the laws and strengthen the movement.

Further throwing the light on the co-operative movement in the country it is worth mentioning that Registrar co-operative societies assumed much more powers, which affected freedom of co-operative movement. The assumption of these powers by Registrar co-operative societies was considered "draconian" by co-operative movement. Further, under this policy frame, there was dual control of state Government and RBI/NABARD over the functioning of co-operative societies. Thus under the pretext of close partnership, there was increased Government control and co-operative management in many cases failed to protect the interests of its members. Keeping in view the demand of co-operative movement to free the co-operatives from the interference and control of the Government, Planning Commission appointed in March, 1990 an Expert Group under the chairmanship of Ch. Brahm Prakash to recommend elements and ingredients of Model Co-operative Law. The suggestions of Model Co-operative Law were presented to the Central Government in 1991 and amendment proposals were cleared by cabinet in the year 2000. Co-operative Ministers have come and gone but nothing concrete could be done for bringing necessary amendments in the existing co-operative law (Sisodia 2000).

Banks and Corporate Governance

Crises and even frauds have become a part of normal bank functioning. This could be corroborated with the facts given in a report published by the International Monetary Fund (IMF) which reveals that over 130 countries comprising almost three fourths of the total membership of IMF had experienced as many as 108 instances of significant banking sector problems since 1980, out of which 41 instances were of the nature of a crises encountered in 36 countries (Lindgren et al. 1996 cited in Capoor 2000). Scam and crises feed on a weak link in the system, not necessarily a co-operative entity. This statement is duly supported by the following: In India, in the early 1990's, Harshad Mehta spotted the public sector banks and Bhupen Dalal found bank of Karad and the Metropolitan Co-operative Bank as their handles. And eight years on, Ketan Parikh exploited another chink in the system, namely Madhavpura Mercantile Co-operative Bank Ltd. (Sen 2002).

Peer pressure of the community to help replicate formal models of corporate governance in co-operative institutions no longer seems to work effectively. As a result a number of co-operative banks have been subject to the influence of pretty political machinations, irregular financial activities and gross mismanagement, which point unmistakably to the need for a regrous system enforceable by law for putting effective corporate governance in place. Some steps taken by the Reserve Bank of India in this regard based on the recommendations of the High Power Committee are worth appreciating. It has for instance, been stipulated that at least two directors with suitable banking experience should be present on the Boards of Urban Co-operative Banks and that the promoters should not be defaulters to any financial institutions and should not have any association with Chit Fund/NBFC/Co-operative Bank or Commercial Bank in the capacity of directors on their respective Board of Directors (Sen 2002).

Co-operatives in the New Economic Era

In the wake of privatisation and deregulation that characterise India's NEP and in view of opening up of India's markets to competition from foreign firms under the new world trade regime ushered in by the World Trade Organisation (WTO), co-operatives will no longer have the protection, support, and patronage of government. They will have to defend for themselves and compete with private firms—both Indian and foreign—for their survival and growth. In our opinion, it is only co-operatives that can protect the poor producer and poor consumer from the adverse effects of free world trade and serve as the safety net for them. The economic reforms have so far bypassed the rural sector; it is only the industrial sector and banking sector that have been liberated from the shackles of unnecessary government rules and regulations. The rural sector still continues to be stifled by several restrictions such as ban of inter-state movement of foodgrains, fixation by the government authorities of consumer price of milk sold by co-operatives dairies in cities, restrictions on adoption of modern technologies by sugar factories, and ban on export of *gur* (jaggery) from producing states to consuming states within the country for months during the *gur* manufacturing season.

With nearly one-third of India's rural population living below the poverty line and with most of the rural producers being small scale unorganised operators having virtually no bargaining power, it is unlikely that the free market model of development will help them. Most of the rural people are simply outside the domain of "markets". So how can the new policy of open and competitive markets help them? (for detail see Singh and Pundir 2001).

Politically, privatisation will prove to be disastrous for the political parties in power at the centre and state levels. If 10 million households (or 50 million people who are members of dairy co-operative) unite and lobby against this policy, no government can afford to ignore their demand unless the party in power deliberately chooses to commit a political suicide. Milk being a politically sensitive commodity, no government can afford to deny supply of adequate and good quality milk at reasonable price to city/urban consumers. With private dairies ruling the roast and with the 'soft' state that we have, there is no way the government can ensure this. Private dairies have no sense of social obligations. There are umpteen examples of private dairies and multinational corporations supplying unsafe and unhygienic milk and milk products and evading payment of taxes and duties. So in view of all this, it seems to us that it is only producers' co-operatives or companies owned and controlled by their members and managed professionally that would promote their socio-economic development in the new era.

All in all, there is enough evidence that the ethical, ideological, social, political, and economic bases of co-operatives will enable them not only to survive but also successfully compete with other forms of organisations in the new era (Rajagopalan 1996:xliv). New forms of co-operation such as Self Help Groups and Producers' Companies and co-operatives in new sectors like rubber and coffee plantations will hopefully be more robust, vibrant and autonomous than the conventional co-operatives.

Challenges and Issues

In recent years changes in the national and international economic environment have posed several challenges for co-operatives and it seems to be imperative to re-examine their role and prospects in the new era. The Government of India has not yet formulated any definite national policy on co-operatives and hence the role of co-operatives in the new regime is ambiguous.

Many studies have shown the heavy hands of government officials create a situation resembling" bureaucratic feudalism" rather than the intended self-reliance. The action by government come after problems are identified. Loan embezzlement and other practices meant members' assets are at risk and government action is needed. (Saxena 1992:7-9). Task force to look at national laws have recommended that the laws be changed so the government officials cannot make equity investment in co-operatives and take control (Planning Commission 1991:4-5). Studies on the successful co-operatives clearly show how autonomy from government officials is a critical factor (Singh 1992:17-24 and Korten 1990).

Some of the emerging challenges / issues before the co-operatives documented by Singh and Pundir (2001:86) seem to be worth mentioning here. They are: (a) How to enable the weak co-operatives to attain and retain financial viability?; (b) How to professionalise their management so that they could meet the unfettered and increasing competition from the private enterprises?; (c) How to liberate them from the shackles of archaic co-operative laws and unnecessary government controls; (d) How to create a congenial socio-economic and political environment and ensure a level playing field for co-operatives?;

and (e) How should co-operatives be re-engineered to enable them to cope with the challenges that they are facing and are likely to face in the new era?

Keeping in view the significance in compliance with the objective of the paper we briefly present some of the important issues and challenges here.

- **Lack of Good Leadership**

Good leadership is a pre-requisite not only for creating and nurturing a co-operative but also for providing a vision, and inspiring and guiding both the members and the management so as to enable the co-operative to achieve its purpose. Every co-operative needs an honest, skilled, benevolent and dedicated leader who should be preferably drawn from the group of cardinal stakeholders (Parnell 1995:53). Good leadership is needed for both members' representatives constituting the Board of Directors/Management Committee and for professionals including managers. In most agri-business co-operatives, the members' leader is designated as Chairman/Chairperson or President. His primary role is to unite the membership, articulate their needs and aspirations and insulate the co-operative from unnecessary interference by politicians and other vested interests. Good leaders also play an important role in attracting and retaining good professional managers and technicians. An outstanding example of this is provided by Amul, whose founder Chairman—late Tribhuvandas K Patel, a leader par excellence—not only attracted Verghese Kurien, a manager par excellence, to work with Amul but also retained him for over 20 years.

In Maharashtra, eminent public leaders including social reformers and political leaders played an important role in fostering and strengthening the co-operatives in general and sugar co-operatives in particular from the very beginning. In the erstwhile Bombay province, the first Chairman of the Apex Bank was Sir Vithaldas Thakarsey and G.K. Gokhale was a member of the first Board of Directors of the Bank. G. K. Devdhar devoted his energies largely to the establishment of rural co-operative societies in the province. Other leaders of standing such as B.V. Jadhav and V.G. Kale also took keen interest in the co-operative movement. Later Vaikunth L. Mehta and D.R.

Gadgil also contributed significantly to the growth and development of co-operative movement in the state, the latter guided and assisted the sugar co-operatives for over two decades (Gadgil 1975:166-168).

When and where good leadership is absent in a co-operative for whatever reasons, a leadership vacuum is created. It is not uncommon when such a vacuum is filled in by the Chief Executive Officer or the top management group who then hijacks the co-operative for self-aggrandisement. Sadly, this is what has happened to most of the co-operatives in India. There is a need to create and maintain pools of potential co-operative leaders to fill in the vacuums at all levels.

- **Lack of Professional Management**

In the new era, co-operatives are going to face growing competition from domestic and foreign companies, particularly in the agri-business sector. The competition poses a major threat to co-operatives that are used to thriving on government-conferred privileges including monopolistic status and huge grants and subsidies. There is ample evidence now available to show that this is already happening in processing and marketing of food products such as milk powder, ice cream, fruit drinks, and so on. In view of this, it is now essential for the survival and growth of co-operatives that they are professionally managed.

One of the main reasons for the failure of co-operatives to attract and retain professional managers is their inability to hire professional managers at the open market rates. Most of the co-operatives in India, especially the primary co-operatives at the village level, are small in terms of size of their business turn over and net profits. Hence they cannot afford to hire professional managers.

The government control and patronage has also become an obstacle to induction of professional managers in the co-operative sector. The co-operatives are not free to hire professional managers; they are forced to follow the government rules for recruitment and promotion of their staff. The government procedure and promotion policy are not only rigid and archaic but also prone to tempering by politicians and other vested interests. Consequently, co-operatives cannot attract and retain professional managers, even if they are willing and able to do so. Besides, the government officers deputed to head co-operatives are not accountable to members of the co-operatives and do not have any stakes in the co-operatives. Accountability to members and not to some remote political or bureaucratic persons is an essential part of democratic governance and professional management of the co-operative. It involves developing and operating transparent accounting and administrative systems and giving an account to the Board of Directors and through them to the members of the co-operative. On the top of it all, they are posted and frequently transferred at the whims of the politicians, particularly the Ministers in-charge, Co-operative Departments. Their average tenure rarely exceeds three years (Singh and Pundir 2001).

- **Poor Board-Management Relations**

Most of the agribusiness co-operatives in India start as small enterprises and rely upon their members to carry out the functions of management. However, as a co-operative grows and its business becomes larger and complex, it requires professional managers. One of the most commonly cited reasons for the failure or poor performance of agribusiness co-operatives is poor Board-Management relations. But since in a genuine member-controlled co-operative, it is the members who elect the Board of Directors who, in turn, have the power to appoint and dismiss their managers, we have to blame the members for the existence of any substandard management. Therefore, the most important task of the Board of Directors of a co-operative is the appointment, direction and monitoring of its managers, and, if necessary, their dismissal and replacement (Parnell 1995:135-6). If the Board is not willing or is not able to do this job, the co-operative is doomed to failure, or at best it becomes manager-controlled and therefore subservient to their personal interests.

There are innumerable examples of co-operatives in India, which are controlled by their managers and not by the elected representatives of their cardinal stakeholders. Such co-operatives, even when they are financially successful, are antithesis of genuine member-controlled and democratically governed co-operatives. Therefore, a pre-requisite for the success of a co-operative is the establishment and fostering of good working relationship between its board of directors and senior management.

- **Excessive Government Control and Political Interference**

Co-operation in India pre-dates the co-operative legislation. Indeed, it may be argued that genuine co-operation has diminished with each succeeding piece of co-operative legislation. This process began with the colonial administration which wanted to ensure that the 'natives' did not make off with funds. To do this, they created the post of Registrar—perforce an Indian Civil Service officer—who did not allow the co-operatives a really autonomous status. After Independence, and particularly in the last two decades or so, co-operative legislation has been rewritten and amended so as to vest with government virtually total management authority and operational responsibility, leaving only accountability with the co-operatives. Consequently, today, in most states, legislation and rules govern what clearly belongs within the bye-laws of individual co-operatives. Government may, *suo motto*, amend the bye-laws of a co-operative; amalgamate or divide co-operatives; hold or not hold elections; veto, annul or suspend a co-operative's decisions; appoint its own officers to manage co-operatives; and nominate, suspend or remove committees' members without cause. Such laws are inimical to the essential nature of the co-operative and professional management. Reservation of managerial positions for civil servants virtually precludes professional management accountable to the members. Insinuating the government into co-operative management opens the door to political interference.

Government contribution to the equity of co-operatives and government guarantees for loans advanced to co-operatives have many serious repercussions such as government interference in the management through their nominated representatives on the Boards of Directors/Management Committees of the co-operatives, taking over of management of co-operatives on flimsy grounds, and appointment of government officers as Chief Executive Officers (CEOs) of apex level co-operatives.

Co-operatives were dragged into the realm of party politics when they caught the attention of unprincipled politicians who began to see them as vehicles for political mobilisation and as the key to vote-banks. The Agricultural Credit Review Committee (1986-89) popularly known as the Khusro Committee referred to the increasing officialisation and politicisation of (credit) co-operatives culminating in virtually depriving them of their vitality as well as their democratic and autonomous character.

There has been a lot of debate on whether government support for co-operatives and government intervention in their management are desirable or not. There is no consensus emerging out of this debate. Government financial support is justified on the ground that co-operatives cannot raise capital directly from capital markets and that their members are poor and hence cannot contribute as share capital all the money that is needed by their co-operatives to run their business efficiently. The latter is especially true in the case of agricultural processing and marketing co-operatives such as sugar co-operatives and milk co-operatives which require crores of rupees for establishing and operating their procurement, processing and marketing facilities. Government interference is justified as a means of ensuring checks and balances, safeguarding the interests of the poor members and preventing misappropriation of public money. However, in practice, the involvement of the state in promoting co-operatives and its interference in their functioning have reduced the co-operatives to being an appendage of the government's development apparatus (Shah 1995b).

Concluding Remarks

Co-operatives occupy an important place in India's economy in terms of their coverage, business turn over and contribution to the economic welfare of their members as well as to the economy of the country as a whole. However, despite this, most of the co-operatives in the country seem to have a dismal future due to a variety of constraints.

The major constraints in the development of co-operatives in the new economic environment include the lack of professionalism in management; an archaic co-operative law, excessive control and interference by government; lack of good elected leadership; small size of business and hence inability to attain financial viability; lack of performance-based reward systems; and internal work culture and environment not congenial to the growth and development of co-operatives as a business enterprise.

We have co-operatives that have succeeded despite the odds. But they are the exception that proves the rule that an oppressive law stifles the soul of our people. Co-operation will only succeed in India if we have laws in every state that allow co-operation to be practiced in its democratic substance, namely, the supreme role of the members and accountability to them.

To conclude, the co-operatives need to be democratically governed by the Boards of Directors elected by their members in good standing, unshackled from the archaic co-operative laws, liberated from unnecessary government controls, and managed professionally, if they are to survive and grow in the new economic era characterised by deregulation, privatisation and globalisation.

NOTE

1. Paper prepared for presentation at a National Seminar on "Reasserting the Co-operative Movement" organised by the Department of Economics, under SAP-DRS scheme and the Indian Society for Studies in Co-operation, Pune, from March 25-26, 2004.

REFERENCES

Apte, D.P., (1996), "Sugar Co-operatives in Western Maharashtra: Causes of Success/Failure," *Indian Journal of Agricultural Economics,* 51 (4).

Attwood, D.W. and B.S. Baviskar, (1987), "Why Do Some Co-operatives Work but not Others? A Comparative Analysis of Sugar Co-operatives in India," *Economic and Political Weekly,* 22(6), June 27, A-38-56.

Bandyopadhyay, S., (1996), "An Evaluation of Performance of a Co-operative Society," *Indian Journal of Agricultural Economics,* 51 (4).

Baviskar, B.S., (1980), *The Politics of Development: Sugar Co-operatives in Rural Maharashtra*. New Delhi: Oxford University Press.

Capoor, Jagdish, (2000), "Urban Co-operative Banks: Problems and Prospects," *Reserve bank of India Bulletin*, July, pp.773-80.

Craig, J G, (1992), "Indian co-operatives in the 21st Century: Breaking the Bureaucratic Noose", Governance and Management of rural Co-operatives, Six distinguished lectures, IRMA, Anand pp. 37-57.

Dharia, Mohan, (2000), National Seminar: The Future of Co-operative Lagislation – Principles and Premises, *Organised by Co-operative Initiative Panel*, 8-9 November 2000, IRMA, Anand.

Dulfer, E, (1974), "Operational Efficiency of Agricultural co-operatives in Developing Countries, FAO Development Paper No 96, Food and Agriculture Organisation of the United Nations, Rome.

Dwivedi, R.C, (1996), "Role of Co-operatives in Rural Economy" *Indian Journal of Agricultural Economics*, 51 (4), pp. 712-727.

Gadgil, D.R., (1975), "Sugar Co-operatives in Maharashtra," in *Writings and Speeches of D.R. Gadgil on Co-operation.* Bombay: Orient Longman Ltd.

Jayalatha, C. S. Varadarajan and K. Lokanadhan, (1996), "Extent of Credit Supply by Primary Agricultural Co-operative Banks in Madurai District, Tamil Nadu," *Indian Journal of Agricultural Economics,* 51(4).

Kurien, V., (2000), *National Seminar: The Future of Co-operative Lagislation – Principles and Premises,* Organised by Co-operative Initiative Panel, 8-9 November 2000, IRMA, Anand.

Marothia, D.K. and A.K. Gauraha, (1996), "Co-operative Management of *Tendu* Leaves: A Micro Analysis," *Indian Journal of Agricultural Economics*, 51(4).

Rajagopalan, R., (1996), "Rediscovering Co-operation: A Connective Summary," in R. Rajagopalan (ed.) *Rediscovering Co-operation.* Institute of Rural Management, Anand.

Sen, Prabal K., (2002), "Urban Co-operative Banks in India: Past, Present and Future, Working Paper 168, Institute of Rural management, Anand, Gujarat.

Shah, Tushaar, (1995a), Making Farmers' Co-operatives Work: Design, Governance and Management. New Delhi: Sage.

Shah, Tushaar, (1995b), "Liberalisation and Indian Agriculture: New Relevance of Farmer Co-operatives," *Indian Journal of Agricultural Economics*, 50(3), July-September.

Shah, Tushaar, (1996), Catalysing Co-operation: Design of Self–Governing Organisations. New Delhi: Sage.

Singh, Katar, (1996), "The Emergence and Survival of Co-operation: A Review of Some Theoretical propositions," in R. Rajagopalan (ed.) *Rediscovering Co-operation.* Vol. III, Institute of Rural Management, Anand.

Singh, Katar, (1998), "The Role of Farmers' Organisations in the Context of New Economic Policy with Particular Reference to Agricultural Marketing and Agro-Processing," *Indian Journal of Agricultural Marketing*, 12(3).

Singh, Katar, (2000), "Challenges for Co-operatives in the New Millennium and Strategies for Coping with Them," *The Co-operator*, 32(8).

Singh Katar and R.S. Pundir, (2000), Co-operatives and Rural Development in India, Research Paper 17, IRMA, Anand.

Singh Katar and R.S.Pundir, (2001), Performance of Co-operatives in terms of their Contribution to Rural Development in India, Proceedings of national Seminar on Co-operative Reforms, 24 and 15 January 2001, National Bank for Agriculture and Rural Development, Mumbai.

Singh, Katar and Vishwa Ballabh (eds.), (1996), *Co-operative Management of Natural Resources.* New Delhi: Sage Publications.

Singh, Katar and Virendra P. Singh, (1998), "Dairy Development in India: Retrospect and Prospect," Research Paper 15, Institute of Rural Management, Anand.

Sisodia, S., (2000), National Seminar: The Future of Co-operative Lagislation – Principles and Premises, *Organised by Co-operative Initiative Panel*, 8-9 November 2000, IRMA, Anand.

3

New Economic Policy and Co-operative Identity[1]

V.B. Kakade

Introduction

The Indian co-operative movement has celebrated its centenary as a mark of its commitment to social cause. The New Economic Policy based on competitive paradigm was accepted as a panacea for economic crises in 1990. The fruit of the NEP shows mixed results. The policy succeeded in attaining higher growth rate, inward flow of foreign exchange, price stability and removal of unproductive controls. However the policy based on market mechanism could not help to increase employment and reduce the poverty and unemployment. The inequality of income widened as the opportunities created by NEP were not shared equally. The historical experience of different countries shows the market mechanism based on competitive forces never helps in solving the problems of the weaker. The co-operative structure offers an alternative institutional structure to resolve the problems created by competitive structure. The co-operative principles have been reformulated without loosing its identity. On this background an attempt is made to review the recent change made in the co-operative principles and argue for co-operative identity on the basis of SWOT analysis of co-operative sector.

SECTION - I

ICA on Co-operative Identity and Principles

The ICA so far has made three times formal statements of the co-operative principles, in i.e. 1937, 1966, and 1995.The Statement of Identity defines a co-operative as "an autonomous association of persons united voluntarily to meet their common economic, social and cultural needs and aspirations through a jointly-owned and democratically-controlled enterprise."

The new co-operative principles are as below:

Voluntary and Open Membership

This principle has changed little from the 1966 version. Basically the co-operatives do not discriminate against potential members based on their inherent characteristics (social, racial, political, religious or gender). Particularly important is the addition of gender as a category in the 1995 principles. It implies that individuals must not be coerced into co-operative membership. It is expected that their participation should be as active and responsible members and should be based on a clear understanding of the values. At the same time, while membership is open, the principle assumes the member is able to use the services provided and is willing to take on the responsibilities of membership. This language recognizes that some co-operatives may close membership based on ability to use the co-operative. The ICA Women's Committee has worked long and hard to have gender added to the list and to ensure that the organization's expectations for co-operative enterprises are clearly expressed. The open membership principle obligates elected leaders, managers and staff to elicit information from the entire membership body (not just a subset of organized opinion) and to understand their members and potential members fully regardless of their religious or political beliefs, their gender or sexual preference or their cultural or social background. The special relationship between the co-operative and the people it serves is a unique characteristic of co-operative business.

Democratic Member Control

The principle of democratic member control defines the way in which members will make decisions. It assumes that members will participate in setting policy and giving broad direction to co-operative activities in a way in which no member has no greater "voice" than any other member. This principle is closely related to the "one member, one vote" principle of the 1966 revision. The new principle, however, gives specific attention to the potentially different voting structures that may be put in place in secondary co-operatives. When co-operatives (rather than individuals) are members of secondary co-operatives, the one member, one vote rule may result in substantial inequities for the individual members of member co-operatives.

Member Economic Participation

This principle deals directly with the very difficult problem of capital acquisition by co-operatives in amounts large enough to compete effectively with vast global industries. Throughout this history, co-operatives have been built on the premise that capital is a servant of the enterprise, rather than the master. Co-operative activities are organized to meet member needs, not to accumulate capital in the hands of investors. In the past, the principle of capital as servant led to a belief that resources generated by profitable co-operative enterprises should be returned to labor, rather than concentrated in the hands of owners of capital, by strictly limiting returns to invested funds.

It has not always been clear what role, if any, is played by non-member capital investment, or investment by members beyond the *"fair share"* required. Although members own millions of dollars that they might invest in co-operatives, the previous restrictions on dividends to be paid on capital did not encourage them to invest beyond the required amounts. Consequently co-operatives have repeatedly been unable to generate equity for capital intensive projects; nor have they been able to maintain the value of invested capital during inflationary times. The strict limitation on dividends to capital has been lifted in the 1995 principles which now imply that co-operatives compensate capital and labor fairly.

In order to retain the democratic nature of the enterprise, members of co-operatives are expected to contribute capital equitably and to democratically control the capital of the business. To retain the community centered nature of the enterprise and the belief that strength comes from pooling resources to engage in mutual self help, there is an underlying expectation that a portion of the co-operative's capital should be owned collectively by all members. Finally, the principle also gives guidance to members on possible uses for surpluses generated by the enterprise. Interestingly, two of the suggested three uses are designed to provide community rather than individual benefits.

Autonomy and Independence

In thirty years since the passage of the 1966 Co-operative Principles, numerous third world countries used co-operatives as an intentional part of their social and economic development strategies. Where there are many instances of successful development through co-operatives, the overall record is mixed at best. Even though the intent was to develop self-reliant member controlled enterprises, government initiation and support was necessary to begin the co-operative ventures. Unfortunately, many of the governments, especially in centrally planned economies, were unable to withdraw their control from the co-operatives. Instead, co-operatives, were controlled by govern-ment functionaries and they became inefficient, bureaucratic and poorly managed, a haven for government bureaucrats. Independence and autonomy was never realized by the government.

The new principle of autonomy and independence emphasizes that co-operatives must be free of intervention from governments or other sources so that the members will be able to control their own destiny.

Education, Training and Information

Education continues to be a priority of the co-operative movement in the new Statement of Identity. The background paper on the principle emphasizes that co-operative education is more than advertising product or distributing information. It is critical to the effective and informed participation of members which lies at the core of the co-operative definition. "It means engaging the minds of members, elected leaders, managers and employees to comprehend fully the complexity and richness of co-operative thought and action." The rewritten principle also highlights the importance of educating the young and opinion leaders about the nature and benefits of co-operation. If co-operatives are to be part of the solution to many of the world's problems, then the people must not only be aware of the concept, but they must appreciate it and be willing to participate in it. Such active involvement will not occur if people do not understand co-operative enterprise.

Co-operation Among Co-operatives

This principle is virtually unchanged from the 1966 Principles. In this principle, the vertical and horizontal integration of co-operatives is expected at all the levels.

Concern for Community

Grounded in the values of social responsibility and caring for others, this new principle gives articulation to the co-operative interest in making contributions to a better society at large. By taking ownership over portions of the economy, co-operative members are saying, in effect, we can meet our needs and the needs of others better than they are currently being met. The co-operatives not only care for their members, but also the non-members including women, old, children, etc.

SECTION - II

The SWOT Analysis of Co-operative Sector

The success of co-operatives is the result of its strong pillars of social principles with practical success. The future of co-operatives depends on understanding these strengths and reducing the weaknesses it has developed over the period. The SWOT analysis helps in this respect to take balance and practical approach. The strength and weaknesses of the co-operative movement shows the present scenario and the opportunities as well as threats helps to plan for future.

The Strengths and Weaknesses of the Co-operatives

The strength of co-operative sector lies in its institutional structure. The co-operatives have played an important role in increasing the wellbeing of its members and of the society.

(A) The Strengths of Co-operatives

1. *Large Economic Base :* The co-operative sector in India has achieved a significant role in economic activities in different sectors. It is evident from the following table.

Indian Co-operative Movement At a Glance all co-operatives-2000-2001

Value Rs. in Million ....

(i) Number of Co-operatives (all levels).........................5,45,354

(a) PrimaryAgricultural co-operatives 139,512

(b) Primary Non-Credit Co-operatives 3,91,370

(ii) Membership co-operatives(all types) ....236.2 Million

(a) Membership of Primary Agrl. Coops .... 157.1 Million

(b) Membership of Primary Non Credit Coops..........63461 Million

(iii) Share Capital (all Levels & all types)............ Rs 1985425

(a) Share Capital of Primary Agrl. Coops........... Rs 93671

(b) Share Capital of Primary Non Credit .... Rs 49325.6

(c) Govt Parti. in Primary Agrl. Coops ....6.65 %

(iv) Working Capital (Credit + Non Credit)........ Rs 34000555

(v) Assets* of co-operatives(all levels)............ Rs 1321,246.63

(vi) Reserves... Rs 179,145.8

(vii) Deposits Rs1,158,664.9

(viii) Coverage of Rural Households...................................67%

(ix) Villages covered by co-operatives 100%

(x) Number of National Level Coop federations 19

(xi) Number of state Level Coop Federations 360

(xii) Number of district Level Coop Federations 2,761

2. *Democratic Structure :* The co-operative structure is based on democratic principles and the members are treated with equal rights and responsibilities. The democratic nature helps in increasing commitments by its members. The capital becomes secondary in controlling the business policy.

3. *Social Commitment :* The profit motive is replaced by social commitment. The social commitment is reflected in its working. The co-operatives deliberately avoid the mal-practices and adulteration or shortcut methods to earn excess profit.

4. *Diversified Activities :* The co-operatives have spread their activities both in terms of area as well as scope. From credit

to housing and dairy to sugar production, the co-operative have spread their activities.

5. *Cost Effective* : The co-operatives are cost effective in terms adopting very simple but effective business pattern. The per unit cost for any activity is substantially low for co-operatives. However this benefit is counter balanced by other factors such low size of turnover and small business.

(B) Weaknesses of Co-operatives

1. *Inefficiency* : The co-operatives in general are inefficient on various parameters such as business per employee. Surplus generated per unit etc. The inefficiency is the result of neglect of business principle and absence of transparent system with accountability.
2. *Surplus Manpower* : The co-operative are over burdened with surplus manpower as it is the case of many public enterprises. The co-operative institutes are looked as employment centers. The leaders of co-operative units normally try to provide employment to their close people.
3. *Low Level Technology* : The level of technology is very low and the inadequacy capital acts as limiting factor in adoption of new technology.
4. *Linkage Problem* : The principle of co-operation amongst the co-operatives leaves much scope for further improvement. The absence of effective linkage reduces the economies of scale. The project "Kiriya Milk Industries of Sri Lanka", headed by Dr. V.Kurien, Chairman, NDDB shows a practical way to create effective linkage. The project aims at trebling Sri Lanka's milk production from 30,000 litres per day to 10,000 litres per day production capability.
5. *Policy Problems* : The co-operative structure and its significance is getting backseat in policy priorities. The NEP based on market competition and foreign capital needs to be corrected. The principle of self reliance needs to be practiced.

(C) Opportunities for Co-operatives

1. *Growing Market* : The market in various developing countries can be tapped effectively through production of goods and services in the co-operative sector. The middle

class of India is nearly 30 cr. and the growth of young population is significant. The multinational have prepared their strategies based on these projections. The growing market of Asian countries in general and of Indian continent in particular acts as fertile land for co-operative development.

2. *Acceptance of Modern Technology* : The adoption of modern information technology plays an important role determining the growth of co-operatives. The adoption of the modern technology can be seen in the experiment of Warna wired village. The WTO rules for export are more stringent and its compliance can be done only with adoption of such high-tech methods. The dairy industry is icon of success of co-operatives in India and its growth may now restrained as the quality of milk is low due to neglect of hygienic conditions in milk production. The private sector is taking major lead in fast adoption in acceptance and use of modern technology which mat leave far behind the co-operative sector. In 1996, Shree Kamdhenu Electronics Private Ltd. (SKEPL) was established as a private limited company. SKEPL provides integrated solutions, marketed under brand name of AKASHGANGA (meaning "milkyway" in Hindi), that automate the milk collection process in village dairy co-operative societies. The company's products include an automatic milk collection system, an electronic weighing scale, a dairy information system kiosk, and a milk analyzer that tests for levels of fat and non-fat milk solids.

3. *Human Capital :* The committed labour force based on co-operative principles is an asset of the co-operative sector. The corporate sector using market incentives for better performance can be adopted in the co-operative sector with some modifications. The success and failure of co-operatives are attributed to the people in the organization. The co-operatives are not only alternative to corporate sector but better alternative due to its human capital.

4. *Competitiveness :* The co-operatives strength lies in healthy competition and not cut throat competition. The adoption of modern tools and techniques along with low cost structure can act as an important pillar for future sustainability.

5. *Quality Awareness :* The co-operatives have their brand image for quality products. The co-operatives can sustain this fea-ture and it can become invisible capital for co-operative sector.

(D) Threats to Co-operatives

1. *Business as Usual Approach :* The lethargy on the part of the members and decision makers is reflected in business as usual approach and neglect of new challenges in the industry. This has resulted in missing the new opportunities.
2. *Vested Interest :* The vested interest group always dominates in the co-operative sector and misuse the co-operative assets for personal benefits. The vigilant members can act as the only remedy for this ill.
3. *Capital :* The limited reward on capital has acted as a limiting factor for growth of co-operatives. The change in co-operative principles from 1995 can solve the problem to some extent. The capital requirement of the co-operative sector is very large due to neglect of modernization and absence of sufficient reserve funds.
4. *Member Alienation :* The success of co-operatives depends mainly on the active participation of the members. The co-operative sector suffers from member alienation which breeds malpractices and encourages the vested interest groups.
5. *Small Business Size :* The scale of operation is very small for large number of co-operatives. It acts as limiting factor in reaping the benefits of economies of scale. The co-operative sector may not be in a position to compete with multinational with global scale of production.
6. *Myopic Approach :* Another limiting factor of co-operative is their myopic approach. Very few co-operative have their perspective plan or long term vision. The small reserve funds, neglect for technological upgradation are the result of this myopic approach.

Conclusion

The co-operative movement on its turn of century can transform itself and its members for better tomorrow. The co-operative identity is not merely as another form of business organization but it acts as an icon for social justice, business with ethics. The modern technology can be effectively used to exploit the economies of scale and effective member control and participation. The co-operative should not become defensive only but more aggressive and needs to sharpen the tools. The SWOT analysis shows that the latent energies can be effectively used to charge the co-operative movement. The adoption of new form, practices and technologies for co-operative identity will give it competitive edge and strength for future growth. The NCU has taken various measures to strengthen the co-operative identity which includes;

1. Democratisation and Professionalisation of Co-operative Management.
2. Lobbying with state Govts and Govt. of India to (a) ensure timely elections in Coops. (b) to amend co-operative laws to provide greater autonomy to co-operatives and ensure their functioning in accordance of Co-operative Principles.
3. Influencing the co-operative organisations to have well defined manpower development and professionalisation policies to improve the quality and efficiency so as to face the market challenges of liberalisation.
4. Tailoring the co-operative education and training programmes based on requirements of co-operative organisations.
5. Convening every three years Indian Co-operative Congress to formulate common view points on various issues.
6. Represents on various co-operative policy formulation bodies and working group to formulate proposals for Five Year Plans.
7. Conducts Research and Studies to Highlights the problems to Govt. of India & other concerned agencies Convene seminars/conferences and workshop on various co-operative subjects to form a common view points of problems and approach the various agencies for necessary action for implementation.

On the background of NEP it is necessary to adopt these measures on war footing basis or it has to face the danger of elimination.

Michael Cracknell summarized the danger as, "Unless the co-operatives can meet this challenge they will end up in down-turn spirals of decreasing volumes of business, deteriorating profitability of their operations, and reduced capacity to pay remunerative and competitive prices and provide useful services to their members, continued flight of members, still further decline in volumes of business."

NOTE

1. Paper presented in Two Days National Seminar on Reasserting Co-operative Movement organized by Department of Economics, Shivaji University, Kolhapur on 25th and 26th March 2004.

REFERNCES

Co-operative/Grocer, January/February, (1996), *Co-operative Grocer* is Published by Dave Gutknecht, P.O. Box 597, Athens, OH 45701.

http://www.indianchild.com/agricultural_marketing_in_india

http://www.digitaldividend.org/case/case_akashganga.htm

http://www.indiadairy.com/ind_profile_factsheet.html

http://www.ncui.nic.in/stat.htm

http://ncdc.nic.in/

Michael Cracknell, (1996), Co-operatives in the Context of Globalization and Liberalization by FAO Co-operatives Consultant.

4

New Forms to Reassert Co-operation

S.T. Bhide

Introduction

India opened up its economy and the forward looking Co-operators like Shri. Mohan Dharia sensed that Indian Co-operative movement would now need rejuvenation to stand on its own feet in the competitive economy as the winds of Globalisation would gain strength. The trend of heavily depend on Govt. for most of the things viz. men, material and money to run the co-operative had to be reversed. Shri Mohan Dharia who was then the Deputy Chairman Planning Commission ; appointed a committee headed by Chaudhary Brahma Prakash in 1990 and pursued the matter for a new legal framewok for Co-operative Societies. The main thrust of the new frame work envisaged then was a liberalized self reliant autonomous, Co-operative Societies without Govt. participation in share capital and consequently expected freedom from Government interference which curtailed their initiatives.This framework of new Model Co-operative law was made available to State Governments. Government of India pursued the matter with the State Governments; but most of the State Governments were reluctant to relax their control on Co-operatives especially in respect of supersession, audit Administration and supervision and turned a deaf ear. Further Govt. of India which pleaded for new co-operative law did not set the example by replacing its own Multi-State Co-operative Societies Act 1984. It was Andhra Pradesh which was the first State to enact a parallel law viz Andhra Pradesh mutually aided Co-operative Societies Act 1995. Andhra Pradesh has then since made good progress in this field of self reliant co-operatives with the guidance of Shri Rama Reddy of the Co-operative Development Foundation, Hydrabad. Only a few other States viz.- Madhya Pradesh, Orissa, Bihar, Jammu – Kashmir, Karnataka, Chhatisgad, Jharkhand and Uttaranchal have parallel Co-operative Societies laws giving more freedom to self-reliant Co-operative Societies. This achievement was mainly because of the vigorous non official pioneering efforts to propogate this new form by Co-operative Initiative Panel Anand headed by Shri. Dharia, V Kurein and L. C. Jain along with the Co-operative Development Foundation of Hydrabad, headed by Shri Rama Reddy. Government of India which was pursuing the State Governments to enact liberalized co-operative law took 12 years to liberalize the Multi –State Co-operative Societies Act which has now come into force in 2002. The whole thrust in this endeavor is to enable the Co-operatives to stand on their own and develop in a free environment in which they should have a level playing field with their competitors viz the individual proprietorships, companies and partnerships etc.

As the scenario became clear that the politicians in the co-operatively developed States like Maharashtra , Gujarat, Punjab, Tamilnadu etc.were reluctant to part with the power they wielded on co-operatives. This was because co-operatives proved to be seats of economic power and stepping stones to catapult many a co-operative leadership into positions of political leadership. It was therefore contemplated by the selfless Co-operators and Government of India that another via media need be found so that co-operators interested in the genuine development of farmers and artisans as a group on their own efforts may be provided with another frame work for co-operatives. Such a frame work should provide for a perfect level playing field with their competitors.

Alagh Committee on Companies Act

A committee was constituted, headed by economist Prof. Alagh. The committee suggested that a new part viz part ix A may be added by amending the Companies Act. The new amendment viz. The Companies (Ammendment) Act 2002 has come into force from last year. These are new types of Producer Companies of Producers of primary products from;

1. Agriculture, animal, husbandry, florcuture, horticulture, pisciculture, forest products, bee keeping, and farming plantation products, re-vegetation and any other primary activity or service which promotes the interest of the farmer and or the consumers; or
2. Produce of persons engaged in handicraft, handloom and other cottage industries.
3. Any product resulting from any of the above activities including by- products of such products.
4. Any product from an ancillary activity that would assist or promote any of the aforesaid activities or anything ancillary thereof.
5. Any activity which is intended to increase the production of anything referred to in clause 1 to 4 above or to improve the quality thereof.

Such companies can be formed by producers of the primary products referred to above.

It would be clear from above that this new enactment provides a level playing field for farmers, artisans for coming together for co-operative production and marketing of their products in competition with others. These organizations are registered under company law as Producer Companies. Though the word co-operative is not there in the name because the said word co-operative can only be used by Co-operative Societies under the laws in that behalf, these producers companies in real spirit and practice are synonymous with co-operative societies.

Aspects of Companies Act, 2002

Let us now look into the Co-operative aspects of this new form of co-operative organization. Section 581(g)(2) of the Companies (Amendment) Act 2002, provides for the principles as envisaged under co-operation.

They are as under :

1. Open and Voluntary membership to all who can use the services of the Producer Company and wish to do so along with discharging the duties of membership.

2. Every individual member has only one vote irrespective of any number of shares he holds.
3. Democratic Management by elected Board. Board shall be responsible to the members.
4. Limited return on capital.
5. Distribution of surplus by the Producers(Co-operative) Company by way of
   (a) Providing for the development of business of company.
   (b) Common facilities for members and others.
   (c) By way of bonus proportionate to the participation by members in the business of the Producer Company.
6. Provision for education of members, employees and others in mutuality and mutual aid techniques.
7. Co-operation amongst producers companies with similar principles at local, national and international level so that the interests of members and their community are safeguarded.

It would be clear from above that these new form of companies would be following the above co-operative principles and still would be able to compete with the private companies with a level playing field as both of them would be governed by the same law in the free competitive economy. Private companies would be mainly guided by the principles of maximization of profits while producer companies will be guided by mutual aid principles. In the long run world turning into a global village, it is the principles of mutual aid aiming at well being of all would win over fierce cut throat competition.

There is a special provision in the companies (Amendment) Act 2002 where under the existing Co-operative Societies of producers referred to above willing to follow the above provisions of mutual aid would be straight away converted into Producers Companies without any "No objection Certificate" or interference from the State Registrar of Co-operative Societies or any other State Authority. Of course there is a provision for discharge of liabilities of creditors and members unwilling to join new company. Such provision is mainly made for smooth conversion of Co-operative Societies into Producer Companies as the past experience of such a conversion viz Development Co-operative Bank into Development Credit Bank (A company) had landed the said bank into court litigation though the thumping majority of members desired it. Co-operative Initiative Panel (Anand). C/o National Dairy Development Board under its leadership is pioneering this new effort to free co-operatives from stringent Govt. controls under State Co-operative laws and is encouraging co-operatives to stand on their own strength.

5

Rediscovering Co-operation Some Issues

R.D. Biradar

Introduction

Co-operation is a joint or collaborative behaviour that is directed toward some goal in which there is common interest or hope of reward. Today, co-operation is projected as one of the modes of governance, the state, the private sector, and household being the other organs.

It is important to distinguish between co-operation as instrument and co-operation as values. Very often co-operatives are promoted by the Government to realize some of its objectives in the name of public interest. Co-operatives have acquired a prominent place in the socio-economic life of people. The co-operative movement has made considerable progress during the post independence period but it has still to go a long way in promoting self reliance amongst under privileged people and bringing them to the main stream. The co-operatives are basically business organizations. They are not distinct forms in matters like expansion, diversification, economy profitability, human resources management, etc.

By and large, the co-operatives do not enjoy monopoly in any sphere of activity today. The new economic policy with (LPG) have brought fresh challenges to the co-operative sector and they must perform well to survive. In this context, this paper brings together the threads of various changes and challenges and shade lights on rediscovering co-operation from the conventional co-operation. This paper also enables the active co-operator as how to cope up with changing and challenging in the world of business by understanding the factors of rediscovering co-operation.

Rationale of Rediscovering Co-operation

Co-operation is a tool of socio-economic change. It is also considered as the most effective tool of economic development. Since the introduction of co-operative societies act 1904; the movement of co-operation has gradually developed and spread over the entire world covering all socio-economic activities. In most of the cases the co-operatives have made grand success, while some have failed to come up to the expected level. It is because of not understanding the rational of rediscovering co-operation. The very rational of rediscovering co-operation is due to shift of change in the world of business in the sphere of socio-economic, techno-political, psycho-cultural factors (refer shift of change table 1). The process of co-operation has found varied expression at different times and diverse cultures. In traditional societies, co-operation was a natural outcome of responding to local needs and was strengthened by bonds of kinship. In the developing countries today, co-operation is often government sponsored but defined as voluntary. In the socialist countries, co-operation may be involuntary to a considerable degree, as it was in earlier USSR.

The goals set for co-operation also different countries. These include economic growth equity promotion, infrastructure provision, decentralized governance and ecological balance etc. It is found relevance not only in management of common property resources, such as forest, pasture, or land held together but also in over coming several contingent situations, such as floods or drought. Co-operation flourished best at the primary level such credit, dairy, urban banks, etc.

The co-operation occurred at various places like worship and at various times like ploughing of land, showing seeds, harvesting of crops etc. The basic question is : how to rekindle this spirit, in which form and for what? Similar several questions should also be answered. More critical among these include :

Table 1 : Shift of Charge in the World of Business (Rediscovering Co-operation)

Before 2000	*After 2000*
• Just Commerce	• E-commerce
• Money	• E-money
• Agri./Industrial Economy	• Knowledge economy
• Socialism oriented	• Free market oriented
• Procedure oriented	• Result oriented
• Govt. recognition	• Market recognition
• Indian market	• Global market
• Inward looking	• Out word in looking
• Urban-Rural market	• Rural-Urban market
• Second wave thinking	• Third/fourth wave thinking
• Simple market	• Complex market
• Twisted economics (No focus on quality)	• Main stream economics (Use of TQM/BPR)
• Consumer satisfaction (with no relationship)	• Delighting consumers E-CRM practices
• Promotion 1. Seniority basis 2. 10.30 am to 5.30 p.m.	• Promotion 1. Merit basis 2. No fixed timing
• Motivation 1. Where is roof	• Motivation 1. Where is the sky

1. What is the political economy of co-operation. Who benefits? Who loses? Where should the state stand vis-à-vis this mode of governance?
2. Should co-operation be injected with the spirit of market culture by making it profit driven? What will be the short run gains? What will be long run implications?
3. What are the cultural dimensions of co-operation? Should religious sentiments be evoked to seek economic co-operation? Will such a strategy ensure salience to the process of co-operation?

Overall, it appears that the process of co-operation is losing its strength and needs to be rejuvenated. It can also be inferred that co-operation as practiced today, is not responding adequately to the emerging needs of society.

In the sphere of research, it stands for interpretation of known facts in the new light, a critical review and revision of what has taken as accepted : a search for deeper meaning of an established idea.

Rediscovering co-operation calls for a new mental orientation. This is said with particular reference to its interaction with the government. In its reincarnated form, co-operation must go by the spirit of community-based governance. While drawing administrative, technical and financial support from the government, this kind of governance has to assert its autonomy in managing its affairs. It must decide as to what is important to it and how is it be achieved. Rediscovering co-operation demands that any project initiated must be gradually transformed into a continuing programme. For the community concerned rediscovering co-operation stands for revival of the old tradition of co-operation. In order to understand the conventional co-operation and rediscovered co-operation, the efforts are made to show it in table no. 2.

It can be revealed from the table no. 2 that, the values viz ; belongingness, sincerity, commitment, dedication, devotion, honesty, loyalty and appropriate use of co-operative principles etc. are declining significantly over the period of time. Similarly operational methods of achieving excellence fall short of supply. It is mainly because of the over all change in the system. Thus it is desirable to understand the new innovative methods of working in rediscovered pattern of co-operation.

Table 2 : A Comparative View of Conventional and Rediscovered Co-operation

Conventional Co-operation	*Rediscovered Co-operation*
• Based on kinship/family ties	• Based on community of diverse components
• Aims at mutual help to overcome a contingent situation	• Aims at development
• Inspired by the sentiment of religiosity and generosity	• Inspired by the idea of mutual gain
• Locus of control is in the hand cf seniors	• Locus of control lies in an elected body

Contd...

Table 2 : (Contd...)

• Integration with higher levels of governance weak	• Strong ties with government for administrative, technical and financial support
• Regional culture as given	• Regional culture used as an instrument
• Govt. role essential	• Govt. role essential
1 Friend, philosopher and guide	1 Manager, controller & director
2 Creator, operator & destructor (GOD)	2 Generator and operational Destructor (GOD)
• Leadership oriented co-operation	• Boss oriented co-operation
• Observed & followed all principles and values of co-operation	• Principles and values of co-operations are not strictly observed & followed

Conclusion

It can be concluded that the success of co-operative movement's is based on rediscovering co-operation. Rediscovering co-operation is the need of hour and enable to perform well in the changing and challenging work of business world. However, the values of co-operation should not be compromised for the development of economy. Further, it can be stated that the charismatic leadership will create the good image for the excellent working of co-operatives. Such leaders inspires and radiates love among the who people believes in saying 'we' instead of 'I' they also know how to do it instead of knowing how it is done. Similarly such leaders never demand respect, fight with their colleagues but they command respect and fights for the problems of their colleagues. So the message for the rediscovered co-operation is to be a leader and not a boss.

REFERENCES

Biradar R.D., (1994), "Basic Values, and Co-operative Principles," The Maharashtra Co-operative Quarterly, Vol. LXXVIII No. 2, Oct-Dec. pp. 25-29.

________, (1991), SWOT Analysis of Shetkari Sahakari Sangh Ltd., Kolhapur, The Maharashtra Co-operative Quarterly, Vol. LXXIV No. 3, January, pp. 115-121.

__________, (1996), Readiness for Reengineering : A Study of Three Co-operatives in Kolhapur; Institute of Rural Management Vol. III Nov; pp. 106-117.

Kurien, V., (1992), "Co-operative the only Hope of Rural India" Sahakarita Sanshodhan, July-Dec. Vol. IV, No. 2, pp. 1-7.

Ravi Shankar A, and Thimmaiah, (1995), "Co-operatives and Liberalization : Challenges and Opportunities" Kurukshetra, Vol. XLIV, No. 2, Nov. pp. 15-16.

Tamni K.K., (1966), "Positioning Co-operatives to the 21st Century" The Maharashtra Co-operative Quarterly Vol. LXXX, No. 4, Jan.-March pp. 6-26.

6

Strengthening Co-operative Institutions Through Corporate Governance

P.A. Koli

India is a large country with divers social, economic, cultural and geographical conditions. It has a federal structure of government with a Union Government and 28 states. Many strategic departments such as defense, finance, foreign trade, etc. have been managed by the both government. Co-operation is such a subject, which is in the jurisdiction of state government. The co-operative laws, the co-oprative structure and the co-operative development vary from state to state. The states have their own co-operative laws. The objectives of such laws are the same i.e. to surve the interest of the members and the public.

Basic Elements of Good Governance of Co-operative Institutions

The performance of the co-operative institutions is influenced by the external as well as the internal factors. The internal factors consists of the board of directors, chairman and the chief executive officer; while the external factors would constitute the co-operative acts, rules and governments resolutions issued by the state government co-operative department. Under this circumstance, it is excepted that the co-operatives should be provided autonomy in their functioning and need to be recognised as member owned, member driven, self reliant, democratic institutions and above all economic enterprises.

Cardinal Principle of Co-operative Governance

The cardinal principles of co-operative governance should be in line with the basic principles of co-operation propounded by the International Co-operative Alliance (ICA) which are universally accepted for the last more that 160 years. The legal framework in the form of co-operative legislation and co-operative policies are based on the basic principles of co-operation.

In Indian context, the existing co-operative legislation and the government policies require a review for making it more member oriented, member driven, member friendly and business oriented. In the present practice, only few efforts have been made. The system of governance in the co-operatives including the size and composition of Board of Directors need to be driven by the purpose and objective of the business. The right board of directors is the one that can best help to deliver the benefits to the members who are at the root of the organisation. The overall system for the direction and management of the organisation, should encompass all the aspects for formulation and execution of the business policy constituting the internal governance of a co-operative.

Indicators of Good Governance In Co-operatives

Some of the well known indicators of good governance in co-operatives would be;

1. Awareness of leaders and members about the principles of co-operation.
2. Awareness about philosophy of co-operation.
3. Honesty of leaders towards the objectives of organisaion.
4. Difference between co-operative and private enterprise.
5. Conscious of Board members about their duties and responsibilities.
6. Extent of delegation of powers to chief executives.
7. Smoothness in communication channels between board members and chief executive.

8. Accountability of the elected representative and professional managers.
9. Level of transparency in decision making process.

The Need For The Corporate Governance In Co-operative Institutions

The principles of corporate governance are not alien to co-operative organisations, rather they are innate to co-operative culture. The concept of corporate governance came into existence since the emergence of joint stock companies. Such companies are formed on Limited Liability and hence they attract the share holders and investors. In such companies there is difference between the share holders (investors). The decision making process is prompt and they are in the interest of a company. No individual and political interference is allowed.

The recent crisis of Madhavpura co-operative and some investment scamp in District Central Co-operative Banks has given rise to the concept of corporate governance.

Corprate Governance : The Practical Aspect

While practising the corporate governance certain principles, organisation will have to be considered such as ;

1. Fixed objectives and set of corporate values.
2. Avoiding conflicts in board of directors.
3. Safeguarding the interest of share holders and stake holders.
4. Protecting the interest of employees.

Similarities and Differences Between Corporate and Co-operative Organisations

The following points will clarify the points of similarities and difference between corporate and co-operative organisations.

CORPORATE	CO-OPERATIVE
Similiarity	
1. Share holders	1. Share holders
2. Outsider Depositor Investors	2. Outsider Depositors
3. Interest is paid	3. Interest is paid
4. No voting rights to depositors	4. No voting right to depositors

Differences

1.	Share are sold in Open Market	1.	No share are sold in Open Market
2.	Chance of knowledgeable Directors.	2.	Lack of knowledgeable Directors
3.	Professional Directors	3.	Less chance of Professional Directors
4.	No Direct Government Relations	4.	Direct Goverment Relation. Many a time Govt. nominee.
5.	No chance for polities	5.	Politics is mixed at every level
6.	Non-dependance on Governance On Governance grants	6.	Dependance of Government grants
7.	Share holders and stake holders keep constant watch on company	7.	Absence of watch by share holders on working of co-operatives.
8.	Flexible Rules and Bye-Laws	8.	Rigid Rules and bye-laws
9.	Fulfillment of Private Goals	9.	Fulfillment of members Goals
10.	Immediate absorbation of new changes	10.	Delay in absorbation
11.	No set values and Principles	11.	Set values and principles
12.	Dynamic in character	12.	Static in character
13.	Professional and Trained management	13.	Lack of professional management

Considering the above plus points available in corporate governance, the co-operatives should also accept the corporate governance keeping their 'one member one vote' principle and accepting the good things of corporate Governance. However, the corporate coverance is possible only at secondary and higher level institutions. The corporate governance is possible only in a big co-operatives such as sugar, spinning, fertilisers, milk unions, urban banks, DCC Banks, Marketing, etc. The is also possible in multi-state co-operatives as well as whose area of operation is more than District level.

Conditions of Corporate Governance

If above corporate aspects wants to be achieved ; the following thing are necessary in the co-operative organisations.

1. Competent and independent Board of Directors.

2. The Board members should be well qualified and having enough knowledge about the concerned work done by their co-operatives.
3. They should not be under any political influence.
4. Board member must be accountable to the profit and loss.
5. The share holders and stake-holders should get sufficient information about the institutions.
6. Scheme of redressal of the grievances.
7. Relevant sub committees to oversee the critical areas of institution.
8. Transparent and fair relationship with customers.
9. Effective system for internal central and vigilance.
10. Inclusion of directors having professional background.
11. The code of conduct prescribing Do's an Don's for Directors.
12. Provision of remuneration to active Board of Directors.
13. Optimum use of Resources.
14. Right man for the Right job.
15. Qualify product and service image among the public.
16. Streamlining decision making process.
17. Continuous research and development.

Thus, the corporate management aims at optimum utilisation of resources, highest returns on capital and indirect and direct participation of share holders.

Conclusion

There are seven principles of co-operation popularly known as Co-operative Rainbow. The reference to the co-operative principles is very significant form the context of corporate governance. If the values and principles of co-operatives and that of corporate governance are crystallized, one can find a common genesis and nucleus. Perhaps, terminology may be different but the basic thought is the same. Unlike in corporate sector, the member of a co-operative organisation has only vote irrespective of his shareholding.

These regulatory provision differentiate co-operatives from corporate sector. Since, 1991, co-operatives are at crossroads, and there is hot discussion on what co-operatives should do to face the liberalized economy? The answer is acceptance of corporate governance keeping the values and principles of co-operatives safe.

REFERENCES

Kamesam V., Co-operative Banks in India : Strengthening Through Corporate Governance. Urban Credit, September, 2002 NAFCUB, New Delhi.

Pandit S., Corporate Governance : Relevance and need for Urban Co-operative Banks. Urban Credit, March, 2002, New Delhi.

Taori V., Strengthening Urban Co-operative Banks Through Corporate Governance, Urban Credit. June, 2002.

Bhoria K., Co-operative Governance with Particular Reference to India. Urban Credit December, 2002, New Delhi.

7

The Challenges Before Indian Co-operatives With Special References to Co-operative Banks

D. Joel Edwinraj

"Without character there is no co-operation" - *Gandhiji*

Introduction

The concept of co-operation is not of recent origin. It began with Adam and Eve. The word *"co-operation"* was derived from the Latin word *'Cooperare'* which means *'working together for a common cause'*. The co-operative movement is the movement for the people, by the people and of the people. The co-operation is the channel through which progress and prosperity of the people can be enhanced. *The birth of co-operative movement in India was in 1904. A century had compled now.* But the growth of co-operative movement in India still unequal. The co-operative movement in India is largest in the world. In 2002, there were 5,45,354 lakhs co-operatives functioning at all levels, 236.226 Million of membership with share capital of Rs.1,98.542.50 million, covering 100 per cent villages and 75 per cent rural house holds with the deposit of Rs.17,75,211.30 million.The co-operatives have now emerged as a vital segment of the economy in our country.

The co-operative banking sector in India has recorded a fast growth since All India Rural Credit Survey Committee Report

1954. The institutional rural credit system has been envisaged as an effective channel for creating an environment for socio-economic development in the society. The institutional rural credit system for agriculture comprises of short-term and long-term co-operative institutions, Commercial Banks, Regional Rural Banks, National Bank for Agriculture and Rural Development Bank (NABARD), and Reserve Bank of India. The institutional credit system for urban areas comprises of Commercial Banks, Urban Co-operative Banks and Urban Co-operative Credit Societies.

This paper is an attempt to identifying the challenges, issues, and major tasks ahead in the co-operatives and co-operative banks.

New Economic Policy

The new economic policy is concerned with the restructuring of the Indian economy. Co-operation is an important sector of the Indian economy and yet it finds no place in the new economic policy. The new economic policy that has now been introduced seeks to move the economy in a different direction. The key note of the new economic policy is ushering in a competitive economy. It is against any special support to any sector because such a support breeds inefficiency in the economy. It is only the competitive economy without any state interference and control which could ensure a rational allocation of resources based on the calculation of cost, prices and profits. The co-operatives will now, therefore, have to all in line with logic of the competitive economy which it is the objectives of the new economic policy introduced in 1991, popularly known as *Liberalisation, Privatisation* and *Globalisation* (i.e.*LPG regime*). LPG with the primary goal of *"growth maximization"* have almost become a universal economic phenomenon.

Liberalisation & Co-operatives

The era of liberalistic trend started with the recommendation of Arthanareeswaran Committee, which called for policy initiatives for professionalization and democratization of the co-operative system and the subsequent recommendation of Brahm Prakash Committee to adopt a liberalized model co-operative societies Act 1991, throughout the country. The challenge of liberalization in the co-operatives coincided with the New Economic Policy initiated in 1991. Popularly known as LPG regime. Deregulation of industrial licencing, liberalization of trade and removable of trade business are the core components of the policy backage implemented since 1991. The co-operative sector has to gear itself to face the economic reform competitive environment in July 1991.

The co-operative system has to build up it professional competence, strengthen its resource base and develop innovative technologies to improve the functioning in various segment of the co-operative sector. This system has to lay emphasis on cost effectiveness in operation and ensuring return from investment made in various economic activities. The policy of 9th Five Year Plan quoted that co-operatives shall be encouraged to grow as self-reliant gross-root economic institutions, to inculcate the habit of thrift and self-help among viable groups to meet effectively the local credit and development needs.

Globalisation and Co-operatives

Globalisation has resulted in increased competition in every sphere of economic activity. Co-operatives is no exception to this matter. The biggest challenge before co-operatives all over the world is to "both survive and thrive" in an era of economic reforms. New investment opportunities are being created. Old business models are under pressure. Increasingly, the goods and services produced by co-operatives have to complete with those coming from other sector. Inputs of science and technology and information technology have to be used to the fullest to boost productivity in the co-operatives. One of the major steps will be to delink these from state control and regulations. In the light of the liberalization process initiated in the country, it is necessary that the co-operatives be delinked from the state control and allowed to function freely based on their professional.

Due to the regulations by the state government in their operations, professional approach to the business activities has been given the go-by many and in the process, they have ceased to be cost and quality conscious in their operations. They also need to diversity into new related product and markets. In order to complete successfully with the private sector the co-operatives have to function as business units and have to be conscious of cost and quality. The success of co-operatives in other countries could be traced to the "value addition". The co-operatives has a crucial role to play in investing in activities that facilitated value addition.

Co-operative Commitments in 21st Century

Co-operative should always be evolving in the future, existing co-operatives will have to change if they are to respond effectively to such problems as the population explosion, the increasing power of the multinational corporations, the crises confronting communities, the problems of environmental degradation and the challenges of adding new constituencies. The most obvious commitment is to sustain and support the co-operative way to doing business. This is not easy because of the strength of the private enterprise model by the media, education, institutions and governments, but it is possible and necessary Co-operators must project a clear picture of what their organizations stand for, how they are operated, and why they are necessary. That picture should be clear in the training given, all those associated with co-operatives, in the advertising co-operative use, in their relations with governments, and their daily activities. Co-operatives will also have to pay much more attention to the legislative frame works within which they function. There will also have to be more effective coalitions among co-operatives than in the past. The possibilities are difficult to over estimate for that to occur, though co-operators will have to consider how second, third and fourth tier organizations are structured.

Ways have to be found to create large concentrations of power that will permit co-operatives to influence significantly the ways in which the international economy is developing. The basis of that power is in local communities, but if full potential can only be realized in the international market place. The future for the international movement, like the past rests in meeting needs. The needs are the simple ones, food, work, saving, borrowing, housing, health, communications and recreation. It is within these specific areas that the future lies its to those areas co-operators must turn if their organizations existing or yet to be born are to fulfill their potential. The *ICA President Mr.Roberto Rodrigues* pointed out, "the time has passed when co-operatives were a third way for socio-economic growth, occupying to space between capitalism and socialism, we have now entered a different era". According to him the co-operatives have to face the common phenomena of LPG (i.e., Liberalisation, Privatisation, Globalisation) deregulation and Multi-National Corporations.

Challenges

The co-operative organization in our country has developed and spread its activities and functions in all spheres of economy like agriculture, poultry, dairy, fisheries, handlooms, banking, sugar, spinning, consumer co-operatives and what not?. That is why this sector has emerged as an important and vital sector of our economy. we have seen that the co-operative have 236.226 million members embracing 100 percent of villages and 75 per cent of household in its fold in the country. But the liberalisation of Indian economy ever since 1991 has brought out drastic structural changes in all sphares of the economy. Global competition creates lot of changes in the strategies of various sectors to improve their competitive spirit and performance. The scope for Indian business sector was widened and opened up to the world market. The Central Government has withdrawn its protective support to the various sectors and they have stand on their own capital base and performance. Hereafter our business sectors should depend upon their own performance rather than depending on government support.

Moreover the government of India is slowly withdrawing its subsidized financial assistance to co-operatives which have to live on their own financial resources and so they are compelled to think in terms of long run stability in the market. So it is clear that co-operatives can exist in the competitive business world only if they are efficient or otherwise they have to quit from the business scene.

How to Face These Challenges?

The co-operatives, in order to face these challenges, should reconstruct their business strategies to function efficiently and to improve their overall profitability.

1. They should develop cost consciousness and reduce the cost of their production at all levels.

2. They should minimize the wastage to ensure maximum efficiency in their operations.
3. They have to develop their own technology in order to compete in global market. In this context, it is essential to adopt the latest technology to improve their efficiency.
4. They can survive in the competitive business world, only if they transact their business activities on more scientific lines.

In order to meet out the withdrawal of government protective support system, they have to search for various alternatives for stabilizing their activities. Then only they can shine as successful organizations. Nothing can come in their way, so co-operative should work very hard. Surely they can survive in the competitive global market out of their own efficiency and performance. The government also expects that the co-operatives should be explosive to the global competitions which can be withstood and stabilized by the co-operatives in a suitable manner.

Historical Perspective of Co-operative Banks

The co-operative credit structure consist of two wings namely short-term and long-term. The short-term credit structure deals with medium-term credit also for agricultural purposes and it is federal in character. It is mostly based on a three tier pattern with State Co-operative Bank at the apex level, District / Central Co-operative Bank at the intermediate level and Primary Agricultural Co-operative Bank at the village level.

The co-operative credit system emerged as the premier institutional agency in the country for provision of agricultural credit. The co-operative credit structure has come a long way since the first Primary Co-operative Credit Society was set up in 1904. At the end of 1980s, there were nearly 92000 Primary Agricultural Credit Societies, 350 District Central Co-operative Banks and 30 State Co-operative Banks supplying short-term and medium-term credit. The long-term credit structure consist of National Co-operative Agriculture and Rural Development Bank's Federation, 19 State Agricultural and Rural Development Banks and 768 Primary Agricultural Rural Development Banks with 754 branches and 1602 sub-branches supply long-term credit. These banks have over the years played a very significant role in making institutional credit.

The credit structure of co-operative banks, namely Production Credit, Investment Credit and Urban Credit given below :

Credit Structure of Co-operative Banks

Agricultural Credit Co-operatives
(Production Credit)

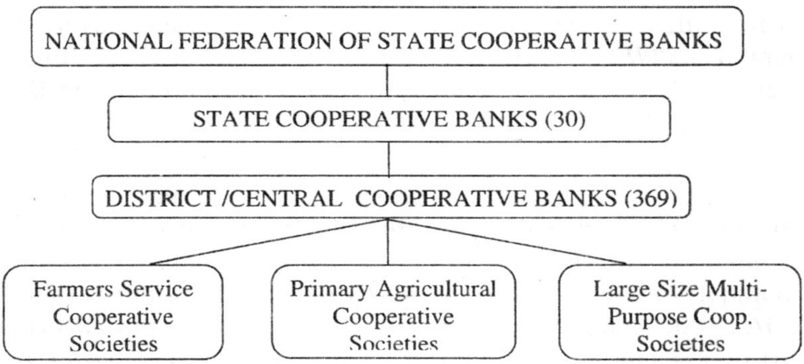

Agricultural Credit Co-operatives
(Investment Credit)

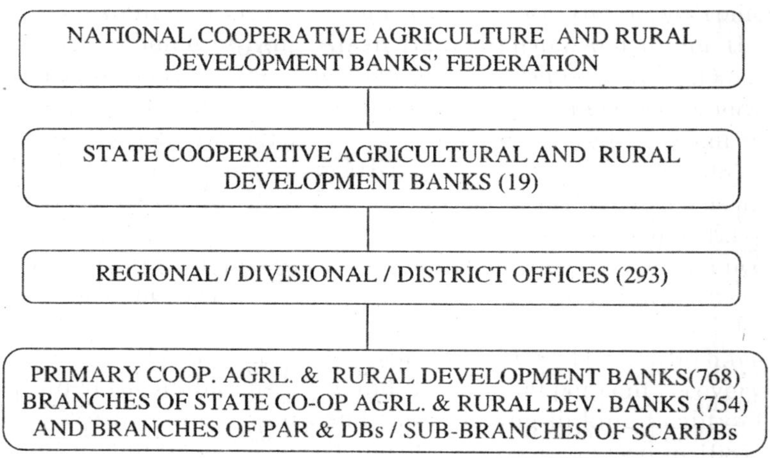

Agricultural Credit Co-operatives
(Urban Credit Co-operatives)

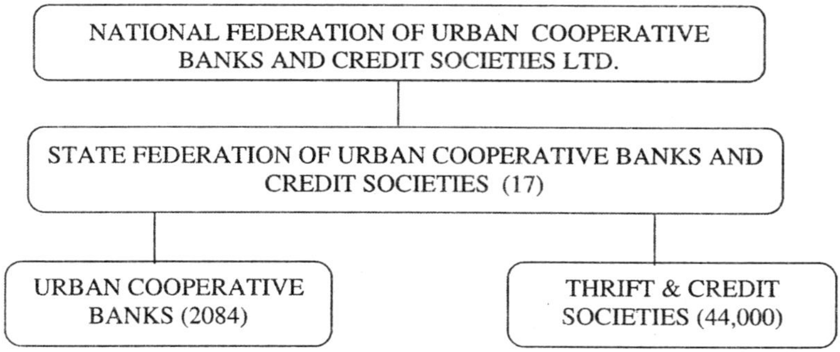

Major Thrusts–Challenges Facing the Co-operative Banks

The main thrust of the new economic policy so far as it concerns the financial sector aims at the opening up of the sector for both domestic and global competition. The major policy concerns which the reforms in the financial sector therefore boil down to deregulation and globalisation and to this end, dismantling all barriers to free operation of the financial system whether it is in the matter of opening of new banks / branches of existing banks. The freedom also empowers the banks to close down uneconomic branches even though they might have been opened earlier. With the special intention of taking the banking services of unbanked areas to serve those sections of the community which had been by-passed by the banking system.

The second thrust is at ensuring that there is adequate operational flexibility and functional autonomy for the banks. The financial sector reforms committee has observed, the approach to the issues of financial sector reforms is to ensure that the financial services operate in a manner that their operations lead to efficient productivity and profitability. The committee had felt that a vibrant and competitive financial system was an essential condition to sustain the reform process in the structural aspects of the real economy. The financial sector reforms impacts on the co-operative banking system in diverse ways. Co-operative banking had, as always been recognized as an integral part of the banking and credit system in the country.

The Reserve Bank of India was being constituted the statute not only provided for the inclusion of a few co-operative banks in the second schedule to the Act, but also placed it on par with the commercial banks for purposes of refinance from the RBI, with the additional provision for extending such refinance on preferential terms to the State Co-operative Banks. The RBI act laid a special obligation on the RBI to promote the co-operative credit and banking system and nurture it so that they developed into financially sound and managerially healthy credit institutions. The achievement of the co-operative banking system has on all reckoning, been significant. The progress registered by the co-operative banking system since then has been phenomenal particularly because of the technological revolution in agriculture transforming it into a commercially viable enterprise, the emerging needs for larger and larger volume of credit. The All India Rural Credit Review Committee (1969) felt that the ever expanding credit requirements, in the new context of the need for a high level of credit, the efforts of the co-operatives had to be supplemented and therefore recommended a role for the commercial banks to supplement the efforts of the co-operative banks. The role of the co-operative credit structure has therefore to be viewed in the above context. The position taken by the Financial Sector Reforms Committee to reckon out the co-operative banks from the purview of the reforms process has become a great challenge to the future growth of the co-operative credit structure.

Future Task

A major corrective measure has therefore to be overhandling of the legislative framework in which the co-operative banks function. The co-operative legislation was, to begin with aimed at facilitating the registration, winding up and related matters so as to protect the system against abuse by unsocial elements. The generous financial assistance provided to the co-operative banks by the Government, the scope of legislation has progressively expanded to enable the Government to take absolute control over the self-government, self-managed co-operative system although the Rural Credit Survey Committee which had recommended state participation to impart financial and managerial strength to the co-operative banks had specifically cautioned that it was not intended that the state participation should dilute in any matter either the self-Government or the member-ownership in the co-operatives.

Co-operative banks could be expected to play its role effectively and the Financial Sector Reforms would be meaningful only if the arbitary powers vested in the Registrar and Government in matters relating to the management and operations of the co-operatives are taken away through appropriate amendments to the co-operative societies Act in different states.

Conclusion

Co-operatives have contributed to the progress of Indian economy in multi-various ways. It is the time the co-operatives shall do some introspection and develop new co-operative approaches and new strategies to reposition themselves in the new emerging scenario in the 21st century. The Government of India still recognize the role of co-operatives in the economic development of our country with social justice. They encourage the co-operative organizations to enter into the fields of floriculture, horticulture and agro based industries. The introduction of insurance reform, the co-operatives will enter into the business of insurance also. The co-operatives can find good revenue generation sources for their business. The policy of liberlisation of economy is against government support. This means, withdrawal of financial help and other protective support, government should relax its rules and regulations in the case of co-operatives for some time, because without government support, co-operatives cannot function well at the movement. In order to meet the challenges, our co-operatives should restructure their business policy and strategies. Similarly in order to face the competition both from private multi-national companies, co-operative organizations should reframe their business activities in terms of buying and selling policies, personnel, technology, the organization structure, involvement of members, the efficiency of the organization. The officials and other persons who are working in the various co-operative organizations should manage the co-operatives efficiently so that they can meet out the problems arising out of competition prevailing in the global business, otherwise the co-operators and the employees in the co-operative will be out of co-operative movement. Pandit Jawaharlal Nehru Said that, "The history of Co-operative movement in India shows that, wherever the movement is strong, it is due the selfless work of dedicated individuals who have steadily resisted the temptation of politics. They have regarded co-operation as an alternative form of serving the people."

The co-operative banking sector would have to strengthen its foundations, keep it self up-to-date in schemes and services as also effective and efficient at the operational levels. Dynamics of economic scenario in India, as a consequence of new economic policy. Leading to privatization and globalisation and on going technological changes in agricultural development, would now throw open several complex policy options in the 21st Century. In the 21st century New Co-operative Movement must think of new strategies and co-operative approaches.

REFERENCES

Bandyopandhyay, A.K and Jayaraman, B, "Globalisation – WTO; Role of Co-operatives Sector", Land Bank Journal-Sept, 2001.

Kamaluddin Ahmed, "Co-operation in Liberalised Economy and Role of Fertilizers Co-operation in New Millenium", The Cooperator, Vol.40, No.7, January, 2003.

Michael Cradanell, "Co-operation in the Context of Globalisation and Liberalisation", FAO Co-operative Consultant, March, 1996.

Kulandaisamy, V, "Strategy for Sustainable Development of Co-operative Movement", The Cooperator, Vol.XXXIX, No.10, April, 2002.

Dr.Frank Ratnakumar, V. Dr.Savarimuthu, A. and Dr.Ravichandran, K., "A New World Through Co-operatives", Rainbow Publications, Coimbatore, 2003.

Indian Co-operative Movement – A Profile 2002, Developed by National Resource Centre of National Co-operative Union of India (NCUI), 2002.

Annual Report of NABARD 2002-2003.

Encyclopaedia of Co-operative Management, Vol.No.1, B.S.Bhatia

The Cooperator, Vol.XXXIX, No.7, January, 2002.

The Cooperator, Vol. XXIV, No. 5, October, 2001.

Sahakrita Samshodhan, Vol. XIII, No. 1 & 2, Jan-June & July-Dec.,1999.

Sahakrita Samshodhan, Vol. XV No. 1 & 2, Jan-June & July-Dec., 2001.

Tamilnadu Journal of Co-operation, Vol.2, No. 11, Sept., 2002.

Co-operative Perspective, Vol. 37, No.2, July-Sept., 2002.

Co-operative Perspective, Vol. 36, No.4, Jan-March, 2001.

8

New Economic Policy and Co-operative Movement in India

Sangram Chavhan

Introduction

Co-operation is a real way of life. Co-operation is a true democratic process. It imbibes human values. Co-operation not only unites people physically but also integrates good qualities of human life. Co-operation is a lamp, which shows us a path in today's changing socioeconomic scenario. It is the only solution to the problem of disintegration of classes which is the outcome of today's market economy, which is purely based on the principle of exclusion. In the process of Globalization co-operation is the only helping hand for the people which otherwise will be thrown out of the development process. Co-operation will strengthen the downtrodden classes and the weaker sections of the society to stand firmly in this changing scenario. Present research paper tries to highlight the opportunities and threats of new economic policy for the co-operative movement in India.

Year 2004 is the centenary year of the Co-operative Societies Act. As we know the first co-operative Act was in existence in the year 1904. In India co-operation has played a significant role in shaping our economy. Especially it is the co-operative movement, which leads in the transformation of rural economy in to a fast developing sustainable economy. Socialistic pattern of society and capitalistic growth both are achieved simultaneously in India up to a large extent, only because of the co-operative movement and powerful co-operative leadership which we had in the past freedom struggle. Co-operative movement provides socioeconomic freedom to poor people and weaker sections of the society. I do not agree with the argument which some of the experts are making that co-operation has failed in India. Moreover I would say co-operation has shown us our weaknesses. Some of the problems which co-operative movement is facing today is not because of its own weaknesses but because of human mistakes, vested interests, individualistic attitude which are rising in the co-operative movement today. But we must bear in mind that co-operation is the only alternative for sustainable development.

If we have to evaluate 100 years of the co-operative movement in India, we have to classify co-operative movement in the following three stages :

1. Co-operative movement before independence (1904 to 1947).
2. Co-operative movement after independence (1947 to 1991).
3. Co-operative movement after 1991.

Co-operative Movement Before Independence

Before independence co-operative movement works as an instrument in achieving the goal of planned economic growth towards welfare state. Co-operative movement tries to strengthen the weaker sections of the society. Co-operative movement has played vital role in rural development process. It works with a mission to reduce socioeconomic inequality. It works for decentralization of socioeconomic and political power. In this period co-operative movement can be viewed as a true freedom movement which tries to provide freedom in true sense.

Co-operative Movement After Independence

Co-operative movement after independence has gained central place in the process of economic development. However it is controlled and regulated by the political power. It was found to be in the hands of bureaucrats. If we critically examine the co-operative movement after independence we found only the quantitative growth in co-operative institutions. The real purpose of co-operative movement is not found to be achieved as per the expectations. The important reason for this is the rigorous control and regulations by the government which retards the freedom of the co-operative movement. Government's intervention in the co-operative movement itself becomes hurdle in the development of co-operative movement in India. Co-operative movement has been exposed to the challenges of free capitalistic economy. Co-operative movement was found to be in the hands of few *gharanas,* landlords and the capitalists.

Co-operative Movement After 1991

After 1991 we have adopted Structural Adjustment Program in which we have already sacrificed the concept of welfare state. This is the major setback to the co-operative movement in India. It seems that co-operative movement is in its last stage. Many people are arguing that co-operation has failed in India. But it was not true. Co-operation has not failed it is the co-operators which have failed. Many of the co-operative leaders, thinkers, scholars have tried to show the real path to the co-operative movement. They have recommended several important suggestions to revive the co-operative movement but government is not giving due consideration to those important recommendations. There is a need to reformulate co-operative structure and co-operative legislation. The Structural Adjustment Program which is primarily based on the three principles, liberalization privatization and globalization has no doubt initiated rapid economic growth but one can not deny the fact that it has not benefited all the people. The industrialists, capitalists, rich landlords, big traders, investors are enjoying fruits of new economic policy at the cost of the weaker section of the society such as workers, agricultural labourer, craftsmen, common service men etc. Process of liberalization opens market for the foreign investors in different sectors, it creates competitiveness in our economy which leads to rise of competitive strength of few Indian industries but on the other side it paralyze larger part of the industrial sector especially small and cottage industries in India. Rural industries are getting major setback by this liberalization process. Our public sector, which was working with the missionary zeal is almost destroyed today. India being signatory to GATT in the year 1994, the agriculture sector too will be increasingly called upon to face the global competition without the protection of high tariff barriers, quota restrictions and large government subsidies. Co-operatives, most of which are in agriculture sector have therefore to face big challenge in future. I hope co-operative movement is having the strength to accept this challenge. Therefore co-operation must succeed. If the economy is liberalized for the globalization the co-operative sector should also be liberalized for global co-operation. Our co-operative movement should be linked with the world co-operative movement so that we could get help from the co-operative strength of the developed countries. But unfortunately this is not happening. The government's policy towards private sector and co-operative sector is totally different. The government, which is talking of liberalization, is imposing heavy restrictions on co-operative institutions because of such dual policy of the government and the negative approach co-operative institutions are struggling for their existence. Since last 35 years we have made 60 reforms in co-operative legislation and the result is co-operative sector has became more and more restricted. So there is a need to decontrol and deregulate the co-operative sector in a positive way.

Government should help the co-operatives without intervention. Government should act like those parents who provide freedom to their children but are always alert about their wellbeing. In India we have larger scope for the development of co-operative movement in different sectors. Especially in the field of agriculture sector, only the co-operative movement can provide the strength to the agriculture to sustain in the process of globalization. India is one of the leading nations in the export of sugar, fruits, flowers etc. Therefore we have to raise the production of these items on co-operative basis. This will also help to minimize the unemployment problem in the rural sector. Here the important point is to be noted that agricultural co-operative movement must be supplemented with irrigation, electricity, transport and communication facilities. Co-operative dairy, co-operative sugar factory etc. are performing well in the states like Gujrat and Maharashtra. The new economic policy also creates a major problem before the co-operative banking sector. The foreign direct investment, foreign banks, nationalized banks and non-banking financial institutions like ICICI pose a danger to the existence of co-operative banking sector. Non performing assets of co-operative banking are increasing day by day very rapidly. There exists a severe problem of over dues in co-operative banks. But if the co-operative banks adopt the modern techniques of co-operative management and try to reduce the rate of interest they can perform well in future. Co-operative banks should also try to provide several kinds of services to their customers. They should adopt new concepts of banking such as E-banking , Telebanking, Mobile banking etc. The major hurdle in the progress of co-operative banking is that the co-operative banks have to function under the control of RBI as well as the Co-operative Act of the state government. Therefore co-operative banks must be solely controlled and regulated by the RBI. Now a days services sector is emerging very rapidly. Near about 48% of our national income comes from the services sector. There is tremendous scope for the co-operative movement in this sector. Services co-operatives will prove to be helpful in achieving socioeconomic equality. Co-operatives have larger scope in the field of transport and housing sector. Co-operatives can also do their best in the field of hospitals, hotels, consumer stores etc. We can't ignore the significant achievements of co-operative movement in India. Co-operative movement in India is the greatest among the world. We are having over 5 lakhs of co-operative societies with the membership of over 20 crs. and near about 2,27,000 CRS. of Rupees as the working capital to advance both farm and non farm credit for agriculture and agro-processing industries. Co-operatives are advancing 40% of the total farm credit and are controlling 60% of sugar production, 23% of the fertilizer production, 30% of textile production, 45% of milk production etc. of our country. But unfortunately political interference and defective co-operation policies of the government is crippling the efficiency of the co-operative societies. If we have to make the benefit of new economic policy and structural changes we must emphasize on the strengthening of co-operative movement in India. The Government should therefore frame a well defined and sound national co-operative policy taking into view the changes that are taking place today in India as well as out side the India. Where there is will there is a way.

REFERENCES

Baidyanath Misra, Co-operative Movement in India (ed) A.P.H. Publishing Corporation, New Delhi, 1997.

The Maharashtra Rajya Sahakari Sangh, The Maharashtra Cooperative Quarterly, Volume LXXXXII, No. 17, Oct-Dec., 2003.

Tata Services Ltd., Statistical Outline of India, 2003-04, Mumbai.

S.G. Bhanushali, Arthic Sudharnancha Kalkhand Ani Sahakari Chhetra, Arthasanwad, Volume 25, Issue No. 1, Apr-June, 2001.

http://www.coopretiveonnet.com

9

Issues In Diversification and Expansion of Business In Co-operative Credit Institution By Restructuring The APCS Into Co-operative Village Banks

V. B. Jugale

Introduction

The significance of Primary Agricultural Co-operative Credit Societies (PACS) in the Indian rural credit market, actuate the policy makers to restructure the PACS rather than a mere reorganization for the welfare of the rural masses within the framework of Financial Sector Reforms (FSRs). PACS, since decades have endured a series of reorganisation prior to their inception. The present co-operative credit system in India is a mere credit delivery system, which is in fact blocked up in an orthodoxy of traditional functioning. Creditworthiness is the basis of loan transactions of almost all financial agencies. That is, one who proves, how loan borrowing is not required, he is granted the credit. During the decades the pattern and practice of rural economy in general and the agricultural economy in particular has undergone a sea-change with a diversification entrusted from productior fronts to that of business fronts. The horizontal linkages of the agri-business have been widened and deepened with multi-facet forward and backward linkages. This tends to restructure the co-operative credit system into the Co-operative Village Banking (Jugale, 1998) which is in fact an opportunity as well as a challenge to the existing co-operative structure. The PACS as visualised initially, are in fact the village banks, which are expected to create a habit of thrift and savings among the rural. Unfortunately they failed to enhance in this front.

The existing PACS are pitiably admired as grass without root agencies and totally contemned. They are accomplish paltry as the agents of District Central Co-operative Banks (DCCBs) mainly engaged in disbursement and recovery of the loans granted by the DCCBs. As a result rise of Self-Help Groups (SHGs) and Poverty Lending Working Groups in India are due to disregard of the co-operative agencies towards the poor people.

Restructuring The Pacs As Co-operative Village Banks

Restructuring the rural financial system has now become inevitable. Particularly restructuring of PACS is empathized to augment the functioning of the agricultural credit system and assumed to fulfil the credit needs of the rural India. The ACRC has rightly pointed out "the essence of basic feature of co-operative banking system must be a larger reliance on resource mobilised locally and lesser and lesser dependence on higher credit institutions. Heavy dependence on outside funds has, on the one hand, made the members less vigilant, not threating these funds as their own, and on the other hand led to greater outside interference and control. Overall this has made the co-operative a mediocre, inefficient and static system."

The present PACS should be restructured as Co-operative Village Banks, which will initiate in mobilising the potential savings from the rural economy. Shivaram Committee was confident enough in this endeavour of the PACS. The Committee felt that, "the PACS should immediately take steps for greater mobilisation of deposits. They should have to adopt an approach and a system that will bring confidence to the rural saver irrespective of whether he becomes the potential depositor of the PACS."

Even the historical perspective at the beginning of the co-operative movement in India has proved the required thrust of the village banking. The term village bank was first used by Nicholson in his report of 1896. Two such banks were established in the erstwhile Madras Province as indicated by him. The idea of establishing Agricultural Banks had been a much discussed subject ever since the Deccan Riots. Sir Wedderburn and Justice Ranade were the first proponents of agricultural banks, which was recommended after conducting an exhaustive survey of Purander Taluka (Pune District). H. Dupenex, after his intensive study of United Province (U.P.), recommended the People's Bank. In 1937, Ambegaonkar and Nanavati in the RBI Bulletin published a theme of "Co-operative Village Banks" which was found out as the best solution for betterment of the rural people. Same title has been reiterated by the author, as a restructured version of the PACS. CVB as suggested by the author is not for solving the problem of indebtedness, but to mobilise the savings and integration of village activities. The bank which fulfils, at once, the requirement of thrift and credit, while promoting in a high degree those qualities which are essential to high national character are the CVBs. They are not formed by the capitalists seeking investments for their funds with the hope of earning dividends thereon...." CVBs are, of the villages, for the villages, run by the villages and banking with the villages. Hence it is advocated in a restructured form.

The specific features of CVBs (Jugale, 1997) are as under:

(i) The cannons of good credit viz. adequacy, proximity, reasonable rate of interest, timely supervision of self management can be served through CVBs.

(ii) A special feature of CVBs will be to ensure mobilisation of rural savings for accelerating the economic growth in rural area. Thakurdas Committee (1950) has rightly pointed out the significance of the rural savings by stating that, "In case of similar people in rural areas, the extension of banking facilities should aim at mobilising small savings and also a part of the income likely to be generated as a result of public investment in various projects."

(iii) Lending at low rate of interest can be made possible through CVBs due to the minimum spread (Margin) of

2 to 2.50 per cent, if CVBs are mobilising their own deposits and disbursing the loans to their members. This is accessible again due to low cost of intermediation.

(iv) An integration of ST, MT and LT credit delivery can be made feasible through CVBs. If the long term deposits have been attracted by the CVBs, it is worth to disburse the long term loans to its members. Normally rural people save for a medium and long period. The Regional Seminar for Asia on Agricultural Credit for Small Farmers, Bangkok (Thailand) (Oct. 1974) has given stress on all credit needs (ST, MT and LT) be met at one place, which has been accepted as criteria for suitability and viability of credit system. Besides the credit facilities must be as near the step door as possible when needed. By integrating the ST, MT and LT loans an adjustments in the type of loans can be made at the level of CVBs for strengthening the repaying capacity.

(v) Direct refinance from the upper agencies like NABARD to CVBs can be made practicable. The middle agencies are swallowing, the margin of about 4 to 4.5 per cent and creating burden on the borrowers.

(vi) The CVBs will thus lead to met all financial needs of farm and non-farm communities in the rural area.

(vii) The repaying capacity of the borrowers can be strengthened through CVBs by increasing the equity, removing the imbalance in resource availability, adjusting the time period of loan requirements, resource planning, enhancing micro-enterprises and by creating proper market links.

(viii) Kisan Credit Cards may be issued by assessing the borrowing capacities of the farmers for consecutive three agricultural seasons.

(ix) Co-operative commonwealth can be attained by establishing vertical and horizontal links in the institutional framework.

Fredrick Nicholson, who was principal supporter of the village banks had enumerated some advantages, which may be taken up as the supportive feature of the CVBs. (i) CVBs as the absolute proximity to borrower can issue loans as and when need arises. (ii) They create local confidence and local capital. (iii) The CVBs know the borrowers and their capabilities. (iv) Supervision on loan utilisation. (v) Cheap credit can be assured through direct refinance. (vi) Profits within the villages. (vii) Agent of the member's other activities. (viii) Unity and integrity can be maintained.

However, some conditions have to be fulfilled for successful operations of the CVBs. For example - (i) Credit availability, (ii) Adjustments of credit terms, (iii) Reduction in the cost of credit, (iv) Assistance for hi-tech agriculture, (v) Whole Village within the ambit of CVBs, (vi) Include every one in the village, (vii) Adherence to co-operative principle, (viii) Sense of belongingness etc.

If the Indian rural co-operatives are not restructured as CVBs, the concept of village banking as it has entered worldwide will substitute the present PACS in India. Hence a model of PACS is required to be designed as CVBs for the development of rural co-operative credit system in India (Jugale, 2000). PACS are entrusted with only loans to land owners and not to the productive poors.

An Exercise of Restructuring : A Case of Mini Kisan Banks In Kolhapur District

The Kolhapur DCCB (Maharashtra State, India) has come up with scheme of Mini Kisan Banks earmarked under the existing structure of co-operative credit system in mid 1980s. It is justified as an innovative banking ideology of the practitioners, within the existing structure of co-operative credit system in Maharashtra. The history of MKBs goes back to the early 1980s, when the Easy Crop Loan Scheme (ECLS) was introduced as an outcome of operational experiences in the crop loan policy. Easy loan indicates the process of way out from the strict adherence to the scheme of crop loan, which had been softened in terms of length of time, process of sanction etc. for the benefit of the farmers. ECLS was applied to selected PACS (Those who have obtained the audit class of A and B) with 100 per cent recovery for corresponding 3 years and those having linking facility of credit to marketing. The scheme of ECLS was revised in 1987-

88. The Board of Directors of Kolhapur DCCB decided to offer the viable PACS to work on the banking lines. Six viable PACS were selected for implementing the scheme of MKB. Out of these only two have adopted the scheme initially. On 2nd January 1996, the scheme of MKB has been revised. At present there are 43 MKBs working in the Kolhapur District (Maharashtra).

The main features of the MKBs are as under :

1. The scheme of MKBs is applied to only viable PACS. Whose audit class remained at 'A' with 100% recovery for more than 3 years.
2. The MKBs are permitted to collect deposits and are allowed to intermediate between savers and borrowers (investors).
3. The scheme of loan disbursement other than the DCCB crop loan scheme can be designed by the MKB, but should get sanctioned from the DCCB.
4. The MKBs have to keep 30 per cent deposit liabilities with the DCCB for which the DCCB charges the rate of interest at 14.5 per cent. Remaining 70 per cent of deposits are used by the MKBs for loan disbursement to their members.
5. The rate of interest on deposits and loans is fixed by the MKBs in consultation with the DCCB.
6. The MKBs are eligible to borrow (cash credit) from the DCCB within their limit after utilization of 70 per cent deposits. Saving account is also opened up for depositing the 30 per cent deposits collected by MKBs.
7. Tallying of asset and liabilities are exercised daily.
8. MKBs are allowed to lend for other than farm activities, the essential provisions prior to this should be made in the by-laws with a scheme of loans disbursement.
9. 30 per cent deposits can be used for M.T. loans and another 40 per cent for short term loans like crop loans.
10. Each MKB has to prepare a schedule of maximum credit limit every year like that of all PACS, for prior approval of the Central Office (DCCB) and individual credit disbursement to its members after approval.

11. Operational guidelines are issued to each MKB for smooth functioning of the scheme.

The idea behind the scheme is to facilitate the farmers by quick services and to facilitate the MKBs to harness the deposits in rural area, so as to provide access of the financial support for making loan business with their members.

The MKB is empowered to constitute a five member committee to deal with the urgent matters and to disburse the loans in time. Every member is given a pass book for his observations and record. In the case of higher loan demands, the MKB can borrow from the DCCB. Exhaustive guidelines have been issued to each MKB for smooth functioning of the system. All types of bill payment e. g. sugarcane bills are routed through MKBs. Cash credit facility upto the limit of 30 percent of the deposits mobilised by the MKB is granted by the DCCB.

The PACS are normally borrowing the Cash Credit at the rate of 9 per cent from the DCCB within their limits and disbursing the crop loans to its members at the rate of 12 per cent with an addition of 3 per cent as their margin. The MKBs are intermediating the deposits and loans other than above mentioned cash credit. For deposits, on an average, they are paying 10 per cent rate of interest, while that on loans they are charging, on an average, 16 to 18 per cent. As a result, the margin of 6 to 8 per cent is retained with the MKBs. In earlier case, the PACS are getting only 3 per cent margin.

To carryout the whole work of MKBs, the Secretaries are being paid extra allowances, along with some assistants depending on the transactions, whose payments are made out of the interest margin. The cost of intermediation of the MKBs has remained less. As a result most of the MKBs are in profit.

The composition of the business consists of crop loans, hire purchase loans (consumer durables) and M.T. and L.T. loans for agricultural implements etc. Crop loan shares 40 per cent of loans and another 30 per cent business is covered by hire purchase (M.T.) and L.T. loans for agricultural implements and remaining amount of deposits are kept with the DCCB as working capital. Crop loan is the major attraction of the members. The L.T. loan borrower has used his loan amount for purchasing tractor, while hire purchase and M.T. loan is used for purchasing TV, Scooter, Cycle, minor agricultural implements and for irrigation installations, etc.

Continuation of the MKB scheme basically depends on the recovery of the loans. It is expected that, the MKB should attain at least 90 per cent of loan recovery. Timely grant of loans is possible through CVBs. On the contrary the PACS system takes much time for grant of crop loans. The quality of lending is quite good. The supervision on loan utilisation is being made by the Board members, because the MKBs are using the local deposits not the DCCB funds.

Table 1 indicate the performance of the deposit mobilisation by MKBs (28) since their nomenclature as MKBs of which 21 MKBs are operating for more than last 5 years. Remaining 15 MKBs have their recent origin, but are performing well. Short term and long term deposits have been mobilised by the MKBs. The annual growth rate of deposit mobilisation is positive with increasing trend therein. Only seven MKBs have not initiated in collecting L.T. deposits. Performance of a few MKBs is noteworthy. Growing L.T. deposits qualifies the MKB to make L.T. investment in rural activities. Moreover, this indicates the credibility of the MKBs. The scheme of MKBs is successful in mobilising rural resources.

Table 1 : Deposit Mobilisation by the MKBs

	Years	*Deposits*			*Annual growth rate*
		S. T.	*L. T.*	*Total*	
1.	**Chhatrapati, Uchgaon**				
	Upto 31/3/1999	15.36	5.70	21.07	-
2.	**Karambali**				
	1996-99 5 years	0.52	4.34	4.86	-
3.	**Nagav**				
	1988-89	-	5.12	5.12	-
	1989-90	-	5.50	5.50	7.42
	1990-91	0.07	5.62	5.69	3.45
	1991-92	0.90	6.46	7.36	29.32
	1992-93	1.05	6.84	7.90	7.33

Contd...

Table 1 : (Contd...)

	Years		*Deposits*		*Annual growth rate*
		S. T.	*L. T.*	*Total*	
	1993-94	1.30	8.39	9.69	22.65
	1994-95	2.66	9.50	12.17	25.55
	1995-96	5.98	10.72	16.70	37.22
	1996-97	8.12	13.98	22.11	32.35
	1997-98	6.08	15.39	21.48	-2.84
	1998-99	9.28	24.24	33.53	56.05
4.	**Shetkari, Shedshal**				
	1998-99	16.92	-	16.92	-
5.	**Yashwant, Rashiwade**				
	1995	0.04	0.52	0.56	-
	1996	3.26	0.57	3.83	583.52
	1997	7.00	0.67	7.67	100.26
	1998	9.73	2.22	11.95	55.80
	1999	6.32	3.95	10.27	-14.09
6.	**Amarapur, Aurwad**				
	1995	1.93	-	1.93	-
	1996	5.76	-	5.76	198.44
	1997	9.19	-	9.19	54.55
	1998	14.58	-	14.58	58.65
	1999	15.67	-	15.67	7.47
7.	**Laxmi, Gadhinglaj**				
	1997	4.79	1.66	6.45	-
	1998	7.43	1.09	8.52	32.09
	1999	13.84	1.02	14.97	75.70
8.	**Dinbandhu, Shedshal**				
	1994-95	1.22	0.19	1.41	-
	1995-96	1.86	1.69	3.55	151.77
	1996-97	3.31	1.13	4.44	25.07
	1997-98	5.14	1.80	6.94	56.30
	1998-99	5.90	2.38	8.28	19.30
9.	**Bharat, Ghalwad**				
	1995-96	6.22	-	6.22	-
	1996-97	6.10	-	6.10	-1.92
	1997-98	7.83	-	7.83	28.36
	1998-99	14.67	-	14.67	87.35

Contd...

Table 1 : (Contd...)

Years	Deposits			Annual growth rate
	S. T.	L. T.	Total	
10. Shriram, Waghapur				
1997	0.07	0.10	0.18	-
1998	0.22	0.10	0.32	77.77
1999	0.10	2.21	2.32	625.0
11 Kedarling, Chuye				
1997-98	-	3.35	3.35	-
1998-99	-	4.48	4.48	11.24
12. Abdullat				
1995-96	7.81	-	7.81	-
1996-97	10.54	1.12	11.66	49.29
1997-98	12.74	3.12	15.86	36.02
1998-99	24.54	2.17	26.71	68.41
13. Jaybharat, Kanwad				
1996	3.70	0.02	3.72	-
1997	3.64	0.47	4.11	10.48
1998	5.77	0.40	6.17	50.12
1999	5.37	0.57	5.94	-3.72
14. Laxmi, Basarge				
1994	-	-	-	-
1997	11.10	1.55	12.65	-
1999	17.52	1.67	19.20	51.77
15. Udgaon				
1993-94	23.36	0.13	23.49	-
1994-95	31.47	0.12	31.59	34.48
1995-96	38.42	0.73	39.15	23.93
1996-97	25.93	1.57	54.50	39.28
1997-98	58.34	2.99	61.33	12.53
1998-99	71.19	4.88	76.07	24.03
16. Janaseva, Padali Khurd				
1995-96	1.62	-	1.62	-
1996-97	1.85	0.10	1.95	20.37
1997-98	4.52	1.89	6.41	228.71
1998-99	6.02	3.38	9.41	46.88
17. Turkewadi				
1998-99	3.52	2.14	5.66	-

Contd...

Table 1 : (Contd...)

Years	Deposits			Annual growth rate
	S. T.	L. T.	Total	
18. Shahu Chhatrapati, Sabalewadi				
1991	1.47	3.96	5.44	-
1992	0.75	4.39	5.14	-5.51
1993	0.60	4.24	4.85	-5.64
1994	0.79	3.72	4.52	-6.80
1995	0.87	3.23	4.11	-9.07
1996	1.47	3.58	4.96	20.68
1997	3.11	3.90	7.02	41.53
1998	4.54	4.36	8.90	26.78
1999	6.39	4.90	11.29	26.85
19. Alas				
1994-95	1.24	0.70	1.94	-
1995-96	1.47	1.74	3.22	65.98
1996-97	9.88	2.42	12.30	281.98
1997-98	14.83	2.96	17.80	44.71
1998-99	21.49	2.59	24.08	35.28
20. Balbhim, Khupire				
1997-98	2.75	0.15	2.90	-
1998-99	3.15	2.90	6.05	108.82
21. Mahalaxmi, Kasaba Sangav				
1995-96	2.29	0.24	2.53	-
1996-97	10.45	1.65	12.11	378.55
1997-98	12.73	4.37	17.10	41.28
1998-99	14.30	9.24	23.55	37.72
22. Amroli				
1995	-	-	-	-
1997	2.12	-	2.12	-
1998	4.45	-	4.45	109.50
1999	6.84	-	6.84	53.78
23. Naganwadi				
1995	0.02	-	0.02	-
1997	1.58	-	1.58	78.00
1998	2.48	-	2.48	0.56
1999	3.91	1.90	5.81	1.34

Contd...

Table 1 : (Contd...)

	Years	*Deposits*			*Annual growth rate*
		S. T.	*L. T.*	*Total*	
24.	**Balbhim, Kasaba Nul**				
	1996	0.22	-	0.22	-
	1997	7.35	-	7.35	32.40
	1998	9.56	-	9.56	0.30
	1999	16.74	-	16.74	0.75
25.	**Datta, Khupire**				
	1995-96	16.69	-	16.69	-
	1996-97	31.45	1.20	32.66	0.95
	1997-98	39.98	4.79	44.78	0.37
	1998-99	57.18	6.78	63.96	0.42
	Total	145.31	12.79	158.10	1.74
26.	**Janaseva, Danoli**				
	1995-96	2.22	-	2.22	-
	1996-97	6.52	-	6.52	1.93
	1997-98	6.60	-	6.60	0.01
	1998-99	11.83	-	11.83	0.79
27.	**Mahaveer, Chokak**				
	31/3/1996	5.12	1.73	6.86	-
	31/3/1997	12.11	4.00	16.12	1.34
	31/3/1998	10.70	7.71	18.42	0.14
	31/3/1999	14.11	10.89	25.00	0.35
	31/6/1999	20.44	10.46	31.91	0.27
28.	**Hirwade Khalasa**				
	1995-96	-	-	-	-
	1996-97	0.36	-	0.36	-
	1997-98	0.22	0.42	0.64	0.77
	1998-99	0.11	0.47	0.58	-0.09
29.	**Ramling, Hebbal, Kasaba Nul**				
	31/3/1996	0.88	-	0.88	-
	31/3/1997	17.51	0.74	18.25	19.73
	31/3/1998	11.64	0.79	12.43	-0.31
	31/3/1999	17.59	1.25	18.85	0.51
30.	**Sarvodaya, Hasur**				
	1995-96	3.08	-	3.08	-
	1996-97	1.99	-	1.99	-0.35
	1997-98	1.65	-	1.65	-0.17
	1998-99	2.30	-	2.30	3.09

Contd...

Table 1 : (Contd...)

Years	Deposits			Annual growth rate
	S. T.	L. T.	Total	
31. Kothali				
1993-94	11.53	-	11.53	-
1994-95	20.12	-	20.12	0.74
1995-96	17.40	0.46	17.86	-0.11
1996-97	37.88	1.45	39.33	1.20
1997-98	36.65	1.52	38.18	-0.02
1998-99	49.35	1.63	50.99	0.33
32. Krishi Sadhana, Kurundwad				
1993-94	10.68	-	10.68	-
1994-95	9.04	0.66	9.70	-9.17
1995-96	6.06	3.53	9.59	-1.13
1996-97	7.38	4.84	12.22	27.42

Table 2 accounts for the performance of the Cash Credit of the MKBs from DCCB. The PACS are very much known for their borrowing from DCCBs. The scheme of MKBs has reduced the borrowings from DCCB. As a result the MKBs are using 6 to 8 per cent margin for their development. Micro finances by the MKBs for Micro enterprises have been developed in the respective rural areas. MKBs are making four types of loan business, (a) Crop loan, (b) Cash Credit (Hire Purchase), (c) M. T. loans and (d) L. T. loans. Crop loan is a regular PACS activity governed by the DCCB. Cash Credit is given under the direction of DCCB for purchase of household consumer durables like TVs and Motorcycles etc. L. T. loans are also given to the villagers (as a special case) for purchase of tractors and other agricultural equipments. The MKBs are free to make their bye-laws regarding the loan disbursement to agricultural activities in their respective village areas duly approved by the DCCB.

It is further observed that, the annual growth rate of borrowings from DCCB in most cases is negative. Crop loan shares major portion of loan disbursement. The trend of borrowing for M.T. and L.T. loans has also declined. This is what the CVBs are expected to do.

Table 2 : Loan Borrowings of the MKBs

Years			*Loan*			*Annual Growth Rate*
	Crop loan	*Cash Credit Hire Purchase*	*M. T. Loans*	*L. T. Loans*	*Total Loans*	
1. Chhatrapati, Uchgaon						
March 1995	1.80	-	-	-	-	-
1996	2.00	-	-	-	-	-
1997	22.00	-	-	-	-	-
1998	25.00	-	-	-	-	-
March 1999	32.00	65.01	-	-	32.00	
2. Karambali						
1996-1999	16.54	18.56	23.07	19.40	42.47	-
3. Nagav						
1988-89	15.58	-	0.33	-	15.91	-
1989-90	17.26	-	-	-	17.26	8.48
1990-91	20.13	-	-	-	20.13	16.63
1991-92	21.69	-	4.40	-	26.09	29.60
1992-93	17.78	-	2.87	-	20.65	-20.29
1993-94	15.70	-	2.40	-	18.11	-12.30
1994-95	24.00	-	0.27	-	24.27	34.01
1995-96	15.94	-	-	-	15.94	-34.32
1996-97	13.22	-	-	-	13.22	-17.0
1997-98	14.56	-	-	-	14.56	10.13
1998-99	18.33	-	6.97	-	25.30	73.76
4. Shetkari, Shedshal						
1998-99	11.33	-	36.45	-	47.78	-
5. Yashwant, Rashiwade						
1995	15.00	-	8.73	-	23.73	-
1996	18.00	-	9.06	-	27.06	14.03
1997	13.17	-	6.22	-	19.39	-28.34
1998	14.94	-	5.56	-	20.50	5.72
1999	15.66	-	4.30	-	19.96	-2.63
6. Amarapur, Aurwad						
1995	22.06	-	19.75	-	41.81	-
1996	23.43	-	18.80	-	42.23	1.0
1997	18.66	-	13.71	-	32.27	-23.35
1998	15.80	-	13.17	-	28.98	-10.47
1999	29.14	-	19.93	-	49.08	69.36

Contd...

Table 2 : (Contd...)

Years			*Loan*			*Annual Growth Rate*
	Crop loan	*Cash Credit Hire Purchase*	*M. T. Loans*	*L. T. Loans*	*Total Loans*	
7. Laxmi, Gadhinglaj						
1997	6.86	-	3.75	-	10.62	-
1998	7.82	-	12.24	-	20.07	88.98
1999	23.09	-	16.90	-	39.99	99.25
8. Dinbandhu, Shedshal						
1994-95	2.16	-	8.22	5.66	16.04	-
1995-96	9.39	-	9.13	9.85	28.37	76.87
1996-97	7.49	-	8.88	16.69	33.06	16.53
1997-98	6.99	-	11.33	17.39	35.61	7.71
1998-99	12.07	-	13.90	14.15	40.12	12.66
9. Balbhim, Ghalwad						
1995-96	3.90	24.76	1.89	3.90	34.46	-
1996-97	20.89	-	0.89	3.15	24.94	-27.62
1997-98	14.83	-	1.54	2.14	18.52	-25.74
1998-99	11.62	-	2.35	1.49	15.48	16.41
10. Shriram, Waghapur						
1997	4.98	-	4.14	-	9.13	-
1998	4.12	-	7.63	-	11.75	28.69
1999	6.35	-	37.51	-	43.86	273.27
11. Kedarling, Chuye						
1997-98	-	20.1	0.48	-	20.49	-
1998-99	-	22.26	10.31	-	32.57	58.95
12. Abdullat						
1995-96	29.62	-	7.86	-	37.48	-
1996-97	15.86	-	15.58	-	31.44	-16.11
1997-98	19.24	-	13.63	-	32.87	4.55
1998-99	17.90	-	28.40	18.54	64.84	97.26
13. Jay Bharat, Kanwad						
1996	16.55	-	10.77	-	27.32	-
1997	15.96	-	11.16	-	27.12	-0.73
1998	13.54	-	14.29	-	27.83	2.61
1999	15.73	-	14.50	-	30.23	8.62

Contd...

Table 2 : (Contd...)

Years	*Loan*					*Annual Growth Rate*
	Crop loan	*Cash Credit Hire Purchase*	*M. T. Loans*	*L. T. Loans*	*Total Loans*	
14. Laxmi, Basarge						
1994	10.25	-	14.02	-	24.28	-
1997	8.45	-	22.13	-	30.58	25.91
1999	7.14	-	28.32	-	35.47	15.99
15. Udgaon						
1993-94	11.06	-	4.35	9.77	25.18	-
1994-95	30.80	-	4.98	13.38	49.16	95.23
1995-96	58.09	-	3.36	9.37	70.82	44.08
1996-67	38.91	-	3.12	7.51	49.54	-30.19
1997-98	57.07	-	3.05	7.49	67.61	36.47
1998-99	50.82	-	12.09	11.31	74.22	9.77
16. Janaseva, Padali Khurd						
1995-96	19.56	-	4.42	-	23.98	-
1996-97	10.45	-	4.45	-	14.91	-37.82
1997-98	12.08	-	1.81	-	13.89	-6.84
1998-99	27.18	-	6.88	-	34.07	145.28
17. Turkewadi						
1998-99	34.38	-	14.83	-	49.21	-
18. Shahu Chhatrapati, Sabalewadi						
1991	17.72	-	3.04	-	20.17	-
1992	18.65	-	4.31	-	22.96	10.51
1993	14.37	-	3.56	-	17.93	-21.98
1994	12.49	-	2.73	-	15.22	-15.11
1995	15.55	-	1.73	-	17.28	13.53
1996	15.70	-	1.51	-	17.22	-0.34
1997	12.52	-	1.95	-	14.47	-15.96
1998	13.69	-	4.81	-	18.10	25.08
1999	12.20	-	8.74	-	20.94	15.65
19. Alas						
1994-95	19.46	8.86	0.28	7.57	28.32	-
1995-96	38.86	11.61	0.19	11.42	50.28	98.21
1996-97	20.97	13.80	1.55	12.25	34.78	-30.81
1997-98	23.25	12.81	0.92	11.89	36.07	3.70
1998-99	25.12	23.41	0.41	23.00	48.54	69.51

Contd...

Table 2 : (Contd...)

Years	*Loan*					*Annual Growth Rate*
	Crop loan	*Cash Credit Hire Purchase*	*M. T. Loans*	*L. T. Loans*	*Total Loans*	
20. Balbhim, Khupire						
1997-98	12.52	-	0.50	8.81	21.84	-
1998-99	6.86	-	1.10	10.36	18.33	-16.06
21. Mahalaxmi, Kasaba Sangav						
1995-96	13.13	-	0.47	5.15	18.76	-
1996-97	16.90	-	2.54	10.93	30.39	61.99
1997-98	27.77	-	6.26	10.58	44.62	46.82
1998-99	26.70	-	3.23	14.05	43.99	-1.41
22. Amroli						
1995	23.09	-	13.61	-	36.70	-
1996	32.01	-	7.74	-	39.75	8.31
1997	27.16	-	5.65	-	32.81	-17.45
1998	35.00	-	12.92	-	47.92	46.05
23. Naganwadi						
1995	19.61	-	7.47	-	27.08	-
1996	21.08	-	8.74	-	29.82	0.10
1997	16.42	-	5.00	-	21.42	-0.28
1998	20.88	-	8.78	-	29.66	0.38
24. Balbhim, Kasaba Nul						
1996	9.27	-	5.41	-	14.69	-
1997	3.80	-	8.74	-	12.55	0.14
1998	3.93	-	6.49	-	10.42	0.16
1999	5.54	-	8.58	-	14.13	0.35
25. Datta, Khupire						
1995-96	11.92	-	3.91	3.84	19.69	-
1996-97	11.29	-	2.72	1.51	15.53	-2.21
1997-98	6.62	-	-	0.60	7.22	-0.53
1998-99	3.48	-	-	-	3.48	-0.51
26. Janaseva, Danoli						
1995-96	2.41	-	9.77	7.36	-	-
1996-97	1.65	-	3.12	1.46	-	-0.60
1997-98	4.43	-	10.33	5.90	-	2.31
1998-99	16.35	-	27.25	11.20	-	1.63

Contd...

Table 2 : (Contd...)

Years	*Loan*					*Annual Growth Rate*
	Crop loan	*Cash Credit Hire Purchase*	*M. T. Loans*	*L. T. Loans*	*Total Loans*	
27. Mahaveer, Chokak						
31/3/1996	7.11	-	1.42	-	8.54	-
31/3/1997	4.39	-	0.79	-	5.19	-0.39
31/3/1998	5.61	-	3.63	-	9.24	0.78
31/3/1999	8.46	1.70	2.67	-	12.84	0.38
31/6/1999	9.98	0.29	2.67	-	12.95	0.008
28. Hirwade Khalsa						
1995-96	22.33	-	9.65	-	31.99	-
1996-97	16.98	-	3.24	-	20.23	-0.36
1997-98	19.39	-	3.76	-	23.16	0.14
1998-99	18.15	-	5.78	-	23.93	0.03
29. Ramling, Hebbal, Kasaba Nul						
31/3/1996	6.58	-	9.01	-	15.59	-
31/3/1997	1.35	-	7.83	-	9.19	-0.41
31/3/1998	4.56	-	4.71	-	9.28	0.005
31/3/1999	3.87	-	5.39	-	9.26	-0.002
30. Sarvodyaya Hasure						
1995-96	19.60	-	3.55	-	23.15	-
1996-97	29.03	-	3.73	-	32.76	0.41
1997-98	32.24	-	3.63	-	35.87	0.09
1998-99	29.85	-	2.81	-	32.66	-0.08
31. Kothali						
1993-94	0.00353	-	2.94	-	12.36	-
1994-95	0.50	-	2.03	-	17.31	0.40
1995-96	5.21	-	6.43	-	23.54	0.35
1996-97	-	-	8.75	-	22.54	-0.04
1997-98	-	-	9.28	-	36.76	0.63
1998-99	-	-	8.83	-	30.77	-0.16
32. Krishi Sadhana, Kurundwad						
1993-94	11.51	-	13.19	-	24.70	-
1994-95	33.70	-	32.47	-	66.17	167.83
1995-96	31.17	-	27.38	-	58.55	-11.51
1996-97	48.09	-	31.44	-	79.53	35.83

It is very difficult to operate the banking activities in the given system of co-operatives. The DCCB is dominating and regulating the funds in almost all MKBs transactions. The rate of interest on S.T. loans (out of deposits) except crop loans is little varying among the MKBs. The borrowers are happy with the MKBs.

The MKBs have to carryout lot of paper work as guided by the DCCBs and for the benefit of DCCB. The entries have to be made at 13 places in various register books. The secretaries are burdened by extra work; consequently they are reluctant to have such credit system.

The MKBs and PACS are the kingpin of the co-operative credit system; they should be emphasized in the overall rural money market. An experiment of the MKBs is a landmark effort of freedom and innovation by the Kolhapur DCCB. Such type of innovations are essential for succeeding the financial sector reforms. Restructuring of rural finance is essential rather than reorganising the co-operative credit system. Otherwise the alternative agencies will occupy the space provided by the existing co-operative credit system. MKBs is a lesson to the policy makers for following the CVB Model, for the development of co-operative credit system in India.

Conclusion

Agriculture sector no doubt is a tough task due to its complexities and as it is in the hands of illiterate and traditional minded cultivators, the complexities further grow. The management of agriculture sector is related to land, soil, water, fertilizer, pesticides and crop management etc. Supply of credit, to carry out all agricultural activities is a pre-requisite, as the complexities are also observed in the rural credit system. Therefore, the entrepreneurship in farm activities is different from that of industrial entrepreneurship. The risk and uncertainties in agriculture sector have direct implications on the risk and uncertainty management of the financial institutions who are issuing the credit to the agricultural sector. The lenders are more safer than the borrowers. The farmers neither have a guarantee of agricultural production due to vagaries of the monsoon, nor they predict a favourable agricultural returns in the form of money income.

The mismanagement of the agricultural credit is normally seen among the farmers, which disturbs the family budget of the farmers. Credit is a bad master if it is mismanaged. It is like, "credit supports the farmers as the hangman's rope supports the hanged". However, if it is used properly, "it can serve as an elevator." Economically, socially and technologically we can improve the positions of the farm and farm families by way of supplying the credit timely, cheaply and adequately. Thus the role of agricultural finance is immense in improving the economic conditions of the farm families.

Co-operatives provide good credit to the farmers, because co-operatives can mobilize rural savings, promotes national thrift, prudence of self control arouse new ideas among the masses, self help and mutual help, remove the isolation, suspicious exclusiveness of the farmers and suggest new departures in the conservative methods of cultivation.

An attempt to raise a logical and rational structure of co-operative credit must involve conceptual, organisational and financially well designed ideology. The continuing need for financial resources of rural co-operatives in India is the result of three elements - prevention of exploitation, investment of fresh resources and steady and integrated growth system. The co-operative structure in India fulfils the principles of better credit. Hence the co-operative structure should be advocated. However the co-operative structure should not carryout the credit disbursement mechanism only. D.G. Karve (1960) has rightly remarked, "Only lending money to the farmers under co-operative regulation cannot be defined as an activity, contributing to economic development." In this respect, to make co-operative credit more effective, a well developed model of Co-operative Village Bank be supported with adequate institutional support, which suits within the framework of financial sector reforms. If not, the concept of village banking for the poors and the concept of local private banks will occupy the empty space in the rural credit system. The MKBs is a right step towards the viable village banking within a framework of co-operative structure. At present the scheme of MKB is running on the line of suggested CVB model. To revitalise the model, it is required to enact the co-operative law and some regulations and permission from Reserve Bank of India is also essential so as to work at par with the banking units. The MKB scheme is a replica of CVB Model. Restructuring the PACS into CVBs is an opportunity rendered under the FSRs. Co-operation as is an alternative to privatization and nationalization suits in the framework of the mixed economy. However, proper mind set is strictly required for restructuring the rural credit system. The strength and ability of the co-operative system lies in, how the sector converts challenges into opportunities.

REFERENCES

Report on Risk and Uncertainty in Agriculture - Chicago.

Choubey B. N., (1968), Principles and Practices of Agricultural Finance, Asia Publishing House.

Fiedler Edgar R. and assisted by Peck Maude R., Measures of Credit Risk and Experience, National Bureau of Economic Research, New York, General Series, 95.

Nelson A.G. and Murray W.C., (1967), Agricultural Finance, IOWA State University, Press, Ames IOWA, USA 5th Edition.

Johl S.S. and Moore C. V., (1970), Essentials of Farm Management, Today & Tomorrow Printers and Publishers, New Delhi.

Singh B.K. & Nantiyal J. C., (1986), An Empirical Estimation of Risk in the Application of Chemical Fertilizers in HYV of Wheat & Paddy in Different Regions of U.P. IJAB, Vol. 4, No. 2, April-June.

Berry, Peter J. & Robinson Liden J., (1987), Port Folio Theory & Financial Structure: An Application of Analysis, Agricultural & Financing Review Vol. 47.

Penson, Johan B. Jr., (1987), Evaluating Financial Trend, in Agricultural and Financing Review Vol. 47.

Nelson A.G., (1957), Credit as a Tool for Agricultural Producer, N. Cent. Reg. Pub. No. 4 and Great Plains Agricultural Council, Pub. No.15.

Jugale V.B., (1991), Theories of Agricultural Finance, Atlantic Publishers & Distributors, New Delhi.

Jugale V.B., (1993), Co-operative Credit in Indian Agriculture: It's Socio-Economic & Technological Impact, Mittal Pub., New Delhi.

Jugale V. B., (1996), Restructuring the Rural Credit System, NABARD Chair Unit, VAMNICOM, Pune.

Jugale V. B., (1996), A Model of PACS, Symposium, Deptt. of Economics, Shivaji University, Kolhapur December.

Jugale V.B., (2000), Towards Village Banking : Working of Mini Kisan Banks in Kolhapur, Monograph-10, UGC-SAP-DRS, Department of Economics, Shivaji University, Kolhapur, March

UNDFW, (1996), Village Banking.

RBI, (1998), Report of the High Level Committee on Agricultural Credit Through Commercial Banks, (Gupta Committee).

Karve D.G., (1960), Failure and Success in Indian Co-operative Movement, Third International Congress on Co-operation.

10

Performance of PACS - An Empirical Evaluation

V. Kulandaiswamy and P. Murugesan

An Overview

Agricultural credit co-operatives constitute the sheet - anchor of co-operative policy and development in India. In the short term co-operative credit structure, which comprises of the three co-operative credit structure, which comprises of the three tier-structure, the primary Agricultural co-operative credit societies (PACS) are at the base, being the foundation for the entire edifice. It is therefore imperative that in any strategy for the development of Agricultural credit co-operatives, major emphasis should be on strengthening the PACS. Besides begin the purveyors of production credit, these grass-root institutions also serve as multi-purpose units providing a comprehensive range of services such as : generating income of the farmers and improving their productivity, delivery of inputs and providing services like processing and marketing, promotion of subsidiary and non-farm activities in rural areas and mobilizing rural savings.

Effective dispensation of services to the rural households hinges on the capacity and viability of the institution; strengthening viability and efficiency is a corollary of effective dispensation of service. The concept of viability has been the main plank of development of PACS since 1960. The All India

Rural Credit Review Committee laid great focus on the promotion of viable units and development of business potentials of PACS.

As a result of the programme of reorganization of Primary Agricultural Credit Societies, the total number of PACS has decreased from 1,34,838 in 1974 - 75 to 92,408 during 1985 - 86, and further decreased to about 92,000 in 1995 - 96. Out of the total number of PACS, 65 percent were found to be viable.[1] The same position continued in 2000 - 01.

The average membership per PACS increased from 293 in 1975 - 76 to 991 in 1995 - 96, though in many states the position is much worse. The average owned funds per society increased from Rs.0.32 lakhs during 1975 - 76 to Rs.1.22 lakhs during 1985 - 86. However the percentage of overdues to demand remained around 41 during the decade between 1975 - 76 to 1985-86. The percentage of PACS making profit to the total number of PACS decreased from 58.1 in 1975-76 to 57.6 in 1990 - 91, and further to 49.5 in 2000 - 01.

The norms of viability had been scaled up from time to time. The working Group on co-operatives for the 5th Plan laid down the norm of Rs.2 Lakhs of loan business as early as in 1973.[2] According to the guidelines of NABARD, a PACS with a loan business of Rs.10 lakhs is normally liable.[3] The Agricultural Credit Review Committee (1989) suggested an optimum business level of Rs.25 lakhs to Rs.30 lakhs and the break-even level of Rs.17 lakhs, for a PACS to be considered viable. Thus the viability norms have been progressively set at higher levels of performance.

Despite these encouraging statistical profiles there exists certain structural and functional weaknesses like low business turnover, poor, share capital base, high cost of operation, dependence on external borrowings, inadequate deposit mobilization, high level of overdues, inadequate member involvement and participation in business and organizational matters.

In the fast changing competitive environment and emerging pluralistic pattern of rural credit system, concrete measures are called for, to improve the viability, operational efficiency, and to enhance the business and management skills of the paid employees as well as elected Board. In the above context the recommendation of the Agricultural Credit Review Committee (1989) appointed by RBI, for strengthening the co-operative credit delivery system and to diversity business activities is a significant milestone in the development of PACS in the country. The ACRC recommended for initiating a programme of Business Development Planning in each and every primary agricultural credit co-operative society in the country under a phased programme, so that during the 8th plan period (1991 - 95) all the village co-operatives emerge as self reliant and autonomous institutions.[4] Subsequently the Pant Committee (1990) and Sankaran Committee were appointed (1991) by the Government of India to highlight the need to take up Business Development Planning in an organised manner and to suggest measures to implement the recommendation of ACRC. Subsequently NABARD entered into memoranda of understanding (MOU) with state and District Central Co-operative Banks and Concerned State Governments for implementing the specific development action plans to revamp the loss making PACS and to improve their viability. In the intervening period, the country witnessed a spate of Banking sector reforms, following the recommendations of Narasimham Committee. The Task force appointed by the Government of India (Capoor Committee July 2001) for suggesting measures for strengthening the co-operative credit system came out with a reform and regulatory framework including structural, financial and managerial reforms. The Task force on Agricultural credit constituted by the planning commission has recommended immediate measures to amalgamate/merge the primary credit societies and also to wind up the defunct institutions.[5] In the Report (December 2001) on Revitalisation Support to co-operative Credit structure, the Joint Committee (Balasaheb Vikhe Patil Committee) has observed that co-operative credit institutions have got an important role to play and they are very close to farmers, artisans and hence it is difficult if their place could be taken over by any other institutional structure for delivery of financial service in rural areas.

The Policy initiatives which have been implemented for more than two decades for consolidation, development and reform the primary agricultural credit sector, should have created some positive impact. It is felt that "there is need for undertaking evaluation of the results emerging from the implementation of BDPS in various states in terms of improvements effected in the operational efficiency and viability of PACS".[6]

The current status of PACS in the macro and level is presented in Table 1. A comparative analysis of performance of PACS at National, and State level reveals that the units at Tamil Nadu level have performed well in all select indicators namely membership, share capital working capital, deposits, borrowings, demand and overdues comparing to National average.

Table 1 : Current Status of PACS in the Macro Level

1. Data relate to per society average
2. Amount Rs. in lakhs

Variables	*All India (2000-01)*	*TN (2000-01)*
Membership	1091	1933
Share Capital	4.06	7.70
Working Capital	43.81	118.51
Loan Disbursement	24.59	58.62
Deposits	10.93	54.27
Borrowings	22.86	56.66
Demand	27.06	49.99
Overdues	9.53	20.40

Source : Indian Co-operative Movement - A Profile 2002, National Resource, NCUI, New Delhi.

Performance : Dimensions and Yardsticks

Performance of co-operatives needs to be viewed from different angles; a multi-dimensional exercise. In the past various committees, experts and empirical researchers have attempted to framework the performance criteria/yardsticks. Starting with the committee on co-operative credit (1960), a wealth of literature is available on the evaluation dimension and criteria.

Scholars across the country and across the world have made fruitful attempts to evaluate the operational efficiency and performance of PACS, in particular or co-operatives in general. Prominent among them include : Okafor F.O. (1979), Dubashi P.R., Krishnaswami O.R. (1987), Mohan Rao R.M. (1988) Suresh

K.A. and Moly Joseph (1988), Sukumaran and Saheena, (1991) Taimni K.K. (1992), Madane M.V. (1992) Bhave G.P. (1992) Mustafa. K. Mujeri (1992), Tushaar Shah (1995) Niranjan Raj Urs (1998), Yashwant Dongre and Narayanaswamy (1999).

A few focused studies on BDP are also available, including studies made by Samar K. Datta and Sanjeev Kumar (1992), Rayudu C.S. (1992) Mohanan N (1992) Sriram M.S. (1992), which have evaluated the performance of PACS in the context of implementation of BDP. A range of Criteria and yard sticks and appropriate analytical tools have been developed by the researchers. Comprehensive inventory of indicators and yardsticks, identified on the basis of the earlier studies, include the following broad aspects : (i) Organisational and Structural (ii) financial and (iii) social.

An Empirical Evaluation

Empricism is the hall-mark of research in co-operation right from the days of All India Rural Credit Survey. Field survey brings reinforcement, reorient or replace the existing perceptions and views. Field survey gives new insights and enriches the knowledge base. The present research paper is a small attempt - a peephole perception of performance of PACS.

The PACS in the selected development blocks of western Tamil Nadu namely Karamadai, Kodumudi and Kotagiri, numbering 30, representing the three revenue districts respectively of Coimbatore, Erode and Nilgiris, are the sample units of the study. "The major theme of research is the performance of PACS - An Empirical Evaluation". The main objective of the study is to evaluate the performance of PACS in its various dimensions using a comprehensive yardsticks of performance, covering a period of 10 years (1989-90 to 2000-2001) with the help of the data collected from all the PACS by means of an interview schedule.

Initially 13 performance parameters were selected based on the relevant research studies and literature. They are : (1) Total membership, (2) Working Capital, (3) Total loan outstanding, (4) Total business turnover, (5) Overdues, (6) Networth, (7) Assets (8) Subsidies and grants (9) Net Profit (10) Transaction cost (11) Manpower Cost (12) Membership of weaker section (13) Loan to weaker section.

The analytical model used by Yashwantha Dongre and Narayana Swamy in a similar study was modified suitably and applied. The methodology adopted is briefly explained below :

As a first step, the absolute values of each variable in respect of each unit of study (N = 30) was converted into standardized value by using the formula. $\frac{x_{ij} - \bar{x}}{sd}$

Where, xij is the average value of the unit for jth variable; and $\bar{x}$ is the grand average of all the units (N = 30) studied . Similarly standard deviation is also found out.

The standardized values for each variable was then converted into score values by adopting a 10 point scale, representing 10th percentile values. The aggregate score for 13 variable for each unit of study will range from 10 to 130.

In order to judge the effectiveness of each of the 13 variable as a performance parameter the score value of each variable was correlated with the total score value, and those variables with 0.3 correlation value were included as effective parameters and the rest were deleted from the analysis. In this process the following eight variables namely; (1) working capital (2) Total loan outstanding (3) Total business turnover (4) Overdues (5) Networth (6) Subsidies and grants (7) Net-Profit (8) Loans to weaker section, were selected and used as performance parameters.

Based on the performance scores in the above parameters, the PACSs were classified into three performance categories, namely poor, moderate and good as shown in table 2.

ANNEXURES

Table 2 : Societies Classified According to Poor, Moderate and Good According to Performance Scores After Variable Reduction

	No	*Percent*
Poor (< = 39)	11	36.7
Moderate (40-49)	12	40.0
Good (>49)	7	23.3
Total	30	100.0

The mean and standard deviation of each of the performance parameter is presented in table 3.

Table 3 : Mean and Standard Deviations of Scores of Selected Variables

	Overall Score								
	Poor (<=39)			*Moderate (40-49)*			*Good (>49)*		
	Mean	*N*	*Std. Dev*	*Mean*	*N*	*Std. Dev*	*Mean*	*N*	*Std. Dev*
Working Capital	2.55	11	1.51	6.75	12	1.71	8.00	7	2.38
Total Loans Outstanding	2.73	11	1.68	6.08	12	2.02	8.86	7	1.07
Total Business Turnover	3.55	11	2.02	5.17	12	2.44	9.14	7	0.90
Overdues	7.45	11	2.34	5.42	12	2.71	2.57	7	1.27
Net worth	3.00	11	2.37	7.08	12	2.07	6.71	7	2.43
Subsidies and Grants	5.09	11	3.53	4.92	12	2.57	7.29	7	1.80
Net Profit	5.45	11	2.94	4.67	12	3.06	7.00	7	2.38
Loans to Weaker Sections	4.27	11	2.33	5.00	12	2.70	8.29	7	2.56

The scoring procedure adopted to classify the PACS into three distinct performance categories, was validated by means of parametric and non-parametric statistical tests namely, analysis of variance (one way) and Kruskalwalli's test respectively.

The results of ANOVA applied for the eight performance parameters as presented in Table 4, show that except subsidies and grants and net profit, the units of study (PACS) classified into three performance categories on the basis of the parameters and scoring procedure adopted earlier, was found to be significantly differ at 1% level.

The results of non-parametric tests shown in Table 5 and Table 6 also give the same results obtained by using ANOVA. Thus the procedure adopted to classify the societies on the basis of their performance as good, moderate and poor is justifiable.

Table 4 : ANOVA Results Comparing Poor, Moderate and Good Societies for Selected Variables

		Sum of Squares	*df*	*Mean Square*	*F*	*Sig*
Working Capital	Between Groups	158.523	2	79.261	24.052	**
	Within Groups	88.977	27	3.295		
	Total	247.500	29			
Total Loans outstanding	Between Groups	167.544	2	83.772	28.289	**
	Within Groups	79.956	27	2961		
	Total	247.500	29			
Total Business Turnover	Between Groups	136.249	2	68.124	16.533	**
	Within Groups	111.251	27	4.120		
	Total	247.500	29			
Overdues	Between Groups	102.142	2	51.071	9.486	**
	Within Groups	145.358	27	5.384		
	Total	247.500	29			
Net Worth	Between Groups	109.155	2	54.577	10.652	**
	Within Groups	138.345	27	5.124		
	Total	247.500	29			
Subsidies and Grants	Between Groups	28.212	2	14.106	1.753	Ns
	Within Groups	217.254	27	8.046		
	Total	245.467	29			
Net Profit	Between Groups	24.106	2	12.053	1.457	Ns
	Within Groups	223.394	27	8.274		
	Total	247.500	29			
Loans to Weaker Sections	Between Groups	73.890	2	36.945	5.746	**
	Within Groups	173.610	27	6.430		
	Total	247.500	29			

Table 5 : Grouping of Sample units on the Basis of Rank

	Ranks		
Variables	*Overall Score*	*N*	*Mean Rank*
Working Capital	Poor (<=39)	11	6.64
	Moderate (40-49)	12	19.25
	Good (>49)	7	23.00
	Total	30	
Total Loans Outstandings	Poor (<=39)	11	7.18
	Moderate (40-49)	12	17.25
	Good (>49)	7	25.57
	Total	30	
Total Business Turnover	Poor (<=39)	11	9.64
	Moderate (40-49)	12	14.50
	Good (>49)	7	26.43
	Total	30	
Overdues	Poor (<=39)	11	21.36
	Moderate (40-49)	12	15.25
	Good (>49)	7	6.71
	Total	30	
Net Worth	Poor (<=39)	11	8.00
	Moderate (40-49)	12	20.25
	Good (>49)	7	19.14
	Total	30	
Subsidies and Grants	Poor (<=39)	11	14.23
	Moderate (40-49)	12	13.58
	Good (>49)	7	20.79
	Total	30	
Net Profit	Poor (<=39)	11	15.36
	Moderate (40-49)	12	13.00
	Good (>49)	7	20.00
	Total	30	
Loans to Weaker Sections	Poor (<=39)	11	11.82
	Moderate (40-49)	12	14.00
	Good (>49)	7	23.86
	Total	30	

Table 6 : Kruskal Wallis Test Statistics

	Chi-Square	*df*	*Asymp. Sig.*
Working Capital	18.574	2	**
Total Loans Outstanding	19.631	2	**
Total Business Turnover	15.965	2	**
Overdues	11.968	2	**
Net Worth	12.790	2	**
Subsidies and Grants	3.354	2	Ns
Net Profit	2.825	2	Ns
Loans to Weaker Sections	8.658	2	**

Conclusion

Of the eight parameters chosen to measure the performance six were found to be very relevant and valid, and may be adopted as performance parameters in similar studies in similar situations.

Of the 30 PACSs studied, those showing good performance were only 7 (23.3%), while 12 units (40%) revealed moderate performance and as much as 11 (36.7%) were found to be poor.

The empirical evidence reinforces the macro-level perceptions and calls for appropriate policy interventions to correct the deficiency by such measures as re-capitalization, amalgamation, bringing down the overdues and improving the overall efficiency.

NOTES

1. RBI, Agricultural Credit Review Committee, Bombay : 1993, P. 220.
2. Ibid., p. 226.
3. NCCT, Training Materials for Business Development Planning in PACS, New Delhi.
4. Viswanathan B. S. Forward Manual on BDP in Primary Agricultural Co-operative, National Resource Centre, NCUI, New Delhi.
5. Dr. Paranjothi. T., Tenth Five Year Plan Approaches Strategies of Co-operative Development, (July – September, 1998, p. 2).
6. Viswanathan B. S. Measures for Revitalising Co-operative Banks, *Co-operative Perspective,* VAMNICM, Pune.

11

Performance Evalution Model For Primary Non-agricultural Credit Societies

Y.S.P. Thorat, Maria Pradeep and Praggya Das

Introduction

The co-operative movement, in its present form, originated in the west in the early 19th century in context of the emerging distributional and market failures of the post-industrial revolution modes of production. Essentially voluntary in nature and initiated by local leadership, these co-operatives assumed forms and organisational structures depending on the nature of the problem to be addressed. Hence consumer co-operatives were started in the UK, agricultural co-operatives in Germany and urban co-operatives in Italy.

The co-operative Movement in India did not emerge voluntarily as a result of the conscious choice of economic units but it originated with governmental policy because of the prevailing socio-political climate of the country. At the turn of the century the socioeconomic conditions prevalent were not conducive for the indebted Indian peasantry- to generate the spontaneity necessary for a grass root movement.

Following the Deccan riots in 1875, the movement, especially as financial intermediation, got initiated in that region, essentially for countering the activities of the money lenders and competing with them in the provision of credit.

During colonial and post – colonial periods in India, the state promoted co-operatives as instruments of rural development. The expectation was that in addition to providing an alternative to village money lenders, co-operatives would mobilise resources for rural development and help to promote social justice.

The Reserve Bank of India (RBI), which was set up in 1935, was given the mandate of conducting research for development of co-operatives in the country. The Rural Credit Survey (1951), which was set up soon after independence, observed that despite the co-operatives having come into existence in the early part of the century, money lenders still accounted for 70 % of rural credit requirements. The government of independent India while perceiving co-operatives to be the principal financial institutions for rural development in the planning model felt that their impact would be negligible until the introduction of state partnership in them. State partnership was both financial and administrative and resulted over time in official and administrative and resulted over time in officialisation of the movement, characterised by control over the day–to-day operations of such institutions by the government. State policy also encouraged a wide range of activities to be brought under co-operatives such as small and village industries, input supply, marketing, processing, warehousing, housing, fishery, dairy, etc.

Thus, for the most part, the experience of rural co-operatives in India was very different from the expectations. In many cases the co-operatives have neither been successful as financial intermediaries nor have they led to an effective promotion of their members interests. However, there are some notable examples of co-operative success in areas such as dairy co-operatives in Gujrat, sugar co-operatives in Maharashtra and the urban co-operative banks in Maharashtra, Gujarat and Karnataka. The growth of non-agricultural credit societies in Maharashtra is also indicative of a movement based on local initiative, which in the main is neither state driven nor state supported.

This study seeks to explore not only original knowledge with respect to particular group of co-operatives in Western India, but also to find results which have important policy implications regarding co-operatives and their development in India at a general level. The extant paper is only one aspect of that study wherein it is intended to assess the performance of the primary non-agricultural credit societies. The performance is examined with reference to a group of Credit Societies located in Kolhapur district in Western Maharashtra.

It has been observed that not only has there been a substantial growth in the number of Credit Societies in this area, but also in contrast to the general experience of co-operatives in India, these organisations have originated on the basis of local level initiatives and also appear to be financially successful. While all the Credit Societies may be "bottom-up" organisations, they exhibit a heterogeneous position in regard to the purposes for which they had been established. A number of them seem to have been set up for gaining political power while others have been set up as feeders for milk dairies, self – help trader's organisations, voluntary savings, loans associatins and women's orgainsations.

Objective

Keeping into consideration the complex role of a co-operative its performance needs to be examined from various aspects, namely, their success as financial intermediaries as also performers of traditional co-operative and social goals, etc. In the present paper, it has been attempted to create a performance Evaluation Model using several critical parameters on the above aspects. The performance evaluation model classifies the Credit Societies as good, satisfactory or poor performers. The paper also tries to assess if there is a conflict among the Credit Societies for meeting their co-operative/social values as against their financial standing on various profitability and efficiency parameters.

Review of Literature

A brief look at the literature available on performance evaluation of co-operatives and on credit rating and classification of firms into certain distinct classes based on their financial performance indicates that the technique of multiple discriminant analysis has been popularly used in the field.

Multiple discriminant analysis technique is used to classfy objects into two or more distinct classes. The problem of classification arises when an investigator makes a number of measurements. The investigator connot identify the object with a category directly but must use available measurements on several objects to first derive a discriminant function, which is subsequently used to classify a new object on the basis of its measurement. Thus using historical data of failed and non-failed firms the discriminant function can be calculated and then used in predicting whether a new firm is about to fail or not.

One peculiar feature of this analysis is that one needs to have a clear definition of sickness of a firm, which may lead to its failure. This is a problem in financial analysis because the definition of sickness itself varies depending on the purpose for which one is defining sickness. It gets even more complex in the case of co-operatives where the performance is not always measured in strict financial terms.

Another technique used in appraising the performance of firm and looking at prediction of failure is the dichotomous classification test, wherein the data are arranged in ascending order and then the array is inspected to find an optimal cut off point-the point expected to minimise the percentage of incorrect predictions. There are no weights assigned to each of the predictor variables as in the case of discriminant analysis.

Another method is of the Net Cash Flow approach and it basically looks at the pattern of flows and concludes that the firm will be sick in the year when the cash flows becomes negative. The pattern of flows of the past years are used here to predict the flows in future and see whether the firm is going to be in trouble or not.

While these two methods appear rather simple, but they are not very popular in financial literature. In case of discriminant analysis, the criticism is that the method does not have a backing of financial theory. The problems encountered in the use of discriminant analysis or any other method is basically related to the definition of performance. This becomes particularly important in the case of co-operatives because, as mentioned earlier, there is apparently no clear definition available.

Regarding the use of variables, a look at the literature on co-operative indicates that most of the studies draw upon profitability ratios to measure performance. The studies by

Gupta and Shekhar (1988), Suresh (1990), Korobw (1977 , Sriram & Rao (1976) have all used profitability ratios.

Sriram and Gopalaswamy have suggested that there is a need to develop surrogates that there is a need to develop surrogates for several non-financial parameters of performance identified in the literature and convert them into some sort of quantifiable factors, which may ultimately be used in constructing a weighted index.

Dongre and Narayana Swamy (1999) have argued that any model used to evaluate the performance of co-operatives must include variables that indicate liquidity, profitability and long-term solvency of business. They have indicated that the evaluation methods developed in the studies of Sidhu and Sidhu (1990), Desai and Nammboodiri (1991), Reddy (1992), Suresh and Vinaikumar (1993), etc. are deficient in one or the other aspect of development and therefore these model may not be fully relevant in the context of co-operatives. They proposed a method, which, can incorporate all the dimensions of development to measure efficiency. Their model is based on scaling technique, suggested by Rao, Bhatt and Bhatta (1991). The scale constructed in intended to measure the poor. They have used almost all variables as shown in the Profit & Loss Account and Balance Sheet so that no important variable is left out. Using scaling technique, they could systematically eleminate insignificant variables. They established the validity of the scale using Discriminant Analysis and Cluster Analysis.

Though Dongre and Swamy's paper looked at the performance of PACs in terms of liquidity, profitability and solvency, they did not build in a dimension to capture the social and co-operative goals of such institutions.

In the present paper, we try to build a scale using parameters that describe, not only the financial part of their performance, but also the social, co-operative and governance aspects of their performance.

Methodology

A. Selection of Credit Societies

As mentioned earlier, the focus of this work is on primary non-agricultural credit societies. Maharashtra alone accounts for about 74 per cent of such societies in India and these societies in Maharashtra are called Path Sansthas or Credit Societies. From among the several districts of Maharashtra, it was seen that the Kolhapur district accounts for about 1/6th of such societies (in number), which capture about 2/3rd of their total business (loans and deposits) in Maharashtra. The sample was selected from a rural area (Radhanagri Taluka) and an urban area (Kolhapur city) of the Kolhapur district. There are 233 Credit Societies in the focus area and the 10 percent sample was chosen by stratified sampling procedure. The strata were formed based on the size of business levels (deposits and credit). 23 Credit Societies were selected on basis of purposive sampling in each stratum in order to obtain a comprehensive picture of different types of Path Sansthas such as women's societies (Mahila sansthas), societies located in inaccessible errains, etc. The work of data collection was done as a part of the larger work of the first author. These Credit Societies are listed in the Table A1 in the Annex.

B. Parameter Selection

To see the performance of the Credit Societies in terms of co-operative/social/governance parameters the following variables were selected.

	Parameter Name	*Parameter Type*
1.	Number of Regular members to total members	Co-operative
2.	Members who have left to total members	Co-operative
3.	Number of small loans (<Rs. 10000) to total loans o/s	Co-operative
4.	Amount of small loans (< Rs. 10000) to total loans o/s	Co-operative
5.	Dividend paid	Co-operative
6.	Surety loans (Amount) to total loan o/s	Co-operative
7.	Small deposits (less than Rs. 5000) to total deposits	Co-operative
8.	Number of small deposits to total deposits	Co-operative
9.	Number of AGMs held	Governance
10.	Attenance in AGMs to total members	Governance
11.	Number of Board meetings	Governance
12.	Attendance in Board Meetings	Governance
13.	Number of SC/ST members to total members	Social

Contd...

Contd...

	Parameter Name	*Parameter Type*
14.	Number of women members to total members	Social
15.	Number of loans to SC/ST to total SC/ST members	Social
16.	Number of loans to women to total women members	Social
17.	Number of Borrowers per Staff	Outreach
18.	Number of Depositors per Staff	Outreach
19.	Amount of loans per staff	Efficiency
20.	Amount of Deposits per staff	Efficiency
21.	Depositors to Operating Expenses	Efficiency
22.	Borrowers to Operating Expenses	Efficiency
23.	Operating Expensts to # of loan issued a/c	Efficiency
24.	Operating Expenses to Amount of loan issued	Efficiency
25.	Non operating Expenses to Working Funds	Efficiency
26.	Operating Expenses to Working Funds	Sustainability
27.	Net Inteest Income to Working funds	Sustainability
28.	Total Expenses to Total Income	Operating self sufficiency
29.	Overdue to Loans o/s	Portfolio quality
30.	Share Capital +Reserve Fund + Other fund	Size
31.	Working Capital	Size

To see the performance in terms of financial parameters on a composite scale, several variables were identified. These variables covered, interalia, the efficiency and sustainability aspects of their performance as financial intermediaries. The variables are as follows.

C. *Methodology of Construction of the Scale*

All the Path Sansthas can be scaled according to each of the parameter separately, which would give their relative performance according to that parameter. In case of most of the parameters the higher the value, the better it is while in case of some (e.g. Expenditure related parameters), the lower the value, the better it will be. This scaling exercise attempts to build a scale that is comprehensive and has multidimensionality as it takes into account all the identified parameters. The exercise has been done using an interative technique as sugges-ted by Rao, Bhat and Bhatta (1991) and used by Dongre and Swamy (1999).

As the variables selected are in different units, firstly all the parameters are brought to common and unit free scale by standardizing them. These standardized them.These standardized values are next converted to scores from 1 to 10 using the decile points of the Standard Normal Distribution. This is done for each parameter. For each sanstha, its scores over all the parameters are added to arrive at the total score. The notation used for the score value of each parameter is given in the Table A2 and their score values in Table A3 in the Annex.

The correlation of these aggregate scores are calculated with the individual score of each of the parameter. The parameters that are highly correlated with the total score are retained and the remaining parameters are dropped. Using these residual parameters we arrive at a new total score. The correlation between the new total score and the set of parameters, which were used to calculate this total score, is again calculated and the process is repeated till each of the parameter in the residual set has significant correlation with the total score. These final total scores are then tandardized and the standardized values are classified in 3 classes using the Standard Normal Tables. The ones with value 1 are weak/poor societies, the ones with value 2 are satisfactory societies and the ones with value 3 are good societies.

Results

A. *Scaling with All the 31 Parameters*

In the first interation 11 parameters were found to be significantly correlated with total score and were retained (Table A4). A new total score is arrived at, by adding the scores of these 11 parameters. The correlations of each of these 11 variables were calculated with this new total score. In this second interation, the variables "Attendance in Board Meetings" and Number of Borrowers per Staff are dropped, as their correlations with the new total score were not significant. The following are the nine parameters.

1. Number of small loans (less than 10000) to total loans o/s.
2. Amount of small loans (less than Rs.10000) to total loans o/s.
3. Number of loans to SC/ST to total SC/ST members.

4. Number of loans to women to total women members.
5. Depositors to Operating Expenses.
6. Borrowers to Operating Expenses.
7. Operating Expenses to # of loan issued a/c.
8. Operating Expenses to Amount of loan issued.
9. Overdue to Loans o/s.

With the remaining 9 parameters which were highly correlated with the total score, the following classification emerges.

Weak :	Rural :	AP, ML
	Urban :	KDN, SR, PrM, SG, SN, PaM
Satisfactory :	Rural :	JB, KWV
	Urban :	BB, KMM, KC, SY
Good :	Rural :	DN, VK, GP, CS, SA, Y, VM
	Urban :	SV, JK

B. *Scaling Using All the Social/Co-operative/Governance Parameters (16 Parameters)*

In the first interation the following parameters, which were significantly correlated with the total score of all 16 parameters, were retained.

1. Number of women members to total members.
2. Number of small loans (less than 10000) to total loans o/s.
3. Amount of small loans (less than Rs. 10000) to total loans.
4. Attendance in AGMs to total members.
5. Number of loans to women to total women mebers.
6. Surety loans (Amount) to total loan o/s.
7. Small deposits (less than Rs. 5000) to total deposits.
8. Number of small deposits to total deposits.

The sum of scores of these 8 parameters led to a new total score. After iteration 2, parameter at serial number 1, 4 & 5 were found to have insignificant correlation with the new total score and were dropped (Table A 5). The classification based on the remaining 5 parameters is as under

Weak :	Rural :	ML, VM
	Urban :	KMM, PrM, SG, SN, PaM

Satisfactory :	Rural :	AP, SA, KWV
	Urban :	JK, SR, KC, SY, KDN
Good :	Rural :	DN, VK, GP, CS, JB, Y
	Urban :	SV, BB

C. *Scaling Using All the Economic/Financial Parameters (15 Parameters)*

On lines similar to above, the scores of all 15 economic/ financial parameters were added to arrive at a total score. The correlations of the scores of individual parameters are worked out with the total score (Table A 6). In the first iteration nine parameters were retained. The sum of the scores of these 9 parameters gives a new total score. In the second iteration the parameters "Number of Borrowers per Staff" and "Operating Expenses to Amount of loan issued" were dropped as they were found to have insignificant correlations with the new total score. The grouping is done as per the following remaining:

1. Number of Depositors per staff
2. Amount of loans per staff
3. Amount of Deposits per staff
4. Non operating Expenses to Working Fund
5. Operating Expenses to Working Fund
6. Share Capital + Reserve Fund + Other Fund
7. Working Capital

The following classification emerges as per the selected economic / financial parameters :

Weak :	Rural :	AP, VK, GP, ML
	Urban :	KDN, BB, KMM, SR, SG, PaM
Satisfactory :	Rural :	DN
	Urban :	JK, KC, PrM, SY, SN
Good :	Rural :	CS, JB, SA, Y, KWV, VM
	Urban :	SV

D. *Scaling Using Only Governance Parameters (4 Parameters)*

The total score was calculated using all 4 parameters of Governance nature. The correlations of individual scores were seen with total score (Table A 9) and the parameter "Number of AGMs held" was removed in the first stage. A new total score based on the three significant parameters was worked out. The correlations of this new total score with individual scores showed that the parameter 'Number of Board Meetings' was not significant. The total score of the remaining two parameters was significantly correlated with its components. This score was based on the following two parameters.

1. Attendance in Board Meetings
2. Attendance in AGMs to total members

The classification based on the above was as under –

Weak :	Rural :	DN
	Urban :	KDN, BB, KMM, SR, PrM, SG
Satisfactory :	Rural :	CS, Y, KWV, ML
	Urban :	JK, SY
Good :	Rural :	AP, VK, GP, JB, SA, VM
	Urban :	SV, KC, SN, PaM

Observation

To get a comparative picture of various classifications, we see the following table :

1 – Weak : 2 – Satisfactory : 3 – Good

The above table gives a classification of 23 Credit Societies as below;

- All Parameter; 8 weak; 6 satisfactory; 9 good
- Economic parameters; 8 weak; 10 satisfactory; 5 good
- Social – coop-gov parameters; 7 weak; 8 satisfactory; 8 good
- Co-operative parameters; 7 weak; 8 satisfactory; 8 good
- Social parameters; 10 weak; 6 satisfactory; 7 good
- Governance parameters; 7 weak; 6 satisafactory; 10 good

It would be interesting to see if these classifications according to several criteria have some element of commonality . For this we compute the following table.

It is observed that the overall rating has more commonality with the co-operative ration than the economic rating. This shows

Table 1 : Classification of Credit Societies on Various Criteria

PS Name	*All Para 9 parameters (2 Iterations)*	*Economic 7 parameters (2 Iterations)*	*Soc-Coop Gov. 5 parameters (3 Iterations)*	*Cooperative 5 parameters (1 Iterations)*	*Social 2 parameters (1 Iterations)*	*Governance 2 parameters (2 Iterations)*
AP	1	1	2	2	1	3
DN	3	1	3	3	2	1
VK	3	1	3	3	1	3
GP	3	1	3	3	1	3
CS	3	2	3	3	3	2
JB	2	1	3	3	3	3
SA	3	2	2	2	3	3
Y	2	2	3	3	3	2
KWA	2	2	2	1	3	2
ML	1	3	1	1	1	2
VM	3	3	1	1	3	3
KDN	1	1	2	2	1	1
SV	3	1	3	3	3	3
JK	3	2	2	2	2	2
BB	2	2	3	3	1	1
KMM	2	2	1	2	1	1
SR	1	1	2	2	1	1
KC	2	3	2	2	2	3
PrM	1	2	1	1	2	1
SY	2	2	2	2	2	2
SG	1	2	1	1	1	1
SN	1	3	1	1	2	3
PaM	1	3	1	1	1	1

that the overall performance of these societies is primarily governed by the co-operative ideals and to some extent by social and governance ideals. Also, the overall performance is governed to a minimal extent by economic ideals.

Table 2 A : Commonality in Classification

Matching	*All*	*Economic*	*Soc-coop-Gov*	*Coopera-tive*	*Social*	*Gover-nance*
All	23	8	14	14	13	11
Eco		23	4	4	9	12
Soc-coop			23	21	11	10
Coop				23	10	8
Soc					23	11
Gov						23

Table 2 B : Commonality in Classification (in percentage)

Matching	*All*	*Economic*	*Soc-coop-Gov*	*Coopera-tive*	*Social*	*Gover-nance*
All	100.0	34.8	60.9	60.9	56.5	47.8
Eco		100.0	17.4	14.4	39.1	52.2
Soc-coop			100.0	91.3	47.8	43.5
Coop				100.00	43.5	34.8
Soc					100.0	47.8
Gov						100.0

It is also seen that the Credit Societies which are good as per economic criteria are not so as per social or co-operative criteria and vice versa. These societies are however good in their Governance ideals. The negative relation of the Economic criteria with the Social – Social – Co-operative – Governance criteria and the positive relation between the Economic criteria with the Governance criteria also emerge out from the following table.

The above also shows that good governance leads to good economic performance, whereas the social/co-operative objectives achieved by these Credit Societies is at the cost of their economic objectives. The Credit Societies are paying the cost of achieving the social/co-operative objectives. They are arriving at a trade off between the ecnomic and social/co-operative objectives.

Table 3 : Ecnomic vs. Social - Cooperative Governance and Governance Scaling

	Social-Coop-Gov				*Governance*			
Economic	*Weak*	*Satisfactory*	*Good*	*Total*	*Weak*	*Satisfactory*	*Good*	*Total*
Weak	-	3	5	8	3	-	5	8
Satisfactory	3	4	3	10	4	5	1	10
Good	4	1	-	5	-	1	4	5
Total	7	8	8	23	7	8	10	23

Verification of the Results

In Section 5 above, the Credit Societies were classified on the basis of several criteria. The technique used for arrivng at the classfication is the scaling technique used by Dongre and Narayana Swamy (1999). As mentioned earlier, with the use of Discriminant Analysis and Cluster Analysis, they had established that the technique gave good results. However, it was felt that we could examine the PSs classified according to economc scaling, by their actual performance. For judging the performance of a business firm on financial parameters, it is important to judge the firm on profit margin, as profit is the central ability of a fim to perform financially. Therefore, the parameter for actual performance of the Path Sansthas was also considered as its ability to make higher Operating Profits.

Excluding the outliers and normalizing the Operating Profits the Credit Societies were classified into three classes. The classes obtained were as under :

Table 4 : Classification According to Operating Profits

Sr #	*Name*	*Op-Profit Scaling*	*Op-profit*	*Economic Scaling*
1.	AP	-3515	1	1
2.	DN	-6337	1	1
3.	VK	-15051	1	1
4.	GP	-27503	1	1
5.	CS	-4213	1	2
6.	JB	50160	2	1
7.	SA	58524	2	2
8.	Y	152880	3	2
9.	KWV	18839	2	2
10	ML	-50118	1	3
11.	VM	3885969	3	3
12.	KDN	-21083	1	1
13.	SV	78661	2	1
14.	JK	8499	2	2
15.	BB	73635	2	2
16.	KMM	15055	2	2
17.	SR	-36296	1	1
18.	KC	366075	3	3

Contd...

Table 4 : (Contd...)

Sr #	*Name*	*Op-Profit Scaling*	*Op-profit*	*Economic Scaling*
19.	PrM	204623	3	2
20.	SY	69813	2	2
21.	SG	-187988	1	2
22.	SN	3168324	3	3
23.	PaM	205705	3	3

We consider the economic scaling as good if the good institutions according to scaling technique are also good as per Operating Profits criteria. It can be seen from the table that there is only one incidence of extreme misclassification (i.e., the good PS getting classified as weak or vice versa). If we have a hypothesis that the technique is good if the probability of extreme misclassification is as low as 1 per cent, i.e. in 99 % of the cases there will be no misclassification, then using Binomial test, it is seen that for the given sample the hypothesis is accepted at 5 per cent level of significance.

We further hypothesize that a technique is good if any type of misclassification is not more than 15 per cent. Using the binomial test, we find that for the given sample containing 7 misclassification out of 23, the hypothesis is accepted at 1 per cent level of significance.

We also tested the classification using a chi-square test of goodness of fit. We have the following classification with Economic Scaling and Operating Profits criteria.

Table 5 : Table for Chi-square Statistics

	Economic Scaling Observed	*Op-profit criteria Expected*
Weak	8	9
Satisfactory	10	8
Good	5	6
Total	23	23

Under the hypothesis that the expected frequencies for weak, satisfactory and good classes are respectively 9/23, 8/23 and 6/

23, we find that the value of chi-square with 2 degrees of freedom at 5 per cent and 1 percent level of significance is respectively 5.991 and 9.210. We therefore conclude that the Economic scaling is as per the expected criteria.

It has been found that the classification technique applied on Economic parameters has categorized Credit Societies correctly into three classes, viz., weak, satisfactory and good. We may therefore presume that the technique provides a good way of classification on other parameters as well.

Summing up

There has been a lot of work done in the literature on the performance of Primary Agricultural Credit Societies, but the performance of Primary Non-Agricultural Credit Societies had not been much explored. There has been a substantial growth of such societies, called Path Sansthas in Maharashtra, were in contrast to the general experience of co-operatives in India, these organizations have originated on the basis of local intitatives and also appear to be financially successful. As they have a complex role to perform, it was necessary to judge their performance on various aspects, as a co-operative, social and economic entity. It was also to be seen if there was any conflict amoung these PSs for meeting their social /co-operative values as against their financial standing.

A set of 31 parameters covering the various aspects of performance of these Credit Societies was chosen. Using scaling technique, their overall categorization was arrived at. Also the Credit Societies so were classified on the basis of their Social, Co-operative, Governance and Economic performance parameters. On comparing these classfications, it was found that:

- Social/co-operative objectives are achieved at the cost of economic/financial goals, i.e. at the cost of its efficiency profitability. Thus there was a clear trade off between the social /co-operative goals and the economic goal.
- Good governance / better manangement leads to better economic goals. Thus vigilance of the members or the responsibility and accountability of management helps in the Credit Societies economic performance. The Credit Societies where Board of Credit Societies Director

participation or member's involvement is good they do better economically. It may imply that the members/ board ask for the Credit Societies performance and examine the same in economic terms and not in terms of their co-operative or social parameters.

- The Credit Societies that are good in co-operative / Social terms may be providing facilities with lower interest margin. i.e. they are giving credit at lower cost to borrowers and providing higher interest on deposits.

REFERENCES

Desai, B.M. and Namboodiri, N.V., (1991), "Comparative Performance of Farmers' Service Societies and Primary Agricultural Co-operative Credit Societies", Vikalps, Vol. 16, No. 4 , Oct. –Dec. pp. 23-30.

Dongare, Yashvantha and Narayana Swamy, M.V., (1999), "Performance Evaluation Model for Primary Agricultural Credit Societies", Vikalpa, Vol. 24 No. Jan. –March pp. 43-53.

Gupta, L.C. And Sekhar Archana, (1988), "Controlling Corporate Sickness, Bangaloe". Oxford University Press.

Korobow et. al., (1977), "Early Warning of Changes in Bank Financial Conditions. In Institutions and Markets in Fragile Environment", Edited by Korobow et.al. John Wiley and Sons.

Rao, Aruna K.; Bhat, ARS and Bhatta, Ramchandra, (1991), "A Methodology to Measure the Efficiency of Business Organisations", Indian Co-operative Review, Vol. 28, July, pp. 237-244.

Reddy, C.R., (1992), "Monitoring and Evaluation of Co-operatives", Indian Co-operative Review, Vol. 29, No.3, January, pp. 208-211.

12

Role of Co-operatives and SHGs In Rural Credit Markets

K.Ravichandran and M.Revathi Bala

Introduction

In India the agricultural co-operative credit system was started with the small beginning in the year 1904 at Tirur village in Tamil Nadu by organizing Primary Agricultural Co-operative Credit Society (PACS). The main objective was to eliminate the role of moneylenders and to provide institutional arrangement for rural credit market. After Independence, Government of India paid much attention for organizing such societies throughout the country. Now this system consists of short- term and long-term credit structures, which are established to meet the different form of credit needs of the farmers. At present, the Indian short–term co-operative credit structure consists of 29 State Co-operative Banks at State level, 367 District Central Co-operative Banks (CCBs) at district level and 93816 PACS at village level. (NCUI: 2001).

PACS are the base level institutions on which the whole co-operative edifice is built. These societies functioning at grass root level have direct contacts with the agriculturists and meet the financial requirements of 9.99 crore members. The PACS provide short-term and medium –term agricultural loan. Short–term loans are issued for the cultivation of crops and consumption purposes, whereas medium –term loans are issued for allied agricultural activities. As on 2001-02 the total loans advanced by this short-term co-operative credit structure was Rs.25698 crores (NABARD: 2002 – 03).

To meet the long – term credit needs of the farmers, the long-term credit structure is functioning with 755 Primary Agriculture and Rural Development Banks (PARDBS) and 19 State Agriculture and Rural Development Banks (SARDBs). During 2000 – 01 they issued loans to the extent of Rs. 1866 crores. (NABARD: 2001 – 02).

Meantime in Tamil Nadu, experiment in Self – Help Groups (SHGs) was done by few NGOs with the support of Tamil Nadu Government in the late eighties. This experiment was proved success. So, It was taken as a laboratory model in other parts of the state and the country. In the year 1989, with the help of IFAD, the Tamil Nadu Government initiated SHGs in 75 Panchayat unions of 8 districts. Then Government of India and NABARD extended support for organizing SHGs in all parts of the country.

Self-help groups are now gaining acceptance as an alternative strategy for credit delivery. They cover the credit needs of small / marginal farmers, landless laborers, rural artisans, women folk and other micro entrepreneurs. In India at present, there are 7,17,360 SHGs linked with banks. They disbursed loans up to Rs.1026.34 crores during the year 2002 (NABARD: 2002 – 03). It is expected that nearly 100 million rural people will get services through 1 million SHGs during the year 2008.

Focus of the Present Study

After globalisation, a great deal of attention has been drawn towards studying the nature and functioning of rural credit markets particularly in backward agrarian economics. The basic philosophy of rural finance is the dispensation of credit at a concession rate through administrative control targeting the rural people engaged either in agricultural or in non-agricultural activities. However, our experience in agrarian credit markets highlighted a number of serious drawbacks in the institutional arrangements for the flow of credit to agriculture. They are the inadequate availability of credit (Somorendro singh: 2001), and unequal distribution of formal credit (Balister & Pankajkumar: 1995), lack of access to formal credit to rural borrowers (N.V.Namboodiri : 2001), absence of supervision over the end use of loans (Jaya S.Anand: 1995), higher transaction cost (K.G.Karmakar:1997), willful default (K. Ravichandran: 2000) etc. These drawbacks alienated the rural borrowers from the formal credit institutions. But these studies could not generalize concrete opinion regarding the actual nature and functioning of agrarian credit markets. Meantime, the growth of SHGs has been natural and draws support from formal credit agencies and borrowers. In this context, the present research has limited objective in that it seeks to analyse the structure and operation of credit markets at micro level. Hence, we address ourselves which institutional source of credit has been accessible to rural borrowers? What is the perception of the rural borrowers on the functioning of the institutions? To which agency they are friendlier? What is the utilization pattern of loan? What are the factors responsible for repaying loan? Which institutional repayment do the rural borrowers delay? To which institution, they are still defaulters? To answer these questions, a study was conducted in Dindigul District of Tamil Nadu among the borrowers of Primary Agricultural Co-operative Banks (PACB) and SHGs.

Objectives of the Study

The study has the following objectives viz.,

1. To study the role of SHGs and PACBs in the rural credit market
2. To study the perception of borrowers on the functioning of PACB & SHG
3. To examine the access, use and repayment practices of PACB & SHG borrowers

Methodology

Survey method was followed for the study. Pre-tested structured interview schedule was used for interviewing the borrowers. A multi-stage random sampling technique was used for selecting the sample. There are 7 taluks in the district. From each taluk one block was selected. Secondly one PACB and one

SHG were selected from each block. In the third stage, 40 borrowers from each block were interviewed which, consists of 20 borrowers of PACB and 20 borrowers of SHG so that the total sample size was 280. Since the maximum number of members in a SHG is limited to 20, the same sample size was taken from the borrowers of PACB.

Focus group discussion was also conducted to elicit information about the perception of borrowers on the functioning of PACB and SHG. Further the study limits its scope only to the behaviour of borrowers in respect of access to credit, its utilization and repayment.

Co-operative Movement in Tamilnadu

It was the Government of Madras appointed one of its senior officers, Sir Frederick Nicholson, in 1892, to study the methods of land and agricultural banks of Europe, and to report how best such institutional models could be adapted to Indian conditions, especially in the Madras Presidency, in order to relieve the rural people from indebtedness. Thiru Sir D Rajagopalachariar, the first Registrar of Co-operative Societies, registered the first co-operative society in India at Thirur village in the present Thiruvalluvar district of Tamilnadu on 30.8.1904 under the 1904 Act. After the enactment of 1919 Act, Co-operation became State subject and first time Madras State Co-operative Societies Act was introduced in 1932. Like this there are many laurels to the co-operative movement of Tamilnadu. The Act, which is now in force in Tamilnadu, is the Tamilnadu Coope-rative Societies Act 1983, and Tamilnadu Co-operative Societies Rules 1988.

However, the growth of co-operative movement at present is not satisfactory. The policies of the successive State Governments have nurtured the co-operatives as quasi-governmental bodies and the members use the co-operatives as shareholders and not as stakeholders. Majority of the PACBs, CCBs, urban banks, spinning mills, sugar mills, consumer co-operatives, marketing co-operatives, industrial co-operatives and weaver's co-operatives are in doldrums. Some of the co-operatives have already been closed. But there are successful co-operatives with motivated membership base. For example the Tiruchencode co-operative marketing society, continuously win prizes at all

India level. The TUCAS Coimbatore has been successful amidst stiff competition in the banking industry. Like these the list of successful co-operatives in Tamilnadu have been exhaustive. The growth of PACBs in Tamilnadu is given in the table 1. The total number of PACS in 1929-30 was 12439. Over the years due amalgamation and restructuring process it has come down to 4582 PACBs. And the current statistics is still lesser than the figure given here due to the winding up of loss making PACBs. What is needed to make co-operatives still vibrant and successful is the restoration of their democratic character, which is negated for them more than two decades continuously. With this background the present study is undertaken.

Dindigul District Profile

Dindigul District of Tamil Nadu is one of the very few districts, which have two distinct agro climatic zones viz., semi and tropical climate and subtropical climate. The district is located between 10.050^0 and 10.09^0 north latitudes and 77.30^0 and 78.20^0 east latitudes. The net irrigated area at 99380 hectares, which is about 42 per cent of the net sown area of 236,457 ha. The district is drought – hit and has a poor ground-water status. It has received less than average rainfall (836 mm) during the last two years. Very small land holdings of less than one hectare accounting for 67 per cent of the total holdings. A wide range of fruit, flower and vegetable, food crops like paddy, maize, pulses and oil seeds like groundnut and commercial crops such as sugarcane and tobacco are grown in the district.

The district has 7 taluks, 14 development blocks and 357 villages covering a geographical area of 6267 sq. km. There are 22 commercial banks operating with the network of 138 branches in the district, 60 per cent of which are located in rural areas. The Dindigul DCCB with its 28 branches as well as 197 affiliated PACB and 6 PARDBs play an important role in financing for agriculture and rural development.

The institutional credit flow in the district has achieved above the targeted level during the past. In the year 2001-02, the credit flow was Rs. 36460 lakhs as against the target of Rs. 3378 lakhs. It is expected that Rs. 43100 lakhs will be disbursed during the year 2003 – 04 for agriculture and other priority sector. (Table 2)

Table 1 : Growth of PACS in Tamilnadu

(Rs. In crores)

		1929-30		*1939-40*		*1945-46*		*1950-51*	
S.No	*Indicators*	*TN*	*India*	*TN*	*India*	*TN*	*India*	*TN*	*India*
1.	No. of Societies (in '000s)	12439	91786	11191	101400	10877	124200	15348	115000
2.	No. of members	0.07	0.31	0.06	0.41	0.07	0.55	0.12	0.54
3.	Average membership per society	54	34	54	40	61	44	78	47
4.	Loans issued	1.83		1.47	7.4	2.66	14.6	6.14	22
		(15.19)	12.05	(19.86)					
5.	Loan Outstanding	5.68	29.73	3.54	23.1	3.28	18.9	8.31	29
				(15.32)		(17.35)		(28.66)	
6.	Share Capital	0.83	10.07	0.55	12.40	0.59	16.5	1.41	8.40
		(8.24)		(0.44)		(3.58)		(16.78)	
7.	Working Capital	6.58	34.93	4.75	30.50	4.70	33.00	9.99	40.95
		(18.83)		(15.57)		(14.24)		(24.39)	
8.	Overdue	0.45	7.34	1.06	10.70	0.38	6.20	0.56	6.00
		(6.13)		(9.91)		(6.12)		(9.33)	

Contd...

Table 1 : (Contd...)

(Rs. In crores)

S.No	Indicators	1960-61		1974-75		1980-81		1990-91		1999-2k	
		TN	India	TN	India	TN	India	TN	India	TN	India
1.	No. of Societies (in'000s)	11021	212000	4778	153000	4778	94000	4618	88000	4582	101545
2.	No. of members	0.24	1.70	0.30	3.60	0.51	5.75	0.59	8.40	0.84	10.84
3.	Average membership per society	213	80	624	239	1055	610	1286	848	1833	1084
4.	Loans issued	30.29 (6.70)	203	73.49 (8.16)	901	N.A	1886	344.22 (7.36)	4679	3468 (14.89)	23297
5.	Loan Outstanding	31.45 (14.43)	218	80.02 (6.79)	1177	363.57 (7.21)	2621	423.72 (6.16)	6877	3987	N.A
6.	Share Capital	4.89 (8.51)	57.45	17.31 (5.84)	296.29	42.35 (13.48)	571.08	58.07 (4.47)	1299.60	316.27 (8.99)	3518
7.	Working Capital	37.24 (13.76)	270.62	123.91 (8.07)	1534.86	364.65 (4.26)	8561.79	162.28 (1.89)	8561.79	5732 (8.99)	42495

Contd...

Table 1 : (Contd...)

(Rs. In crores)

S.No	Indicators	1960-61		1974-75		1980-81		1990-91		1999-2k	
		TN	*India*	*TN*	*India*	*TN*	*India*	*TN*	*India*	*TN*	*India*
8.	Overdue	26.52	44	101.22 (22.11)	503	171.47 (15.80)	1085	134.85 (4.29)	3139	971.13	N.A.

Source :
1. Sinha S.K., (1998), ' Rural Credit and Co-operatives in Inida', Suneja Publishers, New Delhi.
2. Pranab Kumar Chakravarthi, ' Problems of Co-operative Development in India', S. Chand & Co., New Delhi, 1983.
3. *Government of India,* Department of Agriculture and Co-operation, *Co-operative Movement in India – A Statistical Profile 1991, Department of Agriculture and Co-operation.* p-3.
4. TNSC Bank, *Annual Report, 2000, p. 124.*

Note : NA – Not Available.

Table 2 : An overview of the Ground Level Credit Issued

(Rs. In Lakhs)

Particulars	*1996-97*	*1997-98*	*1998-99*	*1999-2000*	*2000-2001*	*2001-2002*	*2002-2003*
Total Agricultural Credit							
Commercial Banks	9120	8028	10071	10311	4595	13858	12796
District Central Co-operative Bank	3055	5037	7341	7331	4746	9986	8830
Primary Agricultural & Development Bank	353	294	312	504	-	707	530
Sub – Total	12578	13359	17724	18146	20624	23051	22156
Other Priority Sector Advances	3632	5576	5479	6062	8944	13409	15084
Grand Total	16210	18935	23203	24208	29568	36460	37240

At present, there are 3485 SHGs functioning of which 2945 SHG functioning in rural areas. Their internal lending amounts to Rs.1473 lakhs. (TCDW: 2002). There are 977 groups linked with bank credit. It is expected that at least 1500 groups will be linked with the bank as on December 2003 with a likely credit off – take of Rs.650 lakhs.

The Results of the Study

Co-operatives and Self – Help Groups

Focus Group discussions were separately conducted between PACB and SHG members to identify their perception on different aspects of PACBs and SHGs. The outcome of the discussions is given in Box: 1

The parameters taken for discussion are not preconceived but emerged out of the discussion with the members. Here the members of SHG are clearer on the different aspects of these two institutions. Because, every member of SHG is involved in the management by rotation and regularly each SHG is involved in rating their SHG as per the indicators given by NGOs and Government Departments. It has been observed that these

Box: 1 : Differences between PACB and SHG

S.No	*Parameters*	*PACB SHG*
1. Constitution	General body of members / Special officers	General body of members
2. Who owns	Government and Members	Beneficiaries
3. Decision–making and management	Special officers and Executives	Members with the help of the animator
4. Systems & Procedures	Based on bylaws /guidelines of Registrar of Co-operatives Societies	Based on experience /Guidelines from NGOs.
5. Supervisory mechanism	Consisting of officials	Consisting of beneficiaries
6. Regulatory mechanism	TNCS Act 1983, TNCS Rules 1988 and bylaws	Societies Registration Act 1860 / self-regulated.
7. Financial resources	External borrowings	Internal savings
8. Functions	Focus on granting loans and distribution of essential articles under PDS	Focus on savings and entrepreneurial Development
9. Savings	No compulsion	Compulsory and encouraged
10. Fulfillment of credit needs	As per procedure	As per need.
11. Relationship between borrowings and savings	Very Low	Very High
12. Utilization of loan	Utilization is not ensured	Ensured
13. Responsibility to repay loan	Particular individual is solely responsible	Collective responsibility of the group
14. Overdue	Regular phenomenon	Unknown phenomenon
15. Experience in rural finance	Rich	Good and growing
16. Member Education	No such programme	Compulsory and Regular
17. Coverage	More than one revenue village	A street /ward
18. Outside dependency	High for financial resources & Management	Emphasis on self help
19. Factors deciding success	Quantitative achievements	Qualitative achievements

rating exercises bred group cohesion, and fix-up responsibility at every individual level. Here the role of NGOs and Government machineries needs appreciation.

Though the Co-operatives represent the application of self-help approach, they have ceased to be thrift-oriented, member-led, autonomous business organizations. Thus, they have grown without the co-operative character. The promotion of thrift amongst members, which was considered as one among the basic characteristics of PACS, has been completely given up, and to the extent, also the principle of member economic participation. The SHGs are autonomous to the core, despite the fact that they continue to draw support from NGOs and banks. Among the host of factors responsible for this full autonomy, the important is that they are informal entities.(K.Ramesha: 1996]

In the absence of democratic management for a quite long time and the failure of member education programmes, the members of PACBs were neither take care about the development of their organization nor interested in continuance of membership. The respondents felt that PACBs were only the extended arm of Government for delivering Government Schemes and programmes whereas SHG was an agency of them to satisfy their common needs and future aspirations. What could not be achieved through co-operatives could be achieved through SHGs; this has been the net realization by respondents. But one thing is apparent that this conclusion was not due to respondents' complete satisfaction over the functions of SHG, but due to the dissatisfaction over the functions of PACBs.

Access to Credit in Rural Areas

Rural money lending has been seen as a lucrative and money spinning activity. Not only the men but also the women informally lend money in rural areas. They have very good network and exchange the information on credibility of the borrowers. Each one also helps the other in recovering the dues from the borrowers. In the study it was found that respondents borrow normally from both formal and informal sources of credit. Although there is a network of formal lending institutions in the rural credit market and restrictions imposed by the Government of Tamilnadu on money lending, the informal sources recorded a mushroom growth in rural areas during recent past. These informal sources satisfy both the investment and consumption needs of the borrowers. An attempt has been made in this study to identify the share of different sources of credit in the total borrowings of the sample respondents.

It was observed that friends and relatives met 70 percent of the credit needs of SHG members. The PACB members approach friends and relatives, village traders, input sellers and moneylenders to their additional credit needs. That is why the average borrowing per members of PACB was Rs.87, 500 whereas it was Rs.11, 000 per members of SHG (Table 3). It shows that informal sources especially moneylenders are still having control over the rural credit market (Sankar Bowmick: 2002).

Table 3 : Source of Borrowings

(Amount in Rs.)

Sl.No	*Sources of Borrowings*	*PACB Borrowers*	*SHG Borrowers*
1.	PACB	(10.29) 9004	–
2.	SHG	–	(9.09) 1000
3.	Moneylenders	(57.41) 50234	–
4.	Friends	(13.45) 11769	51.83 5701
5.	Relatives	(3.59) 3140	27.27 1000
6.	Village Traders	(5.38) 4708	9.09 1000
7.	Input sellers	(9.88) 8645	2.72 299
	Total	87500 (100)	11000 (100)

Interest Paid to Money-Lenders

Moneylenders do not see whether their money is productively or unproductively used. They are very keen in return on their investment. Flexibility in lending and recovery, easy access to the borrowers, maintaining confidentiality of the borrower and his borrowings, friendliness, neighborhood etc., developed an umbilical relationship between the rural borrowers and moneylenders. The moneylenders coming from Dindigul, which is headquarter of the district, offer loans at the doorsteps of the borrowers of PACB. Continuous monsoon failure, absence of non-farm employment opportunities and increasing family expenses were reported as the causes for getting loans from moneylenders. The interest rate prevailing in the study area was Rs.3 to above Rs.10 for every Rs.100 per month. Hence, the average rate of interest per annum is beyond the capacity of the borrower to repay.

However, it was found that the SHG members had been relieved from the clutches of moneylenders to a greater extent after joining in the self – help group. Most of the members felt that the emergence of SHGs made easy access to credit in time. Affordable rate of interest, simple repayment through easy instalments and understandable procedures were the factors made the SHG members to feel satisfaction with this source of credit. But this has reduced only interest burden and not the debt burden (Gautam purkayastha: 2001).

Utilization of Loan by PACB Borrowers

The problem of agricultural finance i.e., overdue is aggravated by ineffective utilization of loans. Credit serves its purpose only when it is used for productive purpose to generate income. In this connection, an attempt has been made to study the utilization pattern of loan by the members of PACB who got loans only for productive purposes. A proper utilization of loans will have propound impact on repayment (Ravichandran K: 2000)

It was found that only 44 per cent of the members fully utilized the loans for the purpose for which it was issued, while 36 per cent of the members partially utilized the loan and 20 per cent of the members completely diverted the loan for different purposes.(Table 4)

Factors Which Led to Full Utilization of Loan

In the crop loan system, there is inbuilt mechanism to verify the utilization of the loan. Every PACB is expected to maintain crop verification register and the officials of the Co-operative

Department should inspect the same. Loans issued for other investment purposes also verified in the same manner. This mechanism has been developed to ensure that the loans are utilized for the specified purpose only. Here, the participation of the borrower is more important.

Table 4 : Utilization of Credit by the Members of PACB

(Figures in numbers)

S.No	*Particulars*	*No. of Respondents*	*Percentage to Total*
1.	Full Utilisation	62	44
2.	Partial Utilisation	50	36
3.	Complete Diversion	28	20
	Total	140	100

In this study, it was found that the lesser-unexpected expenses, awareness on the consequences of diversion, better income through investments and persuasion to use the loan for the specified purpose were found to be the factors, which led to the full utilization of credit. Among these, lesser-unexpected expenses were the major influencing factor. But no one borrower reported that supervisory mechanism of the PACB helped them to utilize the loan fully for specified purpose.(Table 5).

Table 5 : Factors Which Led to Full Utilization of Credit

(Figures in numbers)

S.No	*Particulars*	*No. of Respondents*	*Percentage to Total*
1.	Lesser unexpected expenses	22	36
2.	Awareness on the consequences of diversion	18	29
3.	Better income through investments	17	27
4.	Persuasion to use the loan for the specified purpose	5	8
	Total	62	100

Factors Which Led to Partial Utilization of Loan

The earlier studies conducted on the utilization behaviour of borrowers have identified either the extent of partial utilization with respect to size group of farmers (Kulwant pathania & Yogindar Varma: 1991) (Venugopala Reddy et.al, 1996) or the main factor which led to partial utilization.

So, the present study aimed to identify various factors which led to partial utilization of the loan by the borrowers such as increase in domestic expenses, natural calamities and increase in the cost of agricultural inputs and implements.

Among all the factors, increases in Domestic expenses on the part of the borrowers tend to partially utilize the loan. (Table 6).

Table 6 : Factors, Which lead to Partial Utilization of Credit

S. No	*Participation*	*No.of Respondents*	*Percentage*
1.	Domestic Expenses	20	39
2.	Natural Calamities	17	35
3.	Increase in the cost of agricultural inputs and implements	13	26
	Total	50	100

Purposes for Diversion of Credit

If the loan amount is not utilized for the specified purpose, it is called as 'diversion'. The diversion of the loan may be for productive or unproductive purposes. Though in both the cases, it is misutilisation, the utilization of credit for unproductive purposes may be termed as misutilisation. Here an attempt is made to study the purposes for which loan were diverted. In total 78 respondents were found to be diverted their loan (50 partial diversion and 28 complete diversion) for different purposes.

In the analysis it was found, 48 per cent of the borrowers productively diverted their loan amount such as agricultural expenses, business expenses etc., while 52 per cent of the borrowers unproductively diverted their loan amount for family, medical and educational expenses. The respondents themselves opined that the diversion of loan for unproductive purposes increases their indebtedness. (Modi M.K. & Rai K.N. : 1993 and Venugopala Reddy et.al.,:1996) (Table 7).

Table 7 : Purposes for Diversion of Credit

(Figures in numbers)

S.No.	*Particulars*	*No. of Respondents*	*Percentage to Total*
	Productive Purposes		
1.	Other Agricultural Expenses	23	30
2.	Business Expenses	6	8
3.	Increase in cost of inputs	8	10
	Unproductive Purposes		
1.	Family Expenses	20	26
2.	Medical Expenses	6	8
3.	Educational Expenses	11	13
4.	Unexpected Expenses	4	5
	Total	78	100

Repayment Behavior Among The Borrowers

The strength of the banks lies in the repayment behaviour of borrowers. If the loans borrowed are repaid properly the flow of resources will not be affected. However, the Government waiving policies have worsened the recovery climate. The continuous monsoon failure and absence of non-farm employment add fuel to the fire. As far as Dindigul District is concerned about 31 per cent of the households live below the poverty line. (NABARD, PLP- Dindigul: 2002 – 07). They suffer from lesser sources of income both in farm and non-farm sector. In this connection, the role of SHG is remarkable who satisfied the immediate domestic needs and pools the savings of rural people. The utilization and repayment of the loans are generally excellent in SHGs. Also, they have become income-generating groups by using locally available resources. But misutilisation of loan, defective lending policies, failure to recover the dues in time, failure of supervisory mechanism, willful defaults and political interferences affect the recovery of loans and mounts the burden of overdue to the PACB.

It was found that only 20 per cent of the PACB borrowers have fully repaid their loans. But the SHGs ensured cent percent recovery. The peer group pressure and credit for consumption needs exert a positive influence on loan repayment in SHGs (Girija Srinivasan and P. Satish : 2001) (Table 8).

Table 8 : Repayment Behavior Among the Borrowers

(Figures in numbers)

		No. of Respondents		
S. No.	*Particulars*	*PACB*	*SHG*	*Total*
1.	Fully Paid	28 (20)	140 (150)	168
2.	Partially Paid	56 (40)	-	56
3.	Not yet paid	56 (40)	-	56
	Total	140	140	280

Reasons for Regular Repayment

More than 50 per cent of the PACB borrowers regularly repaid the loan amount to borrow another loan (Rambabu et.al :1991) whereas the SHG members repaid the loan in order to maintain their credibility. Thus, very often face-to – face contacts and team spirit of the people enhance the repayment culture among the SHG members (Table 9).

Table 9 : Reasons for the Regular Repayment

(Figures in numbers)

		No. of Respondents	
S.No	*Particulars*	*PACB*	*SHG*
1.	To borrow another loan	16 (57)	42 (30)
2.	To maintain Credibility	-	78 (56)
3.	Good income from investment	12 (43)	20 (14)
	Total	28	140

Sources of Income Used for The Regular Repayment

Though the 'fully paid' category is very low in PACB, such borrowers have the custom to repay the loan only from the income. But 60 per cent of the SHG borrowers borrow from their friends and relatives to repay their group loans. It indicates that the basic minimum needs pressurized the rural people to borrow from various sources and ultimately leaves them in the midst of poverty (Table 10).

Table 10 : Sources of Income Used for the Regular Repayment

(Figures in numbers)

		No. of Respondents	
S.No	*Particulars*	*PACB*	*SHG*
1.	Income from investment	20 (71)	56 (40)
2.	Borrowings from friends and Relatives	8 (29)	84 (60)
	Total	28	140

Persuasion by The People to Repay

As far as SHG is concerned where there is regular repayment, the chief promoter motivates the members to repay the loan punctually. In the case of PACB, where the repayment is very low, 57 per cent of the borrowers who were prompt repayers repaid the loan by themselves without any pressure or inspiration by the bankers (Table 11).

Reasons for Not Repaying The Loan

Prompt repayment not only ensures the recycling of money for further investment, but also enhances the clientele of the credit institutions. The co-operatives have strong rural base so that they sustain even after the entry of commercial banks in the rural credit network. The main reason for the stagnation of credit flow from PACBs is due to the mounting of overdue which clogs the process of credit recycling. The excessive overdue erode the financial resources of the banks and ultimately cripple their normal working.

Table 11 : Persuasion by the People to Repay

(Figures in numbers)

		No. of Respondents	
S.No	*Particulars*	*PACB*	*SHG*
1.	Friends	10 (12)	-
2.	Family Members	11 (13)	-
3.	PACB officials	15 (18)	-
4.	Chief Promoters	-	46 (33)
5.	By themselves	48 (57)	94 (67)
	Total	84	140

Among the various reasons stated by the borrowers for not repaying the loan in time, insufficient income from investment and unexpected expenses increase the debt-burden of the PACB borrowers, which in turn mounts the overdue position of PACB in the study areas. Also, the Government waiving policies adds fuel to the fire (Table 12).

Table 12 : Reasons for Not Repaying the Loan

(Figures in numbers)

		No. of Respondents	
S.No	*Particulars*	*PACB*	*Percentage*
1.	Insufficient income from investment	28	50
2.	Unexpected expenses	14	25
3.	Family Expenses	4	7
4.	Natural Calamities	10	18
	Total	56	100

Conclusion

The study found that the dominance of moneylenders could still be found in satisfying the credit needs of the members of

PACBs. Even though the SHGs, as an alternative institutional credit sub-system, have overcome this problem, more than 50 percent of the SHG members approach their friends and relatives for their additional credit needs. Also, they are not totally free from debt since they get new loan immediately after repaying the old loan. Some SHGs are concentrating only on micro credit while other SHGs have facilitated more income generating programmes (IGP). The utilization of credit for the purpose for which it was given could not be ensured in the case of the members of the PACB. It tends to unproductive diversion and non-repayment of loan among the PACB borrowers. The peer group pressure, involvement of every member in the management of SHG and face – to – face contacts enhances the proper repayment of loan by the members of SHG. It shows that SHGs have been not only accessible to rural people in satisfying their credit needs and maintaining credit discipline but also emerged as breeding centres of rural entrepreneurs. This is major shift of SHGs from micro credit to *micro finance*. Hence, the 100 years of history made the co-operatives as quasi-governmental organizations, whereas their basic values viz., self-help, self-responsibility, democracy, equality, equity and solidarity have become the business rules of SHGs. So shall we call SHGs as new generation co-operatives?

NOTES

1. Primary Agriculture Co-operative Societies are called as Primary Agriculture Co-operative Banks in Tamilnadu with effect from Government Notification –G.O.Ms.No.507, CO-OPERATION (CCI) DEPARTMENT Dated: 1.9.1987 and Letter No.32651/CG.2/87-1, Dated: 13-5-1989.

REFERENCES

Balishter and Pankaj kumar, (1995), 'A Study of Institutional Finance in Agriculture', *Land Bank Journal*, Vol. 34(1), September, p. 16.

Gautam Purkayastha, (2001), 'Rural Indebtedness in Assam', www.epw.com

Girija Srinivasan and P.Satish, (2001), 'Networking for Micro Credit Delivery', *Journal of Rural Development,* Vol.20(4), October-December, p. 636.

Jaya S.Anand, (1995), 'Utilisation of Long-term Credit: A Case Study', *Land Bank Journal,* Vol. 34(2), December, p. 33.

Karmakar K.G., (1997), 'Supplementary Rural Credit Delivery System – Some Asian Models', *Journal of Rural Development*, Vol.16, July-September, p. 481.

Kulwant Pathania and Yogindar Varma, (1991), 'Impact of Size of Loan and Types of Farmers on Co-operative Credit Utilization', *Indian Co-operative Review*, Vol.29 (2), October, pp. 152-158.

Modi M.K. and Rai K.N., (1993), 'Credit Utilization Pattern on Different Categories of Farms in the District of Kurkshetra, Haryana', *Indian Co-operative Review*, Vol.30(3), January, p. 253.

NABARD, (2001-02), *Annual Report*, p. 127.

NABARD, (2002-03), *Annual Report*, p. 97.

NABARD, (2002-07), *Potential Linked Credit Plan for Dindigul District*, p. 80.

Namboodiri N.V., (2001), 'Potential Role of SHGs in Rural Financing Deepening', *Indian Joural of Economics,* Vol.56 (3), July-September, p. 402.

NCUI, (2001), *Indian Co-operative Movement – A Profile,* New Delhi, P. 19.

Rambabu,Daivadeenam and Eswara Prasad, (1991), 'Repayment Pattern of Agricultural Credit – A Study of Andhra Pradesh in Guntur District', *Indian Co-operative Review*, October, p. 163.

Ramesha K., (1996), 'SHGs: Emerging Co-operatives', In *Rediscovery of Co-operation,* by Rajagopalan R,(Edt), Vol.11, IRMA, Anand, p. 209.

Ravichandran K., (2000), *'Crop Loan System and Overdue'*, Spell Bound Publications, Rohtak, p. 76.

Sankar Bhowmick (2002), 'Structure and Operations of Rural Credit Markets in West Bengal' www.microcredit.com

Somorendra Singh, (2001), 'Trend in Recovery of Loan in PACS', *The Maharashtra Co-operative Quarterly,* Vol. 34(4), April-June, p. 14.

Tamilnadu Corporation for the Development of Women Ltd., (2002), *Agenda of Project Officers' Review Meeting*, Dindigul, p. 1.

Venugopala Reddy and Ratnakar, (1996), 'Credit Utilization Pattern of Farmers', *Land Bank Journal,* Vol.35(1), September, pp. 33-35.

13

Challenges Before Marketing Co-operatives

A.P. Kansal

Introduction

The objective of marketing co-operatives in the agricultural produce marketing system is to effectively compete with firms and /or individuals who earn unreasonably high profits by increasing farmers' bargaining power in the market and thus ensuring incentive price to them. Besides, marketing and processing co-operatives for agricultural produce should also create strong backward linkages towards increasing the productivity of farmers and lowering their cost by pooling the input purchase requirements. Similarly, marketing and agro-processing co-operatives offer possibilities of establishing forward linkages by undertaking processing of raw produce and guaranteed access to market for outputs. Such forward vertical integration offers new marketing opportunities and markets for the benefit of producers through better price realization.

The role of co-operatives in marketing of agricultural produce is manifold. These help farmers to pool their produce and secure a better price in the market. By their presence in the agricultural markets, these provide marketing cover or protection to the farmers. It is in recognition of this role of farmer owned co-operatives that the Government has designated co-operatives as nodel agencies for the price support operations of oilseeds, coarse grains and pulses and marketing intervention schemes for perishables like ginger, pineapples, grapes citrus fruits, onion, potato. In conjunction with public sector organizations like the Food Corporation of India (FCI), Jute Corporation of India (JCI), Cotton Corporation of India (CCI) etc., the coopera-tives provide support as agents of these organizations for purchase of produce directly from the farmers. The commercial purchases of marketing co-operatives seek to set the trend for prices in the market. Thus, co-operatives provide organized support to the farmers and eliminate exploitative practices of the middlemen.

Co-operative Marketing Structure

The structure of Co-operative Marketing Societies consists of the National Agricultural Co-operative Marketing Federation of India Ltd. (NAFED) at the national level, the State Cooperative Marketing Federations at the state level and Primary Marketing Co-operatives at the agricultural market (mandi) level. By and large, the co-operative marketing structure in the states is 2-tier viz. primary marketing societies at mandi level affiliated to state marketing federations at the apex level. Almost all secondary mandi centres in the country are covered by 3216 general purpose and 5585 special commodity co-operative marketing societies. In addition, 157 district/central societies are also in existence in some of the States. General purpose apex level marketing federations have been organized in 27 States and 4 union Territories of Andaman & Nicobar Islands, Delhi, Lakshadweep and Pondicherry with NAFED at the national level.Besides, 22 state level special commodity marketing federations have been organized. In states, having concentration of tribal population, minor forest produce is marketed by large-sized adivasi multipurpose societies (LAMPS) at primary level and Tribal Development Co-operatives/Federa-tions at state level with Tribal Co-operative Marketing Development Federation of India Ltd., (TRIFED) at national level providing marking as well as managerial support to the tribal co-operatives. The organizational and structural process of marketing co-operatives is fully developed and now the stress is on consolidating and streamlining their activities and rejuvenating weak co-operatives to make them self-reliant.

Functions

Primary Marketing Societies: Following are the main functions of co-operative marketing societies:

(a) To arrange sale of agricultural produce of the members by undertaking functions like grading, packing, transportation, pooling etc;

(b) To advance pledge loan;

(c) To procure and supply agricultural inputs and essential consumers goods;

(d) To provide storage facilities to members;

(e) To act as an agent of Government for procurement of agricultural commodities;

(f) To undertake processing of agricultural commodities; and

(g) To act as an agent of the member credit co-operative societies for recovery of production loans.

In actual practice, however, most of the primary marketing societies have confined their activities to marketing of agricultural commodities brought by farmers mostly on agency basis, undertaking procurement on behalf of Government/State Marketing Federation and distribution of agricultural inputs. Some of the societies own processing units and distribute consumer goods in rural areas through village societies. Some societies advance pledge loan to members also. Very few societies have undertaken grading, pooling, transportation, processing and sale of agricultural commodities in terminal markets.

District Marketing Societies : The District Marketing Societies exist in some states where there is three-tire pattern of organization. The societies were organized with the object to coordinate the functions of primary marketing societies both in regard to marketing of agricultural produce and distribution of agricultural inputs and consumer goods. These societies were also to undertake processing where necessary, inter-district trade in agricultural commodities etc. But in actual practice, these are mostly involved in the distribution of agricultural inputs and essential consumers goods. Except in some cases, the extent of marketing operations undertaken by such societies is not appreciable as in many areas; district places are not wholesale markets. Thus, there is very little scope for such district societies to coordinate the marketing of agricultural produce. On the contrary, due to existence of primary marketing society in the mandi or district place, there is unnecessary competition between the primary and district marketing society. These societies, where they exist play a role in the procurement and distribution of agricultural inputs and supply of consumer goods to farmers.

State Marketing Federations : The Co-operative Marketing Federation has a crucial role to play in the development of primary co-operative marketing societies. This federation is organized for undertaking operations on behalf of its affiliated societies, particularly in the field of inter-state and export trade of agricultural commodities and also in the procurement of agricultural inputs and consumer goods required by the farmers. Where large scale processing is required, the state federation may undertake such processing. It may also set up manufacturing units for agricultural inputs for effective service. Other important functions of such federations are dissemination of market intelligence, rendering expert advice on marketing and processing and close liason with concerned State Government Departments. These are also expected to undertake development functions such as assisting its affiliates in construction of godowns, processing units, etc. All these functions necessarily confer upon such federations the duties of coordination, guidance and supervision over their affiliated societies. In practice, however, all the State Federations have not undertaken these functions fully.

NAFED

The main function of national federation is to coordinate the activities of state federations and render expert advice and technical guidance to them on problems relating to co-operative marketing, processing, inter-state trade, export trade, market and price trends, commercial intelligence, business techniques, etc. It may also directly undertake export and inter-state trade and arrange imports of agricultural inputs and other essential articles. Where large scale processing covering more than one state is required, it can set up such processing unit for promotion of interests of farmers. National Federation is undertaking most of these functions.

Need for Integrated Approach

Co-operative Marketing Structure has to compete with private trade which is entrenched firmly in the business. Integration and collective steps in various activities are a must for the structure. Such integration is possible when following basic principles are fully recognized by all concerned at all levels.:

(i) Unhealthy competition and duplication of functions at various levels should be avoided.

(ii) Higher level organizations should always work for the benefit and development of lower institutions and not independently in competition with them.

(iii) Undue concentration of too many functions/resources should be avoided. Gradual decentralization and specialization in different fields should be the aim.

Based on the above principles, mutual relationship and working arrangements are to be developed at the various levels of the structure so as to facilitate integrated approach and rendering better services to the farming community.

Marketing Operations

During the year 2000-01, co-operatives marketed agricultural produce of the value of Rs.9114.98 crores. Nine states of Haryana, Karnataka, Kerala, Madhya Pradesh, Maharashtra, Punjab, Rajasthan, Tamilnadu and Uttar Pradesh accounted for nearly 97 percent of the agricultural produce marketed by co-operatives.

Co-operatives continued to play important role in marketing of fresh fruits and vegetables. During the year 2002-03, value of fruits and vegetables marketed by co-operatives amounted to Rs. 195.65 crores. Major role was played by Gujarat, Himachal Pradesh, Karnataka, Maharashtra, Tamilnadu and West Bengal.

During 2002-03, NAFED undertook price support and market intervention operations mainly in respect of copra, mustard seed, sunflower seeds and urad as a Central Nodal Agency. NAFED also undertook export of onions, niger seed, spices and foodgrains. During 2002-03, NAFED achieved a record business turnover of Rs.2189.88 crores registering an increase of 49.12% over previous year's achievement of Rs.1468.54 crores. Figures of domestic sale and foreign trade of NAFED for 2002-03 were Rs.1874.01 and Rs.315.87 crores respectively. NAFED's presence in mandis through State Federations and lower level marketing co-operatives helped in stabilizing agricultural prices in favour of producers.

Country's economy being pre-dominantly agriculture related, distribution of fertilizer and other inputs is of vital importance. Co-operatives are one of the important institutional agencies for providing fertilizers and other farm imputes to farmers besides credit support. Except in States of Nagaland, Tripura, Mizoram and Arunachal Pradesh where distribution of fertilizer in undertaken by State Agricultural Departments, the co-operatives are actively involved in distribution of fertilizers in all the other States. The organizational set up for distribution of fertilizer varies from state to state. By and large, the structure is two-tier with State Marketing Federation acting a wholesalers at the State level and Primary marketing Co-operatives / PACS as retailers. All the State Marketing Federations and more than 50% PACS/LAMPS/FSS in the country are engaged in the distribution of fertilizers. In addition, commodity societies and their federations are engaged in distribution of fertilizer in some States. During 2000-01, co-operatives distributed 60.49 lakh tonnes of fertilizers (nutrients) representing 31.07% of the total fertilizers distributed in the country. Of this 73.5% fertilizer was distributed by co-operatives of U.P., Punjab, M.P., Maharashtra and Gujarat. Similarly, co-operatives are playing important role in making available other agricultural inputs like pesticides, seeds and implements.

Co-operatives have established 6988 Farmers Service Centers for undertaking wide range of agricultural inputs and also to meet non-credit needs of farmers. Besides, co-operatives have set up 384 Agro custom Hiring Centers for helping small and marginal farmers. Co-operatives are increasingly engaging in established Vermic Compost Units and Bio-Fertilizers Units.

Co-operatives have been playing significant role in the distribution of consumer goods particularly supply of essential consumer items at fair prices to the rural community especially in the remote, inaccessible and hilly areas through 44418 village societies and 9504 branches of such rural co-operatives.

Creation of storage capacity for marketing and supply operations has been taken up by the co-operatives with the assistance of National Co-operative Development Corporation (NCDC). The total storage capacity created by co-operatives increased from 11 lakh tonnes in 1962-63 to 139.57 lakh tonnes by March 31, 2003. Now, over 50,500 primary agricultural co-operatives and most of the marketing co-operatives in the country have constructed godowns with assistance provided by the NCDC.

Co-operatives continued to play an important role as agents of public sector commodity corporations like FCI and JCI. The contribution of co-operative in procurement of Jute on behalf of JCI is significant. During 2001-02, co-operatives procured 69.26 lakh tonnes of wheat through 5530 purchase centres in 5 major wheat growing states.

Problems of Co-operative Marketing Structure

There has been steady growth in the marketing of agricultural produce by co-operatives. Co-operatives have not only achieved the targets set for themselves for marketing of agricultural produce but have been exceeding their targets. Inspite of increase being recorded in agricultural marketing operations of co-operatives year by year, following are major problems of the co-operative marketing structure.

(a) Absence of forward and backward linkages in the structure.

(b) Most of the marketing co-operatives are mainly engaged in supply activities rather then marketing activities.

(c) Very few of them are making outright purchases and selling farmers' produce through pooling.

(d) Co-operative Marketing Societies are undertaking marketing of agricultural produce mainly by handling the produce of farmers on commission basis.

(e) Very few marketing societies are providing marketing finance against the pledge of agricultural produce.

(f) Marketing co-operatives are financially weak and are unable to mobilize adequate working capital for business activities.

(g) In most of the marketing co-operatives, departmental officers are working as Secretary/Manager.

(h) Marketing co-operatives like to engage in the business activities having lesser risks with the result that no long term planning is undertaken at the level of the marketing co-operatives in the service of the farmers.

(i) Co-operative Marketing Structure and various public sector commodity corporations have not developed business links.

The NCDC is making efforts to develop the co-operative marketing structure through planning and providing assistance under its various schemes. There is emphasis on adoption of "Business Development Planning" (BDP) approach in marketing co-operatives. It is hoped that working of marketing co-operatives would improve year by year.

Challenges

In the wake of WTO regime and policy of liberalization and privatization following challenges are facing marketing co-operatives:

The role of marketing co-operatives in bringing value added price to the farmers for their agricultural produce assumes grater importance. The thrust of the programmes in future, therefore, would be to develop functional linkages with PACs for providing marketing, agro-processing, consumer goods and input supplies to farmers through grass root level co-operatives. Similarly, steps would have to be taken for developing integrated approach in co-operative marketing structure. Establishment of agro-processing units and managing those efficiently will be of vital concern to marketing societies to achieve their objectives in the years to come.

Marketing is a very specialized and critical activity in any business organization. The co-operatives would be able to help the members only if they run successfully by providing necessary services to the members and are also able to generate surpluses for redistribution to the members. The issues relating the democratic management, co-operative autonomy, a proper co-operative linkage with larger participation of members are very important aspects which are being highlighted at different forums. An important aspect in co-operative marketing is professional management with proper orientation, expertise, training and motivation. This has been lacking in a large number of marketing co-operatives which needs immediate attention.

It is common knowledge that in rural areas the traders and other people with resources advance loans to farmers to recover the loan when the crop is harvested. In a way, such farmers are tied with such traders/middlemen. It has been noticed that such traders also meet the credit needs for consumption loans like those relating to education, marriage and other religious ceremonies. The co-operatives are not able to provide such services to their members. It is necessary, therefore, that in addition to production loans, the co-operatives also provide consumption loans to the members and establish a linkage of credit and marketing so that the loan advanced are recovered well in time.

In the past, serious attempts have not been made to revitalize the marketing co-operatives. One point approach has been to provide more margin money to such co-operatives but it gets evaporated quickly without adding any business to such cooperatives. Release of margin money assistance after preparing a total rehabilitation package which would involve larger participation from members and other support from the State Government is called for. More induction of margin money will not help. It is necessary, therefore, that to revitalize the marketing cooperatives a time bound and systematic programme is undertaken to work out proper rehabilitation package including provision for managerial and financial input and an integrated view is taken to strengthen such societies.

An exercise has been undertaken by NCDC, NCCT, the Ministry of Agriculture and State Governments to provide training to the staff to prepare 'Business Development Plans' for the marketing co-operatives as also for consumer co-operatives and create a linkage between the PACs, the marketing societies and the consumer co-operatives. Adoption of "Business

Development Plan" approach will strengthen the marketing co-operatives in the country.

A strong co-operative credit structure is also necessary to provide necessary financial support to the agricultural co-operative marketing system in the country. There is an urgent need to train the staff of the marketing societies to help them with the modern tools of management in running the marketing societies successfully. The marketing societies are not able to attract qualified staff on account of poor financial position and on account of the lack of good professional staff, they are not able to run successfully. To arrest this cycle, it is necessary to arrange for proper training for the employees of the marketing societies and adopt a total approach to improve the working of the co-operative marketing societies.Many agricultural commodities are exported to number of countries in processed or unprocessed form. Co-operative marketing societies would be required to explore possibilities of exports of the produce of members, re-orient their operations and integrate functioning ensuring benefits to their members for continuing loyalty from them.

Marketing is the most important function in the economic activities with which co-operatives are concerned and with integrated system of proper pricing policy, marketing infrastructure and actual successful operations of marketing, we can afford to provide satisfactory services to the farmers which will improve their economic status.

Conclusion

Marketing Co-operatives are the hope for the farmers in future. It is high-time that these co-operatives mange their affairs in the service of farming community efficiently and effectively facing the challenges thrown to them in the new environment.

14

Co-operative Sugar Sector : New Avenues For Revenues

G.V. Madiwal, Y.V. Reddy and M.R. Patil

Introduction

Sugar is the first processed article of the diet that every child enjoys with milk. We need Sugar right from morning in bed tea to till at night in sugarcoated tablets. Sugar plays a significant role as a source of energy in our diet. A few of us know about cultivation of sugarcane (raw material), processes of sugar manufacturing and it's by products. After textile industry, sugar industry is the second largest organized agro-based industry in India.

Reference of sugar and its product occurs in Vedas and epics indicated that the sugar was known to Hindus earlier than to any other race. Mr. Columbus introduced sugar cane to American in his second voyage led to the rapid development of sugar manufacturing in tropical America. The other settlers, Spanish, Portuguese and Dutch spread sugar manufacturing rapidly into many parts of America. During the 13th century, sugar cultivation started in all the countries in the Mediterranean. After that Mediterranean became the sources of supply of sugar cane to Europe and Africa.

British rulers made a remarkable achievement in 1922 by appointing the Sugar Commission to observe sugar cane cultivation in India. The sugar scientist revealed that the Indian canes were unfit for white sugar industry. The Coimbattore Breeding station developed a new variety and made possible the growth of sugar industry not only in India but also several other countries. In 1930 the Govt. of India appointed a Tariff Board to examine the position of the sugar industry in India and based on the Board's report passed the Sugar Industry Protection Act, 1932. A clause in the Act protected indigenous sugar industries in India for an initial period of 14 years, till 1st march, 1946.

Global Scenario

Sugar cane is cultivated in 127 countries in the world. Most of them are situated in between 35°S and 35°N of the Equator with altitudes ranging from sea level to over 700 metres and with varying climatic conditions and soils. About one third of the world's sugar production contributed by the five countries viz., Cuba, Puerto Rico, Dominican Republic, Jamaica and Trinidad. The major sugar producers are Brazil, Argentina, Peru and Mexico. In USA the principal sugar cane States are Hawaian Islands, Louisiana and Florida. At a lowest cost of production the USA sugar producers maintaining highest environmental and labour standard. The USA is also a major sugar importer. Here sugar cane harvesting season normally extends 22 to 24 months and some times it extends even 30 to 34 months. The highest sugar recovery recorded in Australia. The Republic of South Africa, Egypt and the islands of Mauritius are the three major sugar producers in African continents. In Asia the major sugar cane producing countries are in India, Indonesia, Philippine and China. In India sugar cane is cultivated in 40.76 lakhs hectors of land. India ranks first with regard to the area followed by Brazil (26 lakhs hectors) and 13 lakhs hectors in Cuba. The International Sugar Organization established under the International Sugar Agreement 1968. After two decades International Sugar Agreement was adopted by the United Nations' Conference on Trade and Development in 1992. India casts 38 votes out of 2000 votes in International Sugar Council.

Role Sugar Industry In India Economy

Altogether there are 506 sugar mills installed in India, unfortunately only 453 mills are functioning. There are 143 mills in India's sugar bowl i.e. Maharastra, followed by Uttar Pradesh, 129 mills. The sugar sector has generated employment for 4 crore farmers in the fields of 40.76 hectors and 5 lakhs in 506 in factories. The Indian farmers are capable to produce 30 crore metric tones of sugar cane in a year. In India early varieties mature in 10 to 11 months and late varieties stands on the field for 12 to 14 months. The Adsali crop stand on the field for 14 to 18 which is grow in Maharashtra and some parts of Andra Pradesh. Normally the crushing season in India extends from October to May. The Southwest monsoon affecting areas start their crushing in October whereas Northeast monsoon affecting regions start their season during late November. Tamil Nadu and some parts of Karnataka get a chance to start their crushing season from June to September and also run their mills about 190 to 200 days above the normal period of 120 to 150 days. During the month of October highest recovery rate is observed.

India produces about 15.53 million tones of sugar every year. The state of Maharashtra contributes 5.34 million tones followed by U.P. 3.73 million tones. Today India is not only self-sufficient but also capable to export to a tune of 0.81 million tones per annum to more than 20 countries. The countries like Pakistan, Bangladesh and Shri Lanka are our bulk buyers. The annual sugar cane price paid to the cultivators by the Sugar mills amounts to Rs.12,500 crore per year. The annual turnover of the Sugar Sector amounts to Rs.20,000 Crore. The Central Excise Department gets an income of Rs.1,400 Crores are the State Governments receives Rs. 800 Crore in the form various cases. Looking at the importance of the Sugar sector the Government of India establish 56 Sugar cane Research stations all over the country.

Co-operative Sugar Scenario in India

Indian sugar industry can be classified into two categories viz. Organized sector (consist of modern sugar factories) and unorganized sector (consist of traditional Sweeteners like gur and Khandsari). The Unorganized sector considered as a rural industry and enjoys much greater freedom than sugar factories. They contribute about 37% of total Sweetener consumption in India. The farmers co-operatives own and operate the lion share of the total capacity of sugar industry. Share of sugar co-operative in the national sugar sector amounts to 59%. The First Five Year Plan (1951-56) could not do a notable improvement in the co-operative sector of the sugar industry. The plan finished with only three co-operative sugar factories on the map of India's sugar industry. The country had to import 0.73 million tones. A ten fold improvement was achieved by the co-operative sector in 1960-61. Indian businessmen and sugar cultivators established 174 sugar mills, out of that 30 factories here in co-operative sector. The total output of sugar was 3.02 million tones and the share of the co-operative was 0.45 millions tones. In 1970-71 there were 73 mills, in 1980-81 149 co-operative sugar factories, in 1990-91 the number shot up to 220 and at the end of the century it was 259 out of 436 sugar mills in India. Today we have 252 working co-operative mills out of 453 (working) mills. About 53 mills in India are not functioning due to several problems.

Problem of Sugar Industry in India

Low Yield of Sugar Cane

Low cane productivity is one of the serious problems that confronts the industry. The Sugar cane yield was 30.9 tones per hector in 1930-31. But the two fold improvement observed after implementation of new varieties of sugar cane like Adsali. In 1994-95 it was 71.3 tonnes per hector and in 2002-03. This year it was 72.6 tonnes per hector. It is very low when it is compared with Peru and Rhodesia which produce 171.4 and 100 tones per hector respectively.

The sugar cane yield across the country varies widely in the range of 40 to 134.2 tones per hector. The Tamil Nadu and Karnataka states stand first and second by producing 134.2 and 91.2 tonnes per hector respectively. Leading states like Madhya Pradesh and Bihar have the lowest yield in the range of 39.3 to 48.5 tones per hector. The Maharashtra and Goa has 89 and 60.6 tones of yield per hector.

Outdated Machinery

Most of the Machineries in sugar mills, particularly in those of U.P and Bihar are out-dated. For the last 40-50 years none of the major repairs or replacements have been made. Low profit often do not allow a substantial depreciation without which the rehabilitation cannot be done.

The Co-operative Sugar Factory, Goa could not make significant gain for the last 30 years. The cumulative effect of accumulated loss did not allow the Mill's management to go for modernization. The factory never experienced major repairs since inception.

Low Rate of Sugar Consumption

The average per capita consumption of sugar in India is only about 17.75 kg per annum, gur and khandsari 8.62 kg per annum (total 26.37kg); one of the lowest in the world. It is 55 kg in Australia, 52 kg in U.K and 50 kg in USA. The high sugar price and substitutes availability in the form of gur in the country, are often responsible for low consumption. Jagarry tea is common in Indian villages.

Competition with Gur and Khandsari Industry

One of the most serious threats faced by the sugar industry is its competition with unorganized sector- gur and khandsari producers. Imposition of high excise duty and control on sugar stock, sugar price and cane price have resulted, decrease in the profit margin of the sugar mills and therefore, they are neither in a position to offer high price of cane to the farmers nor in a position to make payment in time. On the contrary khandsari units are free from such impediments and therefore, even though the recovery percentage of gur or khandsari does not exceed 6 - 7 percent against 8 -10 percent in case of sugar, it is able to offer higher price for cane and payment in time. Infect, over 50 % of the cane grown in the country is consumed by the cottage industry. During the period of low sugar cane production in the country, gur and khandsari producers simply supply their raw materials to the mills, and yet a good return without much efforts.

Government Policies

Neither the sugar cane cultivators nor the sugar mill owners are happy with the implementation of Government policies either by the Central Government or by the State Governments. So far no research has been made on the impact of the Government policies on sugar sector. The Government policies are the key earning drivers of the sugar sector. The government control on the sugar industry extends from procurement of raw material to sale of sugar. Any liberal move in government policies relating to the removal or reduction in levy quota, monthly release mechanism for free market, export thrust, import duty and financial incentives to take over of sick units will have enormous benefits for the sugar industry in the long term. The Central Government regulates sugar price through releases. Presently free sale is 90% of the total production and levy sugar 10%. The overall realization per quintal is much below the cost of factories. The Govt. control policies led to blocked stock of sugar of 12.8 millions tones in 2002-03 which amounts to Rs.16,000 crore.

Other Related Problems are

(i) The idea of sugar complex has not been implemented properly, factories are not permitted to utilize their own molasses;

(ii) obligation have increased to maintain clean air and environment;

(iii) low rate of import duty led to the dumping of sugar from other country.

(iv) due consideration is not given for the promotion of sugar export; and

(v) the Statutory Minimum Price (SMP) is influenced by political wind rather than economic significance.

Suggested Model to Overcome the Problems

In 2005, no states in the world will have a control over the entry of foreign products in their country. The country like China, Japan, USA, are waiting to dump their product in the Indian market for the 'crazy buyers of foreign product'. China has already encroached our toys market. In the mean time the Govt. of India introduced disinvestments policy and sold it stake. In this juncture, the co-operatives are the only hope of the masses to meet the future challenges.The success of the co-operative sugar industries purely depends upon the introduction of the following steps effectively and efficiently.

Corpoerate Patriotism

The co-operative sector is the only field where the members play multi- dimensional role; as a buyer, as a seller, as a producer, as an administrator, as a banker, etc. In case of joint-stock companies, real owners are kept away from the direct participation. The stake-holder are interested in wealth maximization rather than socio-economic development of their company and employees. Lack of corporate patriotism is clearly visible among the members of the joint stock concerns.

The co-operative sector generated 'surety and security' for members. The co-operative sugar factories, in particular, provide a definite market for their entire lot of sugar cane and infrastructure development funds at low rate of interest. A drastic advancement in this direction may push up the status of the co-operative sugar factories among the co-operative sectors.

Merging of the State Boundaries

Most of the co-operative sugar mills in India have problem of short supply of sugar cane. The sugar factories are seasonal in nature. They run 90 to 130 days in a year. Even after considering three shift per day, the total operating time comes less than any other mills which run for 8 hours per day. No unit can maintain its expenditure after utilizing 25% to 33 % capacity but sugar industry is still reaping profit.

The Sanjivani Sahakari Sakhar Karkhana in Goa, could not utilize its full crashing capacity since inception. Goan farmers have been supplying only 40 % of the total cane requirement of the factory for the last 30 years. The factory is depending upon the 60% of gate-cane from karnantaka. The Karnataka farmers are not only interested to supply sugar cane but also interested to become members. The political boundaries of the states do not allow them to unify, being in the same union government. It is high time for the co-operative sugar sector to merge the political boundaries as early as possible without prejudice.

Sugar Industries into Sugar Complexes

The by-products of the sugar industries are (a) Bagasses (30%-35%), (b) Molasses (4%-5%), (c) Press mud (2%-4%), (d) Leaves and Tops (25%-35%) and (e) Boiler ash (0.3%). The cost of sugar continues to be high and due to the neglect of the profitable utilization of the by-products. If the by-products are used the cost of production of the sugar may go down by about 20%. The development of sugar cane by-products industries and their ancillaries may push up the profitability of the sugar industry. The countries like Australia, Brazil, Cuba, Philippines, South Africa and Taiwan have developed numerous industries utilizing the by-products. Some of these countries produce alcohol as main product and sugar as by-product.

All the sugar industries in India have an opportunity to utilize the by-products and the off-season man-days. The sugar mills do not have any operation for 240-270 days in a year. In these days the industries can:

(a) Generate Electricity Power; produce fine writing paper with the help of Australian technology or ready made cattle feed by utilizing bagasses ;

(b) extract alcohol and spirit from molasses; and

(c) wax from filter cake/press mud.

Additional investment in new plant certainly will fetch a large amount of revenue. The industries can compensate the man and machine hours unutilised of in the sugar production unit in off-season. Let us establish co-operative sugar complexes but not just sugar factories in due course.

Recruiting Co-operative Specialist

Only the efficient and expert management can create innovative ideas. Hence there is need to appoint competent man power. The success in performing the functions of recruitment and selection depends on a well-defied recruitment policy. The success of recruitment policy depends upon 'LET' mentality of the employees and THREE 'A's-Adept, Adapt and Adopt.

Let the adept or expert personnel frame the policy;

Let us adopt or accept it, if does not work;

Let us adapt or modify as per our needs.

Majority of Board of Directors occupies the position by virtue of their economic status in the society. The quorum of these directors hampers the innovative ideas of the sugar professionals. The seminar like this may inculcate them to think in right direction; leaving their prejudice and age-old beliefs aside. The well-informed members of the co-operative sugar factories can over turn the problems of selection of directors. Hence the need of the hour is an awareness programme at bottom level.

Export as Viable Option

The countries like Brazil, European Union and Thailand dominate the world export market. Due to the large scale government subsidies and protectionist policy of the respective States, they succeeded in keeping the international price at rock bottom i.e. at Rs. 850 to 900 per quintal, corresponding sugar cost Rs. 1200 to 1250 in India. They never pay Minimum Support Price (MSP) to their farmers. Lot of export incentives and modern technology have these countries at top and in stationary position.

Sugarcanes are crushed under three wheels to extract the sugar juice. In India, unfortunately, sugar industries are under the pressure of three wheels - Cane Price wheel, Quota wheel and Tax wheel. On an average cane constitutes 60% of the total cost of sugar production. The Central and the State Governments notifications on Statutory Minimum Price (SAP) control the sugarcane procurement policy of the factories. The notifications are released in the month of October every year. These notifications are influenced by the sugar politics of the respective states.

In spite of the resistance, Sanjivani Sahakari Sakhar Karkhana, Goa introduced high price for high quality canes, based on recovery rate. Quota system of the Central Govt. led to the pilling up of sugar stock is another problem. For the year 2002-03 it was Rs. 16,000 crore, created an additional burden of 'carrying cost' in the form of interest and maintenance. Quota system is not applicable to gur and khandsari units. The inventory caring cost can be shifted to any other agencies of public distribution system by handovering the stock.

Many sugar units can not bear the pressure of the cess wheel at various stages. In this direction the rational thought of Govt, of Karnataka should be appreciated. The said Govt. had withdrawn the tax burden and created an environment to grow fast with their highest recovery rate which is the vital point of the sugar industries in Karnataka. It is the well organized and with high civic sense members group of the co-operative sugar factories can lead prevailing sugar politics in a right direction.

Conclusion

Ten Avenues For Sugar Revenues

(1) Amicable interstate agreement may abolish shortage of sugarcane problem.

(2) The policy of cane price based on recovery rate gives justice to the efficient farmers and inefficient units.

(3) No more sugar factories but sugar complexes which will generate employment, sales proceeds throughout the year.

(4) Handover the sugar stock to any national inventory agencies and get rid of the nuisance of 'carrying cost'.

(5) Recruitment of trained and adept personnel in co-operative sugar sector.

(6) Implementation of complete freedom and autonomy from paper into practice.

(7) Treating socio-economic impact made by the co-operative sugar industries itself is the tax recovery. Hence recognizing sugar sector as less cess or cessless sector as in the case of unorganized sugar sector.

(8) Self-conscious programme for members to generate corporate patriotism.

(9) Setting of export target and not any import quota.

(10)Following 'LOTUS' policy–keeping politics away being in and around politics. In Short

"Let us drive the growth engine of co-operative sugar factories for prosperity and nation building with self-respect, self-confidence, self-help and mutual help, and self-sufficient."

REFERENCE

M.V. Ram Prasad, Facts for You January, 2004.

T.C. Sharma & O.C. Coutinho, Economics & Commercial Geography of India, Vikas Pub. House Pvt. Ltd., 1995, pp. 326-331.

www.sugarindia.com

15

The Success Story of Warana Co-operative Complex

P. K. Deshmukh and P. N. Gavade

Introduction

This is a success story of a Co-operative Complex, which depicts how dedicated and committed leadership with peoples' participation can convert a barren tract into a throbbing Co-operative Complex. This Co-operative Complex at Warana Nagar is a beautiful township where with the establishment of a Sugar Factory in 1955, a nucleus for further socio-economic development was germinated.

The credit for inspiring and motivating the rural masses to voluntarily come forward and join hands for mutual benefit goes to the outstanding leadership of the Founder-Chairman late Mr. V. A. Alias Tatyasaheb Kore and to his devoted social workers.

With the establishment of the Sugar factory, a focal point for all-round development was formed and a chain of growth oriented activities initiated. The efficient working of a sugar factory mainly depends on two factors, firstly, on regular supply of sugarcane and secondly, on a network of well maintained roads. Warana Sugar Factory (WSF) therefore, gave top priority to bringing more and more land under cane-cultivation by sponsoring and undertaking several lift irrigation schemes on the river Warana. Besides, the factory developed a network of roads in its command area, and constructed several bridges thus linking all the villages with the focal point. All this resulted in the membership of the factory and the area under cane-cultivation showing a remarkable rise. The membership rose from 1768 in 1959 to 19,672 in the year 2000 and the area under cane-cultivation increased from 1066 hectares to 13,157 hectares during the said period.

One of the key factors that has contributed to the growth of WSF is that the management is always vigilant in maintaining the operational efficiency of the factory. A very common measure of technical efficiency in sugar industry is the recovery rate. The total average recovery rate for all the sugar factories in India fluctuates between 9.5% to 10.5%, but the average recovery rate of WSF is 12% with the highest recovery rate of 13.58% in 1962-63.

Another measure of technical efficiency is total sugar losses, in this regard also WSF has a unique position and established a world record in 1963-64 in reducing the sugar losses to the minimum of 1.62%. Yet another measure of operational efficiency is the capacity utilisation. The factory has been operating at over 100% capacity, which implies that mechanical breakdowns are avoided and there is regular supply of sugarcane in adequate quantity. The cane-price paid by the factory to its producer members also reflects on its operational efficiency. The factory has always been on top in giving the highest returns to its members as is evident from the graph appended to the paper.

The consistent progress made by WSF over the years has led to its bagging a number of national and international awards, for instance, in the year 2000, it ranked first in the country in sugar production (14,82,100 quintals), it topped all the factories in sugar export and as regards recovery rate, the factory ranked second in the country (12.64%). The Managing Director of WSF was adjudged as the Best M .D in the year 2001. All these awards speak volumes of the factory's achievements.

Warana Co-operative Market

With the setting up of the sugar factory, there was a gradual change in the local economy and in the attitude of the farmers. Traditional farming gave way to commercial farming and led to its mechanisation. But this transformation demanded larger capital investment and thus the need for an institution which could cater to the credit needs of the farmers arose. This culminated in the setting up of Warana Co-op. Bank (WCB) in 1966. The Bank has been instrumental in mobilising savings in the command area of WSF and in providing credit to the weaker sections, priority sectors and to individuals to undertake activities allied to agriculture such as dairy farming, poultry farming and to small craftsmen, traders, small-scale industries, etc. The fact that WCB has accumulated Rs.126 crores as deposits, has total advances of Rs. 80 crores and membership of 14,971 depicts its efficiency. The Bank has 23 branches and 1 extension counter.

Warana Dairy

The establishment of the sugar factory brought prosperity in its command area. But the leadership found to their dismay that WSF had benefitted only those farmers who had assured water supply for their farms. Thus the gulf between the rural rich and the rural poor widened. The need for uplifting the weaker sections, the landless and the marginal farmers was strongly felt by the leadership. Such a situation demanded the initiation of an economic activity, which would enable the rural poor to uplift their economic conditions. Thus the idea of implementing a Dairy Development project was conceived.

With the setting up of Warana Dairy (WD) in 1968, another avenue was opened for the rural poor to supplement their meagre earnings. WD has enabled thousands of people to buy milch animals by providing them a subsidy for it. This has led to a rise in the membership of WD to 15,500 and the number of milk producers is almost 60,000. Besides, WD has always paid the highest rates to its milk-producers as is evident from the graphs appended to the paper. The average per day milk collection of WD is 2.72 lakh litres and the daily average sale of milk in Bombay itself is 1.45 lakh litres.

Warana Bazar

Although Warana Co-operative Complex (WCC) had a chain of units which enabled the people in its command area to earn a livelihood yet, a longfelt need of this area was a shopping complex which would enable the people to procure all the their essential requirements at reasonable rates. The leadership of WCC was giving a serious thought to the idea of starting a department store at Warana Nagar, but to start such a store in a rural area and to successfully operate it was an uphill task. In spite of the risks involved, the leadership was determined and the first rural co-operative department store of the country viz, Warana Bazar (WB) was started in 1976.The store in a short span has achieved the rare feat of making a record sales turnover of Rs.46.36 crores and ranks fifth in the country next only to Delhi and Bombay. WB has a daily average sale of Rs. 14.5 lakhs. A striking feature of WB is that it has a total membership of 9779 of which 77% are women. Besides, there are 9 women in the Board of Directors and the Chairperson also happens to be a woman.

Growth of Other Activities

After having established the WSF and other institutions, the leadership decided to foster a number of other inter-linked activities in the area. The various co-operatives and other institutions promoted by the leadership in the area are (1) Paper Plant (2) Distillery (3) Poultry Farming (4) Cattlefeed Plant (5) Malted Food Factory (6) Drinking Chocolate Plant (7) Warana Agricultural Goods Processing Unit. (8) Women's Organisation (9) Educational Complex (10) Hospital with 250 beds, etc.

Why Warana Co-operative Complex Has Been a Success?

The study reveals that WCC over the years has evolved as a rural growth centre. The major factors that have contributed to the growth of this Co-operative Complex are as under:

Leadership

Firstly, it is the leadership that has immensely contributed to the growth of WCC. The real challenge before leadership in co-operatives in India is stirring the rural masses out of their age-old inertia. WCC has a fully dedicated and committed leadership. Late Mr. Kore, the Founder-Chairman of the Sugar Factory was the chief architect of this beautiful township. It was his creative urge which inspired the people to participate in collective efforts. It was his vision, integrity and organisational ability, which tremendously contributed to the growth of WCC. He was the moving spirit behind this entire complex. The continuous and uninterrupted association of the leadership with the complex converted a barren tract into a throbbing co-operative complex.

Peoples' Participation

Active participation of the people is a pre-requisite for the healthy growth of co-operatives. But participation of people is something, which cannot be obtained by mere asking, it has to be voluntary and reciprocal. This can best be achieved if different sections of the society get an opportunity to actively participate in the developmental activities and the benefits accruing are shared by the largest number of people and not pocketed by a minority. Peoples' participation thus demands distributive justice and the percolation of benefits to the lowest strata of the society. The policy of the management in WCC has always been to share the benefits of prosperity with the largest number of people and thereby make each and every member totally involve in the movement. The returns given to the cane-growers by WSF and to the milk producers by WD bear testimony to this fact.

Multi- Sectoral Developmental Approach

Thirdly, to make the developmental efforts meaningful, it is imperative to initiate an economic activity, which would, through linkage mechanism, ignite the whole process of rural development. Once the core activity is identified, the approach for further development should essentially be multi-sectoral in nature. The growth of WCC is the result of such an approach adopted by the leadership. Once the sugar co-operative was set up as a core activity, along with this manufacturing sector there was the service sector in the form of Warana Bank, allied sector in the form of Warana Dairy and Cattle Feed Plant, marketing sector in the form of Warana Bazar, human resource development sector in the form of the Educational Complex, by-product sector in the form of the Paper Plant and Distillery. But above all, there is the infrastructure sector in the form of network of roads, transport and irrigation facilities which has made palpable contribution to the growth of this complex. (Refer to the figure appended).

State Participation

Fourthly, State Participation is equally important. Having recognised the role of co-operatives in the socio-economic development of the country, the Govt. extended a helping hand to the movement. But the involvement of the State in the movement should be a temporary phenomenon and should not deprive the movement of its voluntary character.

For establishing the sugar factory, state assistance was a must initially, accordingly, the Govt. contributed Rs. 10 lakhs towards the share capital of WSF. The factory redeemed the entire share capital of the Govt. in subsequent years. State participation very often leads to administrative encroachment and adversely affects the autonomy of the co-operatives, but the Founder Chairman always showed the courage to withstand Govt.pressures and opposed unjustified administrative incursion.

Style of Management

Fifthly, the style of management has also contributed to the growth of WCC. The management has always shown that it is bold, enterprising and is risk-taking. In spite of the risks involved in starting a Consumers' Store (WB) in a rural area, the management showed the courage to start it. Similarly, although no matching contribution to the share capital of WD was made by the State, the management decided to go ahead with the project and today WD happens to be one of the best co-operative ventures of the country.

The management has restricted itself to only framing of policies, there is a clear delegation of executive authority to the managers, there is no administrative encroachment in the operative part of running the business. The management has always tried to promote the interests of both its members and so also its employees. The returns given to the members and the welfare activities undertaken for its employees in an evidence of its approach.

Suitable Conditions

Finally, existence of suitable natural, social and political conditions is also a pre-requisite for the healthy growth of co-operatives. WCC has been a success because of the existence of suitable geographical factors like soil, climate, water resources, etc. Besides, the social and political factors are also conducive. Maharashtra and Kolhapur District in particular, is on the forefront as far as the co-operative movement is concerned.

Apart from all these factors, WCC has been a success because of a number of developmental activities (already referred to earlier) initiated by the leadership for the overall development of its area. The growth of all the these developmental activities besides promoting social welfare and rural development, also enables the leadership to strengthen the allegiance of the members. If one takes into account the multiplier effect of all these developmental activities initiated and undertaken by the leadership in WCC, one has to acknowledge the fact that " there is no other instrument as potentially powerful and full of purpose as the co-operative movement". But can it be so powerful? Can it be so full of purpose? WCC answers these questions.

16

Industrial Sickness : A Study of a Defunct Co-operative Spinning Mill in Tamil Nadu

B Tamilmani

Introduction

Co-operative Spinning Mills (CSMs) are the voluntary associations of either cotton growers or handloom weavers, organised for protecting their economic interests through collective responsibility. They are large-sized economic enterprises promoted with the prime objectives of: (i) producing quality hank and cone yarns; (ii) providing employment to the downtrodden sections of the community; (iii) selling yarn largely to weavers' co-operatives; and (iv) enhancing the socio-economic interests of members at large. These objectives could be gainfully implemented, if the spinning mills are effective in their functioning and administration.

But, the performance report of the CSMs in TamilNadu shows a dismal picture. The net loss incurred by the 18 CSMs (of the total 18 CSMs 4 were closed for about 5 years due to sickness) as on 31 March 2001 was Rs.22 crores and the accumulated loss touched a whooping amount of Rs.352 crores[1]. The menace of sickness (engulfed in the spinning industry) in the recent past is disheartening. All over India, 383 mills (262 spinning mills + 121 composite mills) have shutdown their doors, leaving 4 lakh workers jobless, which includes 50 CSMs[2]. A CSM struck by sickness that finally became defunct is selected for the study.

Objectives

The study was undertaken with the objectives of: i) analysing certain key result areas (KRAs) at the backdrop of the sickness of the CSM, and ii) suggesting suitable managerial measures for curing the sickness and strengthening of the CSM.

Methodology

Case study method was followed. A defunct CSM struck by sickness was selected. Of the 18 CSMs in Tamil Nadu, 4 were defunct for about 5 years. Of the four, one CSM was selected purposively as it was closed recently (1999) and so it would not be much difficult to unearth the reasons for the sickness or closure.

Period of the Study

The study covers a period of 10 years down the line from the year of its closure. The data for 10 years is considered sufficient for a meaningful analysis and interpretation.

Conceptualisation of Sickness

Different government bodies have defined the concept of sickness based on the context and purpose they have referred to. For example, *Reserve Bank of India* defines sickness as, 'one which incurs cash loss for one year and likely to incur cash loss in consecutive years, current ratio less than 1:1 and worsening debt ratio". *State Bank of India* has put it differently without mentioning any criteria as such, those units, which fail to generate internal surplus on continuous basis and depends for its survival upon external funds frequently. *Small Industries Development Corporation* opines, in its way, a sick small-scale unit as one with less than 25 percent capacity utilisation. *Term Lending Institutions* describe sickness as one, which fails to pay four consecutive half-yearly installments of interests and principal, incurs continuous cash losses for two years or erosion of net worth by 50 percent.

The definition of *Sick Industrial Companies* (special provisions) *Act* of 1985 categorically describes three important conditions for considering a unit as sick. They are: (i) the organisation must be more than 7 years old; (ii) its net worth be negative; (iii) it has incurred a cash loss during the preceding three years[3]. We consider this definition for our analysis as it is more appropriate and fit the spinning industry as well.

A Brief Note on the Sick Mill

Misreor Co-operative Spinning Mill was registered on 8th August 1968 and commenced its commercial production on 24th August 1977. It started functioning with a meagre number of 896 spindles of second hand machinery for manufacturing 10s yarn from the waste cotton procured from other sister CSMs. The membership of the mill consists of individuals, the state government, weavers' co-operatives and other co-operative institutions.

Started working with Rs.3.63 lakhs as share capital in 1977, the mill has been able to raise it to the tune of Rs.114.94 lakhs in 1997-98. However a major chunk of share capital was contributed by the government (95 percent). It was the only mill manufacturing 10s yarn and supplying to the weavers cooperative societies. The quality of yarn being inferior, the buyers refused to buy it. Muddling with age-old machines, the mill has never earned profit in any of the 21 years of its existence. The accumulated net loss of the mill on closure was Rs. 1181.41 lakhs.

Analysis of Key Result Areas (KRAs)

KRAs are the activities closely associated with profitability and sustainability of the organisation. In other words, KRAs indicate the priority areas for organizational performance. In the negligence or defective functioning of any one or some of the KRAs would seriously endanger the organization. The KRAs considered for assessing the performance of the sick mill are as follows :

(i) Capacity Utilisation
(ii) Production performance
(iii) Sales Turnover
(iv) Net working result
(v) Audit classification

Let us analyse each KRA with supportive facts and figures given in the table for more understanding.

Capacity Utilisation

Capacity utilisation is an important indicator of the efficiency of operations of spinning mills. It is stated as the proportion of total machine capacity, which has been gainfully utilised for the production of required goods and services. Higher capacity utilization would result in higher production and productivity, and lower cost of production.

The South Indian Textile Research Association's (SITRA) norms of cotton spinning mills is 98 per cent of its machine capacity[4]. The study unit's capacity utilisation is well below the standard norm and it is hanging between 50.71 percent and 79.68 percent respectively of minimum and maximum, during the study period. (See Table 1).

Table 1 : Capacity Utilization

(Figures in Percentage)

S. No	*Year*	*Capacity Utiliza-tion 'A'*	*Growth rate*	*TNCSM's Average 'B'*	*Variance (A-B)*	*SITRA's Norm 'C'*	*Variance (A-C)*
1.	1988-89	57.15	-	84.46	-27.31	98	-40.85
2.	1989-90	68.20	+19.33	85.37	-17.17	98	-29.80
3.	1990-91	75.27	+10.36	88.14	-12.87	98	-22.73
4.	1991-92	79.68	+05.85	81.70	-2.02	98	-18.32
5.	1992-93	75.51	-05.23	87.42	-11.91	98	-22.49
6.	1993-94	56.79	-24.79	84.60	-27.81	98	-41.21
7.	1994-95	60.22	+06.39	77.65	-17.43	98	-37.78
8.	1995-96	50.71	-15.79	71.86	-21.15	98	-47.29
9.	1996-97	51.08	+00.72	69.46	-18.38	98	-46.92
10.	1997-98	62.60	+22.55	77.34	-14.74	98	-35.40
	Annual average	63.72	2.15	80.80	-17.08	98	-34.28

Compound Growth Rate = 0.94.

Source : Data compiled from the various reports of the Mill concerned and office of the DHT.

The comparison of capacity utilization of the study unit with that of the average of CSMs of Tamil Nadu indicates a negative trend throughout the study period. The conspicuous reasons for under-utilisation are: (i) labourers strike and absenteeism, (ii) want of back stuff, (iii) interrupted power supply, and (iv) repairs and maintenance. Under-utilization of capacity has resulted in lower production, low productivity and high cost of production. This has a negative impact on sales and profitability.

Production Performance

Production of yarn is the prime activity of the CSM. Production plan in the mill was determined based on the 'yarn requirements allocation' for weavers co-operatives sent by Directorate of Handlooms and Textiles (DHT). Adhering to the instructions, the mill manufactured 10s, 20s and 40s yarn. An efficient mill would maintain higher production in quantity lowering the cost of production as much as possible. But in the case of study unit, it is otherwise.

The production performance of the mills both in terms of quantity and value was compared with that of the averages of CSMs in Tamil Nadu indicate a disheartening picture. The ideal way of cutting cost is maximum capacity utilisation coupled with production of superior quality. But, the mill experienced with lower capacity utilisation and inferior quality of yarn, an increasing trend in the cost of production every year.

Sales Turnover

Although the study unit enjoyed the 'partly protected market' for their produce, earning of profit was only an illusion. The mill had to follow sales and price policy as fixed by the DHT. Many a times, the yarn price fixed by the DHT was lower than the production cost, resulting loss. The excess of yarn, after having supplied to the Tamil Nadu Handloom Weavers Co-operative Society (Cooptex) could be sold in the open market, but not for an amount less than the price fixed by DHT.

The yarn of the mill, being inferior in quality could not be sold in the open market at the fixed price. At one time the yarn was rejected by the 'Cooptex' itself because of inferior quality. The sales performance of the mill indicates a fluctuating trend

(See Table 2). The comparative picture of sales with production indicates a negative trend in eight out of ten years. The comparison of sales performance of the mill with that of the average of CSMs in TamilNadu indicates a highly negative trend. The causes for poor sales performance were: (i) adverse price policy, (ii) market incompetence and (iii) inferior quality of yarn.

Table 2 : Sales Turnover

(Rupees in lakhs)

S. No	*Year*	*Value 'A'*	*Growth rate in %*	*Variance (A-production)*	*TNCSM's Average 'B'*	*Variance (A-B) 'C'*
1	1988-89	174.29	-	-5.71	771.47	-597.18
2	1989-90	184.75	+06.00	-3.37	802.96	-618.21
3	1990-91	150.06	-18.77	-65.93	876-49	-726.43
4	1991-92	390.91	+160.50	+0.160	1005.10	-614.19
5	1992-93	302.65	-22.57	-68.04	1108.94	-806.29
6	1993-94	262.80	-13.16	-50.50	1112.86	-874.62
7	1994-95	434.54	+65.36	-63.97	1309.16	-874.62
8	1995-96	476.72	-09.70	-60.61	1284.61	-807.89
9	1996-97	442.77	-07.12	+16.50	1260.86	-818.09
10	1997-98	448.23	+01.33	-65.01	1374.85	-926.62
	Annual average	326.77	17.98	-38.31	1070.73	763.95

Compound Growth Rate = 1.35.

Source : Data compiled from the various reports of the Mill concerned and office of the DHT.

Net Working Result

It was a 'loss-making mill'. It incurred a heavy loss all along. Not even in a single year it earned a profit during its whole life period of 20 years. The reasons for loss were: (i) lower capacity utilisation, (ii) technological obsolescence, (iii) lower production and productivity (iv) inferior quality of yarn, (v) high cost of production, (vi) absence of autonomy, (vii) adverse government policy on sales and price, and (viii) economic recession trend. Due to its poor performance the mill has been placed under 'C' audit classification.

Having a high amount of loss to its debt, no serious steps were taken. Despite the daily, weekly, fortnightly, and monthly progress(?) reports are sent to the DHT, it could not find the success track. The purpose of preparation of various reports become waste when they are not properly investigated. Again, the monthly progress review meeting is held at DHT to discuss and review the problems, progress and prospects of the CSMs. Even, with all these periodical efforts no fruitful sign was seen. Therefore, the purpose of reporting and reviewing might have been a ritualistic one, which dissipiates time, money and human resources. The progress review meeting should have been more realistic as the participants Administrators come with ground realities.

Table 3 : Net Working Results

(Rupees in lakhs)

S. No	*Year*	*Net loss of the mill*	*TNCSM's (Average net result)*	*Accumulated loss of the mill*	*Audit classification*
1.	1988-89	-47.33	-103.46	-114.58	C class
2.	1989-90	-23.20	+19.12	-137.78	C class
3.	1990-91	-49.72	+13.09	-187.51	C class
4.	1991-92	-121.19	-118.06	-308.71	C class
5.	1992-93	-121.12	-182.60	-437.84	C class
6.	1993-94	-115.40	-111.46	-653.25	C class
7.	1994-95	-110.39	-177.10	-763.64	C class
8.	1995-96	-124.51	-253.51	-888.15	C class
9.	1996-97	-152.28	-139.84	-1040.43	C class
10.	1997-98	-140.98	-182.60	-1181.41	C class
	Annual average	-100.61	-154.55	-571.33	C class

Source : Data compiled from the various reports of the Mill concerned and office of the DHT.

Prescriptions for Curing the Sickness

Some curative measures are presented here to prevent the sickness from CSMs. These measures must be implemented at full swing, so as to bring an integrated development of the CSM.

Table 3.6 : Audit Classification

Classification	*94-95*	*95-96*	*96-97*	*97-98*	*98-99*	*99-2000*	*2000-2001*	*Total*
A	15	11	11	10	13	13	6	79
	(18099)	(13.92)	(13.92)	(12.66)	(16.66)	(16.66)	(7.59)	(100.0)
	(2.47)	(1.80)	(1.80)	(1.64)	(2.28)	(2.35)	(1.07)	(1.92)
B	77	72	77	78	87	67	5	463
	(16.63)	(15.55)	(16.63)	(16.85)	(18.79)	(14.47)	(1.08)	(100.0)
	(12.66)	(11.82)	(12.60)	(12.77)	(15.29)	(12.09)	(0.89)	(11.24)
C	376	370	356	368	301	84	12	1870
	(20.11)	(19.79)	(19.20)	(19.73)	(16.10)	(4.49)	(0.64)	(100.0)
	(61.84)	(60.76)	(58.76)	(60.23)	(52.90)	(15.16)	(2.15)q	(45.37)
D	139	150	149	129	120	120	10	817
	(17.01)	(18.36)	(18.24)	(15.79)	(14.67)	(14.67)	(1.22)	(100.0)
	(22.86)	(24.60)	(24.39)	(21.11)	(21.09)	(21.66)	(1.79)	(19.83)
Non-Completion	1	6	15	26	48	270	526	892
of Audit	(0.11)	(0.67)	(1.68)	(2.91)	(5.38)	(30.27)	(58.97)	(100.0)
	(0.16)	(0.99)	(2.45)	(4.26)	(8.44)	(48.74)	(94.09)	(21.65)
Total	608	609	611	611	569	554	559	4121
	(14.75)	(14.78)	(14.83)	(14.83)	(13.81)	(13.44)	(13.56)	(100.0)
	(100.0)	(100.0)	(100.0)	(100.0)	(100.0)	(100.0)	(100.0)	(100.0)

Democratic Governance

CSM's are expected to be democratic in functioning. But in practice, they are state-controlled, which provides no place to members. One significant value of co-operation is its 'democracy' which puts members first in decision-making. But, the co-operative democracy was completely taken away by the appointment of 'administrators' (government officials) as the head of CSMs. The functioning of CSM under the guidance of government officials proved to be inefficient and the mills incurred in heavy loss. The reason is 'too much of officilisation of CSMs, loss of autonomy and the adverse policies of government. Authority must be appropriately knitted with responsibility, wherever it is required. CSMs are under the grinding stone of bureaucratic administration in Tamil Nadu.

Democratization of CSMs is a means to rejuvenate them. The decision-making would be more participative in democratic management, and the members would have greater hold in deciding things. The members accessibility and intimacy with their leaders will evoke good understanding and co-operation on either sides. The importance of democratic governance for the success and sustenance of co-operatives (including CSMs) was reiterated by many committees and in many fora. Waiting for clearance even for petty things would affect the democratic management.

Technology up Gradation

The study unit was started with second hand machines that had worked for more than 20 years with those. Expecting to have good quality product from age-old machines is a non-pragmatic proposition. Perhaps, it has led to increased maintenance cost and declining productivity. Technology upgradation is the high need of the hour. CSMs must move with the time on technology advancement, so as to retain the market for ever. I agree that it needs heavy funds, which are highly scarce for the study unit. The capital budgeting proposals of the mill were not sanctioned by the term-lending institutions because of the continued poor performance in the past and the mounting over dues on it side.

Having understood the importance of the technological upgradation in textile sector, the Government of India created a sum of Rs.25,000 crores (Technology upgradation fund) in 1997. The spinning sector was included under the scheme only in 1999 that too after big hue and cry. This could be made use of by the CSMs. It is emphasized here that unless technology upgradation is made, the quality of the product can not be ensured and the maintenance cost will not be cut. CSMs need to remember that in the era of global environment quality alone would speak louder.

Legislative Reforms

The Co-operatives Act of 1983, which has been in vogue in Tamil Nadu, is very much stringent and rigid. The Act is two decades old. There is a sea change in business environment in India and abroad in all business sectors. Unless co-operatives make necessary legislative reforms, they will not be in the race.

Many provisions of the present Act and Rules are restrictive in nature which tend to be impedimented for the growth of CSMs. The act gives enormous power to the bureaucratic style of functioning, which is quite alien and antithesis to the democratic functioning. Administrative authorities by virtue of their power can negate the decisions taken by the board and even go to the extent of superceding the board.

In recent past some states adventuted in passing Self-reliant Co-operatives Acts which are parallel to the existing Co-operatives Act in the states concerned. The enactment of Andhra Pradesh Mutually-aided Co-operative Societies Act 1995 laid the foundation for effective co-operatives. On line with above Act, Madhya Pradesh, Chattisgarh, Karnataka, Orissa, Bihar, Jharkand, Jammu and Kashmir, and Uttaranchal have parallel Acts[5].

The salient features of the Act are making the co-operatives more autonomous, dynamic, members economic enterprises, free from state control, free to formulate and amend their own byelaws, more freedom in mobilization and investment of funds, audit by charted accountant; and the process of registration is very easy.

An increasing number of co-operatives are being enrolled under the self-reliant acts. Among the states Bihar takes the leading role. The Government of Tamil Nadu must consider the importance of making co-operatives more autonomous and understanding the enactment of such suitable acts is the need of the hour.

Financial Planning & Control

Effective procurement of funds and their judicious utilization warrants proper financial planning and control. As finance is the life-blood of the CSMs, but highly scarce, a scientific application in this regard is required. Their capital structure is composed of owned funds and borrowed funds. Owned funds include equity and reserves. A major portion of equity comes from the state government and the question of reserves does not arise in study unit, as the mill has not earned profit in any of years of its existence. Borrowed capital consists of long-term borrowing from term lending organizations and working capital from the concerned 'District Central Co-operative Banks'.

Preparation of periodical performance reports on cost and returns is merely a ritualistic phenomenon, yielding no result. High debt due to low debt serving capacity, erosion of working capital all made to a greater extent of financial indiscipline. The will has experienced all along with heavy financial crunch. CSMs are in general constrained of fund raising to meet their financial obligations. One suitable suggestion is made here that co-operative law could suitably be enacted to facilitate CSMs to raise funds in the from of: (i) collecting deposits, (ii) mobilizing equity, (iii) issuing bonds & debentures, (iv) raising corpus funds in the form of donations, grants-in-aid and others.

Professional Management

Placing the skilled and technically competent personnel to the suitable jobs is the objective of professional management. Professionalism would help certainly to function better. In CSMs, a large number of officials and operatives remain unskilled. No doubt, professionalisation of managerial cadres at all levels in CSMs would cost heavier and time longer. But for this, CSMs should not stick to the concept of "ever unchanged". They need to adapt themselves to the changing scenario. As a first step, professionalisation could be introduced in the top level of KRAs namely production, marketing and finance. Then gradually the whole spectrum of functional areas must be brought under the fold of professionalism.

Periodical management development programmes must be arranged for all the managerial cadres in the outdoors, to motivate the personnel of CSM's. Management education and placing operative level personnel in the decision making process would go a long way in the effectiveness of CSMs.

Conclusion

Closure of the mill is a highly destructive decision, which throws away the socio-economic objectives into dust bin. Perhaps, closure is the immediate option that floats on the surface of the mind. But we must submerge into the problem 'to deal with it'. Almost anything can be brought within comprehension through 'analysis'. A clear understanding of the sickness and appropriate prescriptions taken in time must help cure the sickness. Prescriptions are practical suggestions meant for action. Prescription slips kept in pocket has never cured illness.

NOTES

1. Information Folder on Performance of Co-operative Spinning Mills in TamilNadu, Directorate of Handlooms and Textiles, Chennai.
2. AIFCOSPIN, 37th Annual Report, 2000-01, Mumbai: All India Federation of Co-operative Spinning Mills, p. 2.
3. T. Ravi, Management of Sickness, p. 27.
4. S. Mohan, Financial Performance of Co-operative Spinning Mills, Allahabad: Saithanya Publishing House, 1997, p. 18.
5. CIP, The Link, Anand: Co-operative Init'iative Panel, May-June-2003, p. 2.

17

New Strategies For Co-operative Dairy Development In The Era of Economic Liberalization & Globalization

Samwel Kakuko Lopoyetum

Introduction

In developing countries like *India* and *Kenya* there is paramount need to permit co-operative dairy sector and organizations to perform its functions and decision-making process with greater autonomy and independence, particularly in the era of LPG's. The vision 2010 that is being advocated and implemented by the National Dairy Development Board (NDDB) should aim at fostering the required planning, execution and control of activities with micro- level approach in the era of LPG's, and economic Liberalization. The dairy co-operative sector needs to improve the quality of its products and utilize many other relevant production methods and modern marketing strategies. As a whole, the dairy co-operative sector would assume themselves as dynamic force in enhancing rural industrialization and commercialization of dairy activities (sector) in rural areas and all the villages. The promotion of farmer's socio-economic welfare and livelihood would need self-governance and sustainability of dairy co-operative societies and they can tie over the harsh realities of open market environment and huge competition unleashed by the LPG's era. It is worthy to blend the opportunities brought about by the free market economic system and make availability of their products felt in the open market economic enviroment. They must take advantages of economic liberalization (EL) and globalization (G) of the national economy. In the era of open market economy, dairy co-operative sector must improve its productivity and profitability to survive, offer affordable services to members, as such can ultimately lead to sustainability of dairy co-operative industry in the era of liberalization and Globalization.

Indian dairies are often being referred to as primitive and unable to manufacture modern processed dairy products. The liquid milk demand of urban consumer is met by reconstituted milk powder imported from various regional and international sources. Moreover, the per capita availability of milk has increased from 112 Gms in 1970-71 to 203 Gms in 1997-98 and stands at 214 gms/day as against 300gms/day recommend by Indian Council of Medical Research (ICMR).

Moreover, a large number of internal and external problems are directly affecting dairy co-operative sector such as: the animal productivity remains very low averaging 1.5 litres/day, low purchasing power of the vast majority of the consumer, dairy sector is not producing milk and milk products EXPECTED TO MEET the international standards. Again, constraints such as inefficient milk production, inefficient milk procurement, inefficient transportation, non-adoption of modern milk processing system; inefficient storing and distribution system has extremely affected the dairy co-operative sector. Similarly, unimproved cattle herd, poor herd quality, low milk yield, lack of fodder (cattle feed), inadequate veterinary services, low viability and low profitability have hampered the growth and development of dairy co-operative sector in developing countries such as *India* and *Kenya.*

Most of the milk is in the hands of very small and economically poor milk producers located in rural areas, with small land holdings. Dairy farmer depends on seasonal agricultural crops for their fodder and cattle feed. Milk production is subsidiary occupation and provides employment opportunity, dairy co-operative sector is faced with inadequate technical skills, which leads to low milk productivity, inadequate support for marketing and Distribution of milk and milk products. Ultimately, inadequate technical support for breeding and health cover, and also milk shall remain a perishable commodity if not stored properly during the Marketing and Distribution process. All these dairy factors need thorough improvement and even further improvement of co-operative dairy management and administration is needed in order to compete in the era of economic Liberalization and Globalization.

Thrust Areas of Dairy Co-operative Sector in the Era of LPG's

The total milk production increased from 78 million tonnes in 1999-2000 to 81 million tonnes in 2000-01, the milk powder (including infant milk food) increased from 2.25 lakhs tonnes in 1999 to 2.30 lakhs tonnes in 2000, production of condensed milk increased from 11,000 tonnes in 1999 to 11050 tonnes in 2000. More than 70000 Dairy co-operatives organizations are covering over 7000 villages and dairy co-operative organizations which are run by the women constituting now 21% of the total dairy co-operative societies and set to increase by 2010. The main thrust areas remain to be (i) The dairy Co-operative Enterprises shall remain to be the major socio-economic tool for the removal of poverty (ii) Dairy Co-operative Enterprises shall provide ample opportunities, and chances for self - employment and gainful employment (iii) It provide income generation opportunities to the marginal, small dairy farmers and rural community. (iv) It act as a dynamic socio-economic mixed shield and for better improvement of the weaker section of the community. (vi) Rural dairy co-operatives organizations shall continue to provide and supply fresh milk to urban milk consumers. (vi) It provides adequate milk to improve Nutritional standards of the Human being, particularly children and old – age groups. (vii) There is an urgent need to improve Hygiene, cleanness and quality of milk & milk products. (viii) Intensification and Extensification of Better milk yielding breeds of cows in the Rural areas. (ix) Complete revamping and reworking of the production and marketing system of dairy sector in India by introducing New Revolution in the Dairy Sector. (x) There is shortage of fodder production in most of the Districts, therefore, Dairy co-operative union and primary milk producers co-operative societies must improve the supply of fodder & find innovate or better ways of fodder production activation process through establishment of feed factories and fodder Banks.

Need for Diversification of Business Activities in District Milk Producers Co-operative Unions and at the Level of Primary Milk Producers Co-operative Societies

The District Milk producers Co-operative Union must diversify its operations and functioning. It must improve the availability of cross-breed animals, recomend high yielding animals, they must intensify and extensify Artificial Insemination (AI) services, must improve the provision of concentrates feeds to farmers, improve fodder production and milk collection operations, improve milk distributions, venture into production of different milk products, improve organization of most of the PMPCS & must provident adequate technical inputs. The union is collecting milk from its members and selling unprocessed milk (whole milk) to meet the share of milk demand in most parts of the Districts. By effectively and efficiently collecting milk from PMPCS, they are directly boosting their business performance and profitable working of the primary milk producer's co-operative societies. They must initiate programmes to enhance milk production at the District level through effective and efficient dairy extension services, dairy animal breeding programmes etc., in collaboration with the department of Animal Husbandry. The most Efficient and Effective ways of harnessing the livestock wealth in most of the rural and urban areas can be through co-operative dairy sector, private sector, self-help and voluntary business organizations. It would generate adequate income and gainful employment to the enormous number of dairy farmers. The cattle feed is largely based on the crop residues, open grazing system, collection of fodder from places and obtaining concentrate feeds from the PMPCS stores. The union must adopt the instruments of the Backward and forward linkages and fill gaps between demand and supply of milk in the District. It must sensitize dairy farmers on the cost of production of milk, seasonal fluctuations, the quantity and quality of the milk produced. The union must arrange for prompt payment i.e., weekly or fortnightly as desired by the PMPCS and ensure lower rates (prices) of concentrated cattle feed, than the prices offered by private supplies / businessman. In Procurement and marketing operations of milk union, the critical areas are milk Quality control, packaging of Milk and Milk products, branding, Advertisement, milk pricing, milk payment and milk processing. The union must ensure that all these factors are effectively and Efficiently managed and controlled to ensure profitability & ensure survival (sustainability) in the era of the open market economic system & globalization.

In the era of LPG's, there is an urgent need to encourage the new formation of strong and viable Primary Dairy Co-operative Societies (PDCS), strengthening and improvement of their working conditions and enhancement of their profitability, viability, sustainability and business results of primary milk producers co-operative society to feed the increasing population with milk & milk products. There is an urgent need for inculcating the collective efficiency in primary milk producer's co-operative organizations and District Milk Producers Co-operative Union. Dairy sector is known for granting permanent income and generating gainful employment opportunities to the small, marginal farmers. Dairy co-operative organizations encourage members to supply milk through co-operative societies and, they can mobilize necessary support from dairy farmers and farmers associations. The PMPCS can ultimately improve the socio-economic conditions of the dairy members.It is an effective agent of socio-economic transfor-mation of both rural and semi-urban areas of developing countries such as *Kenya* and *India*.

Encouraging the Role of Self – Help Groups (SHG's) in Dairy Business Activities As a Form of the New Generation Co-operatives

Nearly all Self – Help Groups are promoting socio – economic Development in most of the Districts by making a lot of contribution towards generation of Income & Employment opportunities. The SHG's promoted by NABARD have been launching large number of specific programmes for women empowerment and capacity building measures which have provided active partnership support among developmental agencies. For example in Dindigul District there were 3485

Self–Help Groups operating with 53380 women as members. The creamery unit run by Chemparutti self–help groups is promoting and doing dairy Business activities by obtaining loan under SGSY schemes to undertake keeping of milk animals and undertaking dairy Business activities. This SHG's are engaging themselves on the income generating activities and providing employment to its members. They undertake training activities for its members. Their members take their own milk produce that are produced to the creamery centres, where they are paid on the basis of cream extracted from whole milk. The value of cream is noted in the Register on daily basis and the account is maintained by the members in specific banks and Repayment of loan is fixed by the group i.e. Rs. 1000 per member. They provide a number of prompt services to dairy members such as;

(i) Member Doorstep delivery of the cattle feed concentrates and other Essential Services.

(ii) They reduce the transportation cost, which would have been exorbitant to the dairy members.

(iii) Payment of milk is on the basis of Butter Fat (BF) content (cream content)

(iv) They offer very good price for milk supplied to the creamery center

(v) No delay of payment of milk price, therefore they adopt timely settlement of dues: *(Source: Field Investigation in Dindigul District).*

The major Expectations of dairy farmers was gauged and tabulated as seen in table 1. It is understood that majority (92 percent) of the respondents emphasized on the restructuring and revising of the milk price once in six months, 80 percent of the respondents required prompt payment of milk price, 50 percent of the respondents demanded and expected expansion of local market sales, 43 percent of the respondents demanded the arrangement of loans facilities and 25 percent of the respondents are interested and expecting the regular conduct of election. Therefore, most of the respondents are demanding & expecting milk price restructuring & reviewing. It is followed by expectation and demand for prompt payment of milk price.

Generally, dairy farmers are more conscious on the milk price than other factors such as cost of milk production.

Table 1 : Expectations of Dairy Co-operative Members In The Era of LPG's

S. No.	*Details of Expectation*	*No. of members (N = 60)*	*Rank*
1.	Prompt payment of milk price	48(80)	2
2.	Arrangement of loan facilities and other financial facilities	26(43)	4
3.	To conduct co – operative elections	15(25)	5
4.	Expansion of local market sales	30(50)	3
5.	Restructuring & Revising the milk price once in every six months	55(92)	1

Source : Field Investigation carried out in the Dairy Co-operative society located in Dindigul district rural area.

Factors Responsible for Gearing up Dairy Co-operative Sector to Face Economic Liberalization and Globalization

The dairy co-operative sector must gain dynamic competitive advantages in an open market economic system in order to meet the challenges posed by globalization and Economic Liberalization. Thus, this paper has identified the following factors, which are significant for gearing up the growth and development of dairy co-operative sector such as.

(i) The natural importance given to milk and milk products consumption with the rising income levels of rural and urban communities from time to time.

(ii) The largest cattle population (wealth) and ability of women – folk, Energetic and enthusiastic youth getting involved in the better animal husbandry management practices.

(iii) More importance is given to the quality of milk and higher prices for hygienic milk on t he basis of Butter Fat and SNF Components.

(iv) The New Generation Dairy Co-operative Farmers (NGDCF) is highly educated making use of the latest sciences, information and technology, quick adoption

Table 2 : Services Marketing mix of Milk Co-operative Processing Industry: Strength and Weakness in the era of Economic Liberalization

Services Marketing Mix	*Strength*	*Weakness (w)*
1. Product	Multi product, Availability of raw materials (milk), Establishment of control laboratory (Commissioner of Milk), Not adulterated milk, product a availability is average.	Quality of product are low, percentage of BF is very low, inadequate milk products, less standardization of milk, milk yield is very low, quality of milk is very low, no knowledge of the milk products, sell of liquid milk, inadequate quality control measures, lack of new product development, innovation, no common branding, no attractive package, no functional value, moderate quality, awareness of products low.
2. Price	Policy of prompt payment, policy of payment on BF/SNF, revision of the procurement price (Buffalo & Cow milk), different selling price a metro.	Inadequate price, absence of competitive price policy, lack of consistent price structure, haphazard controls and subsidies, milk is sensitive to price, rural markets desire low to medium price products.
3. Place (Distribution)	Supply of inputs at the door step, milk procurement and marketing of milk, sale of milk, wholesales, dealers through retail outlets, dependents on the village shops, shandies, transportation is average.	Cost of collection of milk is very high, long distances, places, untimely delivery, insufficient transport facilities, poor distribution, unconnected distribution network, no market segmentation.
4. Promotion	Financial Assistance (NDDB), existence of federation to do promotion, Introduction of	Improper linkage to banding and financial institutions, inadequate advertisement and

Contd...

Table 2 : (Contd...)

Services Marketing Mix	*Strength*	*Weakness (w)*
	schemes OFI, OFII, OFIII, vision 2010, sales promotion measures are effective, use of traditional media (Puppetry, street theatre.)	publicity, limited funds for advertisement, less sales promotional measures, not gives importance to customers / relationship, personal selling is expensive, prevalence of more language and dislects.
5. Participation (People)	Producers oriented, supervision and control of societies as per their own laws, technical expertise i.e., NDDB staff, NDRI	Untrained and non professionals, illiterate, traditional, superstitious, poverty of diary farmers, lack initiatives, indebted farmers, no proper training to employees, political interference's, appointment of special officers, excess staff, lack of technological know – how, not familiar milk products, dairy terminology used difficult.
6. Processes	Additional facilities given by NDDB, subsidy-given by the government, adaptation of new technology, use of better dairy processing system	Products manufactured far from the point of production Use of less sophisticated machines, accumulated losses, increase in r aw materials costs, delayed audit, unhygienic dairy conditions, inadequate use of modern technology, lack of innovation.
7 Physical Evidence	Assets / Own building, infrastructure, equipment's.	Inadequate machines and equipment, poor infrastructure for processing, transportation system is expensive

Source : Dr. S. K. Lopoyetum (2002) GRI.

of advancement of science and technology. They will take dairying operations as full time business activity in the era of LPG's.

(v) The veterinary services, Artificial Insemination (AI) and health cover of animals are privatized and the Government veterinary hospitals are continuously providing free animal health services.

(vi) The WTO and International Organizations (MNC's) are following very stringent quality requirement for export purposes, which can enhance dairy performance in the Indian rural economy.

(vii) The removal of subsidies by western countries can provide chance to India Dairy Industry to compete in the World Global Dairy Market. India and New Zealand are two countries without much subsidies and gradually withdrawing.

(viii) It is estimated that, the basic food segments will grow by 100 percent by 2005 and an addition of 25 lakh households, therefore, generally shifting to higher levels of food consumption patterns. There are inclinations of deviating from ordinary food substance to processed value added foods.

(ix) The extended shelf-life of dairy products by using advanced methods of food preservation (UHT) and cost effective packaging system, controlling the quality of milk products would have a srong bearing in the Twenty First Century or New Millenium.

Dairy Co-operatives in the era of Economic Liberalization and Globalization

A very large number of dairy farmers are directly involved in the Dairy Co-operative Societies (DCS) which would double in the 21st century with the emergence of New Generation Co-operative Dairy Farmers and the emergence of self-help groups. There was phenomenal increase in milk production by treble to 663 million tonnes between 1970 and 1995, which would be enhanced in the forthcoming decades. There would be Declined dependence on imported dairy commodities. There is huge prospects of sustainable growth and generation of adequate rural employment in the 21st century. Transfer of income from urban to rural areas/equitable distribution of incomes would be streamlined in the years to come. There is spin off rural economic development through operations floods programmes of NDDB i.e., OFI, OFII, OFIII, and other new dairy development programmes such as vision 2010. By creating technological consciousness and awareness among 75 percent of 'OF' beneficiaries who are landless, marginal and small farmers, there is strong possibility of dairy sector moving forward in a big way in the era of Economic Liberalization and Globalization. In fact, the vision 2010 plan of NDDB is geared towards production of milk and milk products in different milk shed areas and dairy regions of the country in large quantities in the forthcoming years.

Notwithstanding modernization and advancement of science and technology in the 21st century, there will be tremendous social empowerment and emancipation of rural poor leading to significant improvement in their socio–eco–political environment. Women particularly, would be the largest beneficiaries of the 21st century dairy co-operative sector. Presently, the animal husbandry and dairying industry contribute to about 8-10 percent to the GDP of the country, which would be enhanced in the ensuing decades. The creation of efficient milk processing capacities and growth of dairy equipment industry has helped in the development of dairy co-operative industry. In fact, India has also exported expertise in dairy co-operative enterprise to countries such as Sri Lanka (Kiriya Milk Industries of Lanka Limited etc), setting up of Modern dairy Processing plant in Kyrgyz republic. Also, *Zimbwabwe* and *Kenya* is nowadays keen in borrowing *the Anand pattern / model* and in due course of time they will follow suit.

Need for Hygiene Cleaningness and Sanitization of Dairy Equipments

In the era of Economic liberalization and LPG's it is essential to maintain hygienic conditions in the dairy units else their products may not be accepted at the world standard level. Sanitary and phyto-sanitary (SPS) measures (non-tariff measures) must be given top priority by the dairy co-operative organizations. Even the WTO and the European Union countries insist on bacteria – free milk and milk products. The dairy co-operative sector must be conscious of quality standards acceptable in Global Dairy Market.

In addition to tariffs barriers, there are many Non-tariff barriers over which directly and indirectly affect dairy Industry in India. The Non-tariff barriers are imposed under Technical barriers to Trade (TBT) and even European Union insists that milking cows must be mechanized to avoid contamination and they must use portable water in Dairy Processing factories. They must also use filtered air, steel machinery, and advance methods of Dairy Technology. In this way, they are protecting Human Health, animal health, plant life and Environment at large.

The most serious problems in the rural areas are milk-stones accumulation in the milk containers/equipments. The milk – stone is the accumulation of dried milk solids and salts from hard water & washing solutions. It consists largely of calcium phosphate, milk proteins; precipitate coagulated and baked – on by heat. The milk – stone consist of moisture 2.7% to 8.7%, Fat 3.6 to 17.7%, Protein 4.4 to 43.8%, Ash 42 to 67.3%. The rural dairy farmers can be educated and trained on sanitization process. They must leave the surface of the milk containers free as possible from milk residues & viable organisms. They can use detergents (two or more types of detergents) such as Alkalis (Sodium Hydroxide/Sodium Carbonates, Phosphates, Bicarbonates), Acids (Phosphoric, Tartaric, Citric, Gluconic, Mild Acids for milk – stone removal, use of not more than 1% of Conc. of Nitric acid in stainless steel surfaces). It is essential to prepare chemicals with Higher Cleaning Efficiency.

Methods & Procedures for Sanitization that can be Opted by the Dairy Co-operative Societies

The procedure of sanitization depends on the hardness of water and type of the soil prevailing in the region. There are three methods of washing viz. Hand–Washing, Mechanical Washing (Can–washing & Bottle–washing) and cleaning–in–place or in–place–cleaning (IP). In India, most dairy organizations use sodium carbonate, which lower the cleaning efficiency than Tri–sodium silicate. The procedures for sanitization that can easily be followed by dairy co-operative units are:

(i) Drain and Remove all the loose and other matter from the milk containers / equipments.

(ii) Do pre-rising with cold or tepid water to remove remaining milk solids.

(iii) Use hot water rinsing to remove traces of detergents.

(iv) Sanitizing to destroy all pathogens and almost all Non-pathogenic organisms.

(v) Draining and drying must be done to prevent bacterial growth and corrosion. Never use Towel cloth of any kind, provide adequate drying and ventilation process to the containers and equipments and developing.

Bench Marking Strategies and Methods of Improving Dairy Co-operative Sector

The District Dairy Co-operative Development Strategies can be undertaken at two levels viz at DMPCS & at PMPCS. The strategies must be based on: (i) Procurement and marketing strategies (ii) Processing and operational strategies (iii) Organizational control & management (iv) Uses of better Strategy of milk production and productivity of animals (v) better Strategies of animals feeds and fodders (vi) Use of better Dairy Extension services and Animal Health Cover (vii) Adoption of Anand pattern of dairy co-operatives (viii) Strategy of prompt milk payment (ix) Effective and Efficient use of common community grazing land. (x) Improvement of milks Quality by giving proper education and training to the dairy farmers. (xi) Providing financial assistance and loan facilities to the dairy farmers.

Best Strategies and Approaches to Enhance Management & Business Operations of Dairy Processing Co-operative Societies.

The best strategy may be defined as the best plan of action to achieve the specified objectives under competitive circumstances particularly in the era of economic liberalization and Globalization. Strategies are dynamic in nature and subject to modification. Adoption of strategies is a continuous process. The term strategy has military connotation and used widely in the field of management and administration of business, because they are fought like wars and counter-wars in different environmental situations. The following are some of the most viable strategies, which can be adopted by co-operative marketing and dairy processing organizations. (1) The researcher is advocating for Efficient and Effective organization and methods (O&M) in dairy co-operative sector. (2) Modernization of dairy co-operative sector by using the latest methods of Manufacturing and processing of milk and milk products. (3) Use of Appropriate and Intermediate Technology. (4) The NDDB & Federation and unions can have dairy business on Joint ventures & Collaboration basis. (5) Promotion of Inter – Co-operative Dairy Products Export Trade, (6) Use of improved Storage and Grading system, (7) Use of low cost Packaging and effective labeling, practices (8) Dairy co-operative must aim at Cost focus strategy, (9) Dairy co-operative can adopt Focused Niche market strategy in domestic market and external markets. (10) Application of Product Differentiation strategy as marketing strategy of dairy co-operative products. (11) Enhancement of competitive and adoptive approach in dealing with the dairy co-operative affairs. (12) Adoption of value Addition Techniques, especially in co-operative products and services, (13) Inculcating the culture of Professionalism and enhancing Human Resource Develop-ment in dairy co-operative organizations. (14) Promotion of Dairy Business Diversification, (15) Implementation of Internal Checks and Controls, (16) Use of Information Technology (IT) and Communication, (17) Creativity and Innovative Strategies, (18) NDDB's and Federations (States) and dairy unions can adopt Consultative strategies strictly on business terms (19) Adoption and use of 4 P's marketing strategies and 7P's service marketing strategies by all dairy co-operative units, (20) Computerization and Automation of Dairy Co-operative Processing manufacturing sector, (21) Integration and Collaboration strategy (Strategic Alliance) of dairy co-operative at local level, regional level, state level, National level and international level. (22) Use of Management quality circles (MQC) and (23) Finally exploration of the use of viable Combination strategy.

Conclusion

There is an urgent need for initiating New Dairy Revolution through Co-operative Sector in India. The success of the dairy co-operative organizations depends on a number of factors that could be classified as internal or external. Moreover, extreme efforts must be taken to ensurė competitive dairy sector in the era of economic liberalizations and globalizations. They must face the competitive dairy market in the global environment by producing the best dairy products. The quality of the products produced by the co-operative sector must meet the international standards in terms of the nature and the standards laid down by the WTO and other quality standards laid down by the most reputed organizations. In order to meet the higher quality standards of the dairy products, all dairy co-operative organizations must adhere to the phyto-sanitary and hygienic production requirements of the milk and the milk products. The NDDB, as an apex organization must set out a separate wing which would promote and link the dairy sector with the international standard requirements and at the same time make arrangement to appoint an authority which would look in to the quality of milk and milk products. Finally,the dairy co-operative dairy sector must also promote the production of clean milk and also improve the milk parlor an d the milk processing plant..

REFERENCES

Ananthakrishnan, C.P., Pandmanabhan, P.N., (1992), *"Dairy Farming and Milk Production"*, Shri Laxmi Publications, Madras.

Attwood, D.W., Baviskar, B.S., (1988), *Who Shares? Co-operatives and Rural Development,* Oxford University Press, Delhi.

Kulandaisamy, V., (1982), *"Co-operative Dairying in India"*, Rainbow Publication, Coimbatore.

Maxcarenhar R.C., (1988), *"Strategy for Rural Development – Dairy Co-operatives in India"*, Sage Publication, New Delhi.

Deepak Shah and Asok Shah., (1996), *Impact of Dairy Co-operative on Marketing Pattern of Milk – A Case of Study,* Indian Co-operative Review 33 (3).

Shiyani R.L., (1996), *An Economic Inquiry into the Impact of Dairy Co-operatives on Milk Production,* Indian Journal of Agricultural Economics 51 (3).

Subburaj B. S.K. Lopoyetum and R. Karunakaran, (2001), *"Members perception on the social impact of Dairy Co-operative societies in Dindigul District; A Survey,* Indian Co-operative Review, 39 (1), pp. 40-53.

Subburaj B.S.K. Lopoyetum and R. Karunakaran, (2001), *"Members Perception on the Social Impact of Dairy Co-operative Societies in Erode District; A Survey"*, Co-operative Perspective, Journal of Co-operative Management (Quarterly Journal Vol. 36, No. 4, pp. 30-41.

Katar Singh of Mukunda Dar., (1982), *Impact of Operation I at the Village Level – Research Report,* Anand IRMA.

Gupta S.K. *"Dairy next millenium the challenges"* Yojana Vol: 43 (11), Nov. 99.

Anjani Kumar, (1998), "Milk production Function and Factor Demand in Milk Production" The Bihar Journal of Agricultural Marketing Vol. VI. No. 4, October

Shrode R.B., (1999), *"Dairy in India"* Rural India Vol. 62 (9).

Singh Mohar. etal., (1998), "Constraints Faced by the Dairy Seeking Information Regarding Improved Dairy Forming Practices" Rural India, Vol. 61 (9-10).

Nath Abbay etal.(1998) "Milk Procurement a Challenge for Personnel of Milk Union" Rural India, Vol. 61 (6).

Koli. P.A., (2000), "Can Milk Co-operative Sustain in 21st Century" Indian Co-operative Review Vol. XXX VIII, No. 1.

Hage, N.C., (2001), "WTO Challenges for Indian Dairy Farmers", Yojana.

Mohinder Singh & Anilkumar, (1996), *"Technological Interventions in rural dairy development; A study"*, Kurukshetra.

Selvaraj, V., (2002), *"Marketing of Dairy Products through E - Commerce"*, Kissan World, Vol. 29.

Subburaj, B., *"Indian Dairying – Its Prospects"*, Tamilnadu Journal of Co-operation, March, 1997.

Subburaj. B. Ravichandran. K. And Samwel Kakuko Lopoyetum, (2003), *"Appropriateness of management strategies; Are they myth to co-operatives"* The Cooperator, Vol. 40, No. 8.

Iyer L.L., (1973), *"Fifty Years of Dairy Development in India Tasks Ahead"* Indian Dairy man, Vol. 25, No. 12.

Suryamurthy, (2001), *"Milk Marketing Strategies"* Tamil Nadu Journal of Co-operators Vol. 1, No. 8.

Samwel Kakuko Lopoyetum, (1999), *"Indo – Kenya Dairy Co-operative system; Scope for Dairy Co-operative Development and Replicability strategy of Indian Model in Kenya"* Co-operative Perspective, Journal of Co-operative Management. Vol. 34. No. 3.

Samwel Kakuko Lopoyetum, (1999), *"Computer Application in the Management Administration of Co-operatives"* Tamil Nadu Journal of Co-operation Vol. 91. No. 4.

Srinivasan Gowda, M.V., (1994), *"Co-operatives in the New Economic scenario, Agenda for liberalization"*, Southern Economist, p. 21.

18

Housing Co-operatives in the 21st Century

A.S. Joshi

Introduction

The Co-operative movement in India has completed 100 years and it is the largest in the world. There were 5.50 lakh co-operatives in India having membership of more than 280 million. The co-operative movement is playing distinct and important role in socio - economic development in the country. It has made notable progress in various sectors e.g. banking , textile, sugar co-operatives, dairy co-operatives, labour co-operatives, housing co-operatives, etc.

Housing Need

Food, clothing and shelter are the prime requirements of human being and housing is one of the basic needs. Lack of adequate housing is a problem all over the world but it is serious in developing nations. Now a days, a shelter does not mean just a primitive shelter but the adequate quality of houses. In our country, the new National Housing and Habitat Policy announced by the Government of India in the year 1998, recognizes that "Shelter is a basic human requirement which needs to be met on priority basis. Estimates for the year 1991 by the NBO indicate that there was net shortage of about 31 Million housing units in India. The existing stock of houses is classified into four categories.

(1) Pucca Houses
(2) Semi - Pucca Houses
(3) Kutcha
(4) Un- serviceable Kutcha

Estimates of Housing Shortage In India

It can be seen from table 1 that the supply of housing is not keeping pace with the population growth, the condition of housing is very poor in rural areas. There is an increasing shortage of houses in rural and urban areas. The condition of housing is poor in urban area and it has resulted in the growth of slums. As per census of India 2001, the total slum population was 40.3 million. This problem is serious because deterioration of old houses, increased demand for new houses. population growth, urbanization, lack of repair and maintenance of existing housing stock, scaricity of finance and building material resources.

Table 1 : Estimates of Housing Shortage In India 1991-2001

S. No.	*Estimated Item*	*In Million Number*					
		Rural		*Urban*		*Total*	
		1991	*2001*	*1991*	*2001*	*1991*	*2001*
1.	Households*	113.5	137.0	47.1	72.2	160.6	209.2
2.	Housing Stock	106.2	127.8	42.6	64.8	148.8	192.6
3.	Usable Housing Stock	92.9	111.5	36.7	56.7	129. 6	168.2
4.	Housing Gap	20.6	25.5	10.4	15.5	31.0	41.0

* Adujusted for Congestion.

Source : National Building Organisation.

The problem of housing shortage is complicated, crucial, and important and complex. It differs from place to place, state to state and time to time, It has quantitative and qualitative aspects.

Role of Housing Co-opearatives

The problem of housing shortage can be solved by private, public and co-oprative effort. Housing co-operatives are considered the most appropriate agencies which can help the Government in meeting the targets set under National Agenda. The policy provides that co-operative sector is to be given preference in allotment of land and house sites to encourage group housing by this sector.

The Government should encourage for private housing by way of tax reliefs, cheap building material, and financial facilities. Even in public sector some efforts are made to solve housing problem. Co-operatives have attracted the attention of social reformers, economists , sociologists and poiticians, since its inception as a form of business organisation. Housing co-operatives are people's organizations based on self- help, self - reliance and community participation. In the coming years, co-opratives including housing co-opratives will be regarded as purely economic and business enterprises.

Benefits of Co-operative Housing

The modern concept of housing does not limit the scope of housing to provision of shelter alone, but a comfortable shelter with such surroundings and services, as would keep a man healthy and cheerful throughout his life.

The main benefits of co-operative housing are :-

- A housing co-operative is neither a public nor a profit seeking organisation.
- Contrary to public housing, co-operative housing provides opportunities to its members to control the house designs at the planning stages.
- Co-operative housing satisfies not only the quantitative but also the qualitative aspects of housing.
- Housing co-operatives, besides, generating a sense of responsibility amongst users for post-occupancy maintenance, also provide the necessary mechanism for effecting it.
- Project cost of housing co-operatives is minimised
- Loans are arranged for their memebers get collective responsibilities for the repayment of loans.
- The members of a co-operative society have get the right to vote and participate in the affairs of the society.
- A co-operative, is a small community that undertakes several social activities such as organising special programmes, arranging health services, improving the

ecology of its area, improvement in social behaviour and mental health, etc.

Other co-operative economic activities such as consumer co-operatives, banks, clubs and other common services which are needed by the community can be established by a housing co-operatives in an economical manner.

The housing co-operatives contribute to national development. Housing co-operatives can also foster national integration both as an end in itself and as a means of promoting national development. Housing co-opratives by fostering intimacy, cohesion and good relationship at the neighbourhood level can create conditions conductive to character building of the younger generation who can then be expected to better handle the responsibilities of nation building, in the future.

History of Housing Co-operatives

The Co-operative housing movement was started nearly 95 years ago in this country. Mysore State (Now Karnataka) was the first to take lead in forming the first housing Co-operative society in 1909 known as the Bangalore Building Co-operative Society Ltd., This society served as a model and inspiration for future co-operatives. Bombay also took the initiative in the matter by forming a non - official body in 1913. This was known as Bombay co-operative Housing Association for the purpose of carrying on propaganda in favour of the co-operative housing movement. The pioneer in the initiation of co-operative housing in India was late Shri. S.S. Talmakhi.The Saraswat co-operative housing society at Gramdevi in Bombay was organised through his patient and persistent efforts in 1915. Although the co-operative housing movement was statrted in the beginning of twentieth century, its progress till 1950 was considered to be negligible. In the real sense of the term ; the progressive era of housing co-operatives started with the launching of First Five Year Plan in 1951, wshich emphasized the importance of co-operatives in the economic development of the country.

The progress of housing co-operatives in the country can be judged from the statistics given in Table 2.

There are four types of primary co-operative housing societies.

Table 2 : Progress of The Co-operative Housing Societies In India

Year	*No.of Primary Housing Co-operatives*	*No. of Members (in Millions)*
1959-60	5564	0.32
1963-64	9896	0.62
1967-68	13834	0.90
1971-72	20234	1.37
1975-76	27646	1.74
1979-80	34052	1.86
1983-84	40000	3.00
1993-94	72040	5.93
1996-97	75698	6.16
1998-99	90000	6.50
1999-00	92000	6.80

Source : Statistical Statements relating to the Co-operative Movement in India,Government of India / Reserve Bank of India and Registrar of Co-operative Societies.

(1) Tenant ownership housing societies

(2) Tenant co-partnership housing societies.

(3) House Mortgage societies.

(4) House construction or House building societies.

At State level Co-operative Housing Federeations were set-up in most of the States and at the national level the National Co-operative Housing Federation of India (NCHF)was also founded in the year 1969.

Consequently, the co-operative housing movement started growing rapidly. The number of primary housing co-opratives, which was 5564 in 1959-60, has increased to 90,000 in 1998-99, with a membership of 0.32 millions in the year 1959-60 raised to 6.50 millions in the year1998-99. In the year1999-2000 there were 92000 primary housing co-operatives with the membership of 6.80 millions. In the last forty years the housing co-operatives increased upto 16.5 times. The number of State level apex Co-operative Housing Federation has increased from 25 to 26. About 25 lakh housing units have been constructed under the aegis of housing co-operatives in the country and a large number are under construction. Every year, about one thousand new societies are registered and more than one lakh members join the umbrella of housing co-operatives. Apex federations have provided housing loans of about Rs. 5959 crores upto 31.3.2000 to their primary co-operatives. These apex federations, besides raising funds through share capital contribution, deposits, etc. raise long- term loans from financing institutions like LIC, HUDCO, NHB, Commercial and co-operative Banks. The stracture of housing co-operatives is as under.

Housing Co-operatives In India

National Co-operative Housing Federation (1)

State Co-operative Housing Finance

Societies /Federations (26)

Primary Co-operative House

Building /Group Housing Societies(92000)

Members (6.80 Million)

It is seen from the chart that there were 92000 primary co-operative societies in the year 1999-2000 along with the membership of 6.8 millions.Therewere 789 primary co-operative societies for SC / ST. In order to solve the need of the houses of the low caste people Government & co-operative department should take active steps to solve the need of the people. In the year 1999-2000, 20,83,482 house were completed and the houses 4,46,280 were under construction.

Housing Co-opratives And Maharashtra

A large number of co-operative housing societies have come up in the principal cities of Maharashtra mainly because of acute shortage of housing. The adoption of co-operative method to provide housing is not new in India. The first society formed in Bombay was Bombay Co-operative Housing Association. But the movement of co-operative housing did not gather momentum till 1950. In the year 1948-49 there were 486 co-operative housing societies. The number of co-operative societies increase upto 2006 in the year 1957-58. By the end of March 2001 there were 52330 co-operative housing societies in Maharashtra.

As per table 3 it is found that the development of primary co-operative housing societies in Maharashtra is slow and steady. Year after year there is an increase in membership, share capital, and houses constructed during the period. In the year 2001 there are 52,330 primary co-operative societies along with 18,56600 membership.They have constructed 116000 houses during the year.There were nearly 56.88 % housing co-operatives in Maharashtra as compared to total co-operative societies in India.

The District Kolhapur is known as District of Co-operation. We must pay great tribute to Chattrapati Shahu Maharaja for his various efforts for the development of the co-operation. For the development of co-operative movement in the kolhapur state the efforts of Mr.Bhaskarrao Jadhav, Mr. J.P.Naik, Shri S.S.Shirke, Shri M.S.Todakar etc. were responsible for the development of co-operative movement in Kolhapur District. The efforts of leaders like Shri Tatyasaheb Mohite, Shri Tatyasaheb Kore, Shri. A.B.Naik, Shri Dattajirao Kadam, Dr. Ratnappa Kumbhar(M.L.A.)were responsible.

Tasks Before The Housing Co-operatives

With liberalization of Indian economy and withdrawal of Government support, there is a big challenge before the co-operatives. The co-operative sector must adjust to changing situation. The following measures can be taken.

1. Government role may be limited to creating an favourable environment.
2. Housing co-operatives should be regarded as purely economic enterprises.
3. Financial Support / Subsidies from Government may be given only to weaker sections.
4. Co-operatives will have to find ways to moblise capital for their project from internal and external sources.
5. Co-operatives have to face competition in the market by adopting professional management, use of modern technology.

Table 3 : Primary Co-operative Housing Societies

(Rs.in lakhs)

Item	*1961*	*1971*	*1981*	*1991*	*1999*	*2000*	*2001*
Societies	1,495	7,425	15,640	33,913	48,560	50,284	52,330
Membership	765	2,909	5,317	11,315	17,967	18,192	18,566
Share Capital	420	1,204	2,682	5,295	10,888	13,187	13,372
Owned funds	538	1,527	3,206	7,153	15,404	17,871	18,595
Brrowings outstanding	1,283	7,419	21,100	49,161	77,413	82,537	1,20,883
Working capital	2,504	13,143	35,081	97,923	4,35,001	4,64,396	4,94,807
Loans outstanding	N.A.	N.A.	2,480	1 8,699	2,60,972	2,74,540	2,75,574
Loans overdue	N.A.	N.A.	198	3,169	10,061	10,749	11,773
Houses and Tenaments constructed during the year (00)	32	54	107	317	1,063	1,105	1,160

Source : Co-operative Movement at a Glance in Maharashtra 2001.

Need For Removal of Constraints

The following things need to be done to improve the working of housing co-operatives.

1. A separate model law of housing co-operatives as finalised under the National Housing and Habitat policy should be finalised as early as possible or there is need to amend co-operative law for the smooth working of housing co-operatives.
2. Housing co-operative face the problem of land shortage. The Government should make land available to housing co-operatives.
3. Stamp Duty and Registration fee must be exempted. Double taxation must be avoided.
4. Housing complexes built by housing co-operatives should be approved by state Level Apex Co-operative housing federation.

Conclusion

In order to face the emerging situation and translate their vision into action co-operative housing societies, enhance managerial ability, increase resouce moblization, creation of co-operation among the co-operatives and policy for development of housing co-operatives to face the present and emerging situation.

The achievements in the field of co-operation are note worthy. They are useful for prosperity and nation building co-operatives should strengthen their power for visionary approach. The more and more housing Co-operatives should be formed in rural areas also, so that the rural populations will not migrate to cities. Similarly, the members contribution in the cost of house may be reduced up to 10 to 15 per cent of the total.

19

Growth of Co-operative Institutions in Goa

M.R. Patil

Background

The idea of co-operation in India is as old as human beings. Our joint family living system is an excellent example of practical co-operation and the members of such joint family earn and spend jointly. The real spirit of co-operative movement sprouted in India with the enactment of the 1904 Co-operative Societies Act. The main aim of co-operatives during the pre-independence period was to substitute money lenders so as to provide financial relief to the farming community. Importantly, during the post-independence period, the aim has been to make the co-operatives a powerful instrument for economic development. Since independence, a co-operative sector has been recognized as one of the most significant segments of Indian economy and the movement was spread to the nook and corners of the country. Presently, there are more than 5 lakh co-operative societies with a membership of 23 crores. This sector covers 100 percent of total villages and 75 percent of the rural householders. More than 15.47 million individuals are employed in this sector. Today, the co-operative movement has emerged as one of the largest movement in the world.

Goan people started co-operative activities particularly in the credit areas in the form of "communidades" centuries ago as early as the Portuguese came to Goa. Goa was liberated from the Portuguese regime yoke on 19th December, 1961 and remained union territory alongwith Daman and Diu for several years. On 30th May, 1987, it was delinked from the union territory and was conferred a statehood. Goa state has an area of 3,702 sq. kms. and population of 13,43,998. About 50 percent of the population is rural. Administratively, the state is divided into two district (North Goa and South Goa) and eleven talukas. Tourism, industry, agriculture, fisheries and co-operation are the mainstay of Goan economy. The co-operative movement in Goa began late with the institution of the Office of the Registrar of Co-operative Societies on 17th November, 1962. The Nagargaon Group Vividh Karyakari Sahakari Seva Society Ltd., Nagargaon, Sattari Taluka and Valpoi Group Vividha Karyakari Sahakari Seva Society Ltd, Valpoi, Sattari taluka in North Goa district happened to be the first and second societies registered with the Registrar of Co-operative Societies on 4th March, 1963. At the end of the first co-operative year, on 30th June, 1963, the department had registered 62 co-operative societies of various types having a total membership of 4942. The movement has now gradually expanded and embraced co-operative activities of all types. Presently, the Goa state has only tow tier co-operative structure. At the Apex level, the Goa State Co-operative Bank and at the base or village level, primary co-operative societies. The Maharashtra State Co-operative Societies Act 1960, with necessary modification has been made applicable to the state of Goa since 18th December, 1962. After several years of Goa being conferred a statehood, the Government of Goa has passed the Goa State Co-operative Societies Act, 2001 and the framing of co-operative rules is under progress. In 1981, the Goa State Co-operative Union, an Apex co-operative institution in the state, was established for all types of co-operatives. As on 31st March, 2003, there are 2035 co-operatives of all types with a total membership of 7,55,379 which represented more than 56 percent of the total population of the state. The different types of co-operative institutions in the state of Goa can be viewed from Table 1.

Economic Significance of Co-operative Institutions

The co-operative institutions in the country have indeed continued to play an extensive role in the process of economic

Table 1 : Different Types of Co-operative Institutions in the State of Goa as on 31-03-2003

(Rs. In Lakhs)

S. No.	*Type of Society*	*No. of Societies*	*Member-ship*	*Working Capital*
1.	Goa State Co-op. Bank	1	8854	65810.01
2.	Urban Co-op. Bank	7	261870	93828.53
3.	Urban Co-op. Credit Societies	120	215577	26130.44
4.	Salary Earners Co-op. Credit Societies	254	60603	7573.34
5.	Consumer Co-op. Societies	96	42823	1271.88
6.	Dairy Co-op. Societies	158	25050	749.12
7.	Farming Co-op. Societies	6	259	0.86
8.	Fisheries Co-op. Societies	7	1508	48.63
9.	Housing Co-op. Societies	1166	27189	18717.72
10.	Industrial Co-op. Societies	39	3183	207.93
11.	Marketing Co-op. Societies	9	9908	451.82
12.	Poultry Co-op. Societies	2	58	0.59
13.	Processing Co-op. Societies	5	6180	5149.40
14.	Service Co-op. Societies	87	85616	4725.16
15.	Transport Co-op. Societies	3	57	0.86
16.	Labour Co-op. Societies	14	456	38.11
17.	Panivatap & Agri. Requisites Societies	47	3350	31.78
18.	Sangh & Union Federation	3	993	865.59
19.	General Co-op. Societies	11	1845	40.76
		2035	755379	225642.53

Source : Office of the Registrar of Co-operative Societies, Panaji, Goa.

development and growth under the present global economic environment. The co-operatives are a distinct form of organizations and they can not be matched with any other private/public institutions. Virtually, there is no substitutes to the co-operatives to serve the masses and protect the interest of the weaker section of the society from all kinds of exploitation. The distinguished characteristics of the co-operatives can be seen in their working and operation. These institutions are the autonomous association of persons united voluntarily to meet their common economic and social needs and aspirations through a jointly owned and democratically controlled enterprises. These essentially function based on the universally accepted set of co-operative values and principles. The 50th All India Co-operative Week celebration held during 14th to 20th November, 2003, focused on the theme that the co-operatives are growth engine for prosperity and nation building. These institutions have provided an employment about 15.47 million individuals and around 14.39 million people are self employed through co-operatives in India.

The co-operative enterprises that are promoted by the members and for the members, not having any vested interest keeping the profit motive as secondary, committing to the welfare and well being of the members in particular and community at large in general, play certainly a pivotal role under the ongoing liberalizing, privatizing and globalising economy. These co-operative institutions have made an entry into various key economic activities like industry, agriculture, finance, consumer, housing, dairy, poultry, fishery, marketing, et al. and have been contributing to the welfare of the weaker sections of the society. Considering the importance of these organizations, the new Multi-State Co-operative Societies Act 2002 and the formulated National Co-operatives Policy have provided a greater autonomy to co-operatives. The co-operative institutions have been equally playing an important role in the process of economic development of the state and their contribution in the state's economy is of paramount importance. In recognition of the co-operative institutions in the process of economic development, a study on the growth and progress of co-operatives in the state of Goa assumes greater importance. Against this background, an attempt has been made in this paper to introspect the growth trend of all types co-operative institutions in the state of Goa.

Objectives of The Study

The broader objective of the study is to examine the growth and progress of the co-operative institutions of all types with regard to the selected parameters viz., number of societies, membership, share capital, working capital, deposits, loans advanced, loans outstanding and profits, for the period from 1988-89 to 2002-03.

Data And Methodology

The present study relates to 15 year period from 1988-89 to 2002-03 based on secondary data. The necessary data with regard to the selected variables is gathered from different sources in the following manner: The data for the period from 1988-89 to 1998-99 is obtained from the Statistical Pocket Books (yearly publication), Directorate of Planning, Statistics and Evaluation, Panaji and the data for the period from 1999-2000 to 2002-03 is collected from the yearly statement of co-operatives, prepared by the Office of the Registrar of Co-operative Societies, Panaji, Goa. The co-operative year 1988-89 is taken as the base year as it happens to be an immediate succeeding year in which Goa was conferred statehood. In order to accomplish the objective of the study, the collected data for the said period was analysed and the growth rates of selected parameters were computed by using the following Linear Regression Model written as under:

$$Y = b_o + b_1 x_1 + U_t$$

where Y = dependent variable

b_o = constant (Y intercept)

b_1 = regression coefficients (slope parameter)

x_1 = independent variable

U_t = error term

Results and Discussions

The computed regression coefficients (growth rates) of the selected variables with regard to all the different co-operative institutions, urban co-operative banks and urban credit including salary earners co-operative societies for the period from 1988-89 to 2002-03 are presented in Table 2, 3 and 4 respectively.

From the Table 2 it can be witnessed that the number of societies have registered on an average 36.77 percent growth during the study period which is obviously considered to be an impressive growth. This clearly shows that the co-operative movement has really received a very good fillip in the state and the alertness about benefits of co-operatives among the people has been promoted effectively. As far as the total membership was concerned, considerably, a better growth was observed i.e. 28.15 percent during the whole period. This undoubtedly speaks about the people's attachment, faith and trust in the co-operative form of organizations particularly in fulfilling their socio-economic needs and requirements. The attachment and belongingness is indeed high as these co-operatives are promoted by themselves. The funds mobilized in the form in the form of share capital has recorded exceptionally good growth i.e. 53.09 percent during the study period revealing an encouraging contribution of the members towards share capital of their co-operatives. This liberal generation of funds will certainly enable the societies to serve the members better. The funds generated by the co-operatives in the form of deposits has shown reasonably good growth i.e. 10.85 percent during the study period. This encouraging deposit mobilization obviously recognizes the vital role of locally based and promoted co-operatives in stimulating and inculcating the savings habit amongst the members as well as non-members. This small portion of generated savings certainly supplements the size of capital formation which is considered to be very precious and essential for the nation's economic development and growth. The loans advanced by the co-operatives to the members was noticed to have registered an excellent 44.15 percent average growth during the study period. This clearly disclosed that the co-operative institutions advanced their mobilized financial resources to various income generating economic ventures that are undertaken by their members. This showed that the co-operative institutions also play a major role in creating employment opportunities whereby enhancing the size of income level of the weaker section of the society. The advanced loans stood outstanding, has recorded 12.60 percent on an average annual growth during the study period emphasizing on a continuous close monitoring of deployed funds as the growth of outstanding advances was observed to be within the reasonable limit. The societies were found to have showed 14.40 percent average growth in their profits which speaks about the poor performance in their profit maximization. One of the genuine reasons for this low profits could be due to their service orientated approach rather than profit making ambition. It is also equally true that many of the societies were noticed to have incurred losses during the study period. The total number of societies that have posted losses for the co-operative year 2002-03 were 281 and the societies with no profit and no loss were 247. One of the reason among others could be lack of interest and conflict among the members of the managing committee on the one hand and lessening interest of the members in the affairs of the society on the other.

Table 2: Growth Trends of Selected Variables of all Co-operative Institutions (1988-89 to 2002-03)

S.No.	*Variable (Y)*	*Regression Coefficient (%)*
1.	Number of Societies	36.77
2.	Number of Members	28.15
3.	Share Capital	53.09
4.	Working Capital	17.74
5.	Deposits	10.85
6.	Loans Advanced	44.15
7.	Loans Outstanding	12.60
8.	Profits	14.40

It can be observed from Table 3 with regard to the urban co-operative banks' functioning in the state. The number of banks have registered almost a negative growth over a period of time i.e. 0.10 percent indicating a total stagnation in the growth of urban co-operative banks in the state. Presently, there are only 7 co-operative banks that have been operating in the state. It is important to note that of the seven banks one is women co-operative bank, which has been serving the socio-economic needs of the women community. The reason for stagnant growth in the number of banks is due to the small state having a population about 13.50 lakhs and these banks have established a wide branch bank network all over the state of Goa. It is also important to note that the average population per bank branch office in the state is the lowest in India being less than 4000. The membership of the banks has registered 10.80 percent average growth which is considered to be reasonably good. A lower growth in the membership might be due to a few banks operating in the state. An another obvious reason for this low membership growth is because of an encouraging growth in the number of urban credit as well as salary earners credit co-operative societies which by and large fulfill the same needs and requirements as the urban co-operative banks meet. The share capital has recorded 12.80 percent growth during the study period which is not satisfactory. This showed poor efforts on the part of the banks in encouraging the members to contribute more and more towards the banks' share capital so as to have a strong equity base. The growth of deposits was observed to be very low during the study period i.e. 6.01 percent. This low deposit growth could be due to the changing perceptions of customers as well as a sharp increase in the banking network in the state. The growth of total loans disbursed was noticed to be satisfactory as deployment of funds is largely influenced by the size of funds generated. The total deployed funds stood outstanding, was found to have registered unreasonably high growth i.e. 34.70 percent which is not satisfactory. This clearly showed a very low recovery of disbursed funds. This trend of loans recovery will certainly bring the banks under risk and uncertainty. The working capital and profits have registered 16.87 percent and 20.87 percent growth during the study period. The growth of these two variables was observed to be satisfactory during the study period.

Table 3: Growth Trends of Selected Variables of Urban Co-operative Banks (1988-89 to 2002-03)

S.No.	*Variable (Y)*	*Regression Coefficient (%)*
1.	Number of Banks	00.10
2.	Number of Members	10.80
3.	Share Capital	12.80
4.	Working Capital	16.87
5.	Deposits	06.01
6.	Loans Advanced	13.80
7.	Loans Outstanding	34.70
8.	Profits	20.87

The Table 4 reveals that the number of urban credit and salary earners co-operative societies have registered 17.86 percent average growth during the stud period indicating consistently a good growth over a period of time. The membership of these societies has showed reasonably satisfactory growth i.e. 12.83 percent. The growth of share capital of these societies over a period of time was observed to be very poor. This could be due to non-attraction of the members towards shares of the societies. Moreover, whatever the share capital the societies could generate is because of the linking of loans advanced to the share capital. It means, the member borrower has to contribute 5 to 10 percent of the loan availed towards the share capital of the respective society. The deposits of these societies was observed to be reasonably good as the basic aim of these societies is to help the members in terms of meeting their immediate financial needs without much procedural delay. Therefore, whatever the deposits, the societies have raised, is considered to be good. There was a declining growth observed over a period of time as far as loans disbursement was concerned. This poor growth of advances might be due to an increasing options and alternatives that are extended to customers by other financial institutions. Especially, during the latter years, the commercial banks have drastically changed their lending policies. They have now shifted from financing for industries to financing for consumers. This revamp in their process has come in the wake of an unreasonably mounting Non Performing Assets (NPA). The total loans disbursed stood outstanding registered 16.47 percent average growth during the study period indicating an unreasonable hike in the outstanding loans. The working capital and the profits have registered 16.47 percent and 20.42 percent growth respectively during the study period. The growth in working capital over a period of time is considered to be good. In case of profits, though there is a satisfactory recorded growth, yet many societies have incurred losses during the study period.

Table 4 : Salary Earners' Co-operative Societies (1988-89 to 2002-03)

S.No.	*Variable (Y)*	*Regression Coefficient (%)*
1.	Number of Societies	17.86
2.	Number of Members	12.83
3.	Share Capital	07.02
4.	Working Capital	16.89
5.	Deposits	10.89
6.	Loans Advanced	10.72
7.	Loans Outstanding	16.47
8.	Profits	20.42

Conclusion

The foregoing analysis has examined the growth and progress of co-operative institutions in the state for the period from 1988-89 to 2002-03, with regard to the selected physical and financial parameters. The analysis revealed the following concluding remarks: (1) The total number of co-operative institutions and their membership during the study period have registered really a remarkable growth and all the financial parameters of these societies except profits and deposits have also posted a very good growth; (2) As far as the urban co-operative banks were concerned, all the variables except the number of banks, deposits, loans outstanding were found to have registered reasonably good growth; (3) The urban credit and salary earners co-operative societies were noticed to have made a good progress in the areas of number of societies, membership, deposits, credit deployment, working capital and profits. Intoto, it can be said that the co-operative institutions of all types have been really progressing.

20

An Evaluation of Urban Co-operative Banks In India

R. B. Teli

Historical Perspective

The UCBs cater primarily to the needs of lower and middle income class people, residing in urban, semi-urban and metropolitan centres to rescue them from the clutches of moneylenders and also they have inculcated a habit of thrift and savings in them. Inspired by the success of Urban Co-operative Credit Movement in Germany and Italy, some middle class Maharashtrian families settled in the erstwhile Baroda (now Gujarat state) started a mutual aid society named "Annyonya Sahakari Mandali" on 5th February, 1889, under the guidance of Late Shri. V.L. Kavathekar. The enactment of Co-operative Credit Societies Act, 1904 and the extension of B.R. Act in 1966 gave the real impetus to the movement. The first urban co-operative credit society was set up at Canjeevaram town in Madras province in October, 1904. Subsequently, The Betegiri Co-operative Credit Society" in Dharwar District in the undivided Bombay Province and "The Bangalore City Co-operative Credit Society" in the erstwhile Mysore State was registered in October 1905 and December 1905 respectively. After passing the Co-operative societies Act, 1912, the co-operatives were organized at a fast rate. However, the Urban Co-operative movement did not receive the impetus till Maclagan

Committee (1915) recognized it's importance as seen from the fact that Urban Co-operative Societies (602) constituted a meagre (4.4%) of agricultural credit societies (13745). The Seed of Urban Co-operative Movement was sown by the Maclagan Committee.

During the banking crisis and after first war the progress of Urban Co-operative Societies was not slowed down. It was realized that these societies were eminently suitable institutional agencies for mobilizing local savings and to provide financial accommodation to those who were in the clutches of money lenders. The Indian Central Banking Inquiry Committee (1931), observed that "The duty of these Urban Banks should be to try to do for the small trader, the small merchant and the middle class population what the commercial banks are doing for the big trader and big merchant."

First survey was made by RBI, in 1961, which commended the working of UCBs and pointed out that the government did not pay much attention for the development of non-agricultural sector. Varde Committee (1963) expedited the growth of UCBs by it's valuable suggestions. Damry Committee (1968) admitted the key role of UCBs in providing finance to small-scale industries. R.G. Saraiya Committee (1972) sponsored UCBs to undertake housing loans to their members. It also advised ceiling on individual borrowings. Madhav Das Committee (1979) stood a landmark in revolution of UCBs. The implementation of various recommendations of the Madhav Das Committee and subsequent creation of the separate Urban Bank Department (UBD) in 1984, for regulation and management of their working, has given a great impetus to the growth of UCBs. They were enjoying special privileges, but now no such privileges are available. They are on their own to compet with commercial banks in all the spheres of banking.

The NEP has created opportunities for the growth of UCBs, provided they prepare themselves for the competitive challenges ahead of them. RBI appointed the Marathe Committee (1993) to examine the licensing policy of new UCBs and accepted the recommendations of this Committee and liberalized the licensing of UCBs. As a result, during the period from May 1993 to 1999, RBI issued 537 licenses to new UCBs. Similarly branch licensing policy for UCBs was liberalized w.e.f. 8/1/1996. Under this polity, over 3300 licenses were issued for opening new branches.

Further, RBI appointed, the Chitale Committee, to review the auditing related matters. In July,1996, this Committee submitted its report and RBI decided to implement the recommendations.

In order to review the activities of UCBs, the High Power Committee (HPC) was appointed, in May,1999, under the chairmanship of Shri. K. Madhavarao, to evolve objective criteria to determine the need and potential for organization of UCBs, to review the entry point norms, branch licensing, area of operation, feasibility to introducing capital adequacy norms for UCBs, weak banks, conversion of co-operative credit society into UCB and to suggest necessary legislative amendments to B.R. Act and State Co-op. Acts, for strengthening the Urban Banking Movement. Based on the recommendations of HPC, the RBI revised the entry point norms w.e.f. August,2001. The main thrust of the policy on strong capital and corporate governance. It was that there should be at least two directors with suitable banking experience or relevant professional qualifications.

HPC has suggested that the continued financial stability of UCBs cannot be ensured unless they are subjected to the discipline of maintenance of prescribed minimum Capital to Risk Assets Ratio (CRAR). RBI examined the Committee's recommendations and it has decided to implement CRAR norms to UCBs in a phased manner over a period of 3 years with effect from 31/3/2002. Scheduled and non-scheduled UCBs should achieve CRAR norms of 8% and 6% respectively. Both are expected to achieve the same level of CRAR, as applicable to commercial banks by 31/3/2004 and 31/3/2005 respectively. Non-Scheduled UCBs will have to maintain 6%, 7% and 9% CRAR by 31/3/2002, 31/3/2003 and 31/3/2004 respectively.

UCB movement in India has passed about 115 years, in 3 stages. *The First Stage,* which is establishment stage, started from the 1889 to 1980, in which most of the UCBs existed in urban cities of the country. *The Second Stage,* which is developing stage, started from 1980 to 1991. During this period UCBs developed their banking business. *The Third Stage,* which is competitive stage just after the NEP (1991). In this stage, the UCBs has to face stiff competition from commercial banks, foreign banks, private banks, private financial agencies, government financial agencies and money lenders those who are standing on the same platform where UCBs were operating their business.

Analysis of The Operations of UCBs In India

As on 1st March,1966, when the B.R. Act 1949 was made applicable to Co-op. Banks, there were 1106 primary (Urban) co-op banks in the country in 1966-67. This number of UCBs increased to 1306 in 1990-91, showing an average annual growth rate of 1.15% and the percentage increase in 1990-01 over 1966-67 stood 18.08%. The operations of UCBs have shown considerable progress during the period of 25 years from 1966-67 to 1990-91. Owned funds have increased form Rs. 58 crore to Rs. 1481 crore as on 30 June, 1991, as on 30 June,1967 showing average annual growth rate of 15.27%. Both the deposits and loans outstanding have registered a significant increase from the low levels of Rs. 153 crore and Rs. 167 crore respectively as on 30th June, 1987 to Rs. 10157 crore and Rs. 8003 crore respectively as on 30th June, 1991. During the same period, working capital increased from Rs. 222 crore to Rs. 13,990 crore showing an average annual growth rate of 19.25%. The credit-deposit ratio was declined from 109.15 to 78.79.

Performance relating to operations of UCBs in India from 30/6/1991 to 31/3/2000 covering decade has depicted in *Table 1* and *Graph 1.* The table and the graph indicate that UCBs in India continue to register a steady growth in respect of different variables. It is seen that nearly 78% of working capital was of the deposits and 11% of owned funds. It means UCBs were self-reliant and very few banks needed borrowings from other banks during the period under review. Actual number of UCBs has increased from 1397 in 1991 to 2050 by 31st March, 2000, showing 1.47 times increase and percentage increase was 46.74%. Owned funds, deposits and advances, which were 1481 crore, Rs. 10157 crore and Rs. 8003 crore respectively in 1991, it increased to Rs. 9312 crore, Rs. 71,183 crore and Rs. 45,993 crore respectively in the year 2000. During the same period, working capital has increased to Rs. 90,301 crore as 31-3-2001, as against Rs. 13,990 crore as on 30/6/1991. The borrowings stood at Rs. 1475 crore as against Rs. 376 crore in 1991. They formed only 1.73% in 2000 as against 2.82% in 1991. Their deposit have shown highest compound growth rate of 21.49% during the decade under study.

Table1 : Indicating Performance of Urban Co-operative Banks In India For The Period From 1990-91 To 1999-2000

Rs. in Crores

Year	No. of Reporting UCBs. No.	Working Capital	Owned Funds	% of Owned Funds to W.C.	Deposits	% of Deposits to W.C.	Borrowings	% of Borrowings to W.C.	Loans Outstanding	% of Loans Outstanding to W.C.	C.D. Ratio
1991	1306	13390	1481	11.06	10157	75.86	377	2.82	8003	59.77	78.79
	(0.50)	(17.46)	(17.91)		(17.29)		(0.80)		(17.66)		
1992	1401	14742	1766	11.98	11108	75.35	544	3.69	8713	59.10	78.44
	(7.27)	(10.17)	(19.24)		(9.36)		(44.30)		(8.87)		
1993	1399	18007	2224	12.35	13531	75.14	565	3.14	10132	56.27	74.88
	(-0.14)	(22.15)	(25.93)		(21.81)		(3.86)		(16.29)		
1994	1400	22037	2723	12.35	16769	76.09	604	2.74	12172	55.23	72.59
	(0.07)	(22.38)	(22.43)		(23.93)		(6.90)		(20.13)		
1995	1431	25977	3239	12.46	19711	75.88	664	2.55	14520	55.90	73.66
	(2.17)	(17.88)	(18.94)		(17.54)		(9.93)		(19.29)		
1996	1501	31744	3848	12.12	24165	76.12	758	2.39	17908	56.41	74.11
	(4.89)	(22.20)	(18.80)		(22.60)		(14.15)		(23.33)		
1997	1653	39570	4695	11.86	30714	77.62	619	1.56	21550	54.46	70.16
	(10.13)	(24.65)	(22.01)		(27.10)		(-18.33)		(20.34)		

Contd...

Table 1 : (Contd...)

Year	*No. of Reporting UCBs. No.*	*Working Capital*	*Owned Funds*	*% of Owned Funds to W.C.*	*Deposits*	*% of Deposits to W.C.*	*Borrowings*	*% of Borrowings to W.C.*	*Loans Outstanding*	*% of Loans Outstanding to W.C.*	*C.D. Ratio*
1998	1502	52229	5985	11.45	40692	77.91	886	1.70	27807	53.24	68.30
	(-9.13)	(31.99)	(27.47)		(32.49)		(43.13)		(29.03)		
1999	1587	66985	7314	10.93	52617	78.55	1040	1.55	34172	51.01	64.94
	(5.66)	(28.25)	(22.20)		(29.31)		(17.38)		(22.89)		
2000	1781	85000(p)	9312	10.96	71183	83.74	1475	1.73	45993	54.11	64.61
	(12.22)	(26.89)	(27.31)		(32.29)		(41.83)		(34.59)		
Average Annual Growth %	3.36	22.40	22.22	8.21	23.37	77.23	16.40	2.39	21.24	55.55	72.05
C.G.R.	3.15	20.30	20.18		21.49		14.61		19.11		

Source : 1. Statistical Statements Relating to Co-operative Movement in India, RBI Bombay.
2. Supplement to RBI Bulletin Dec.2000.
3. Dr. Roy P.P. "Management of UCBs", Himalaya Publications, New Delhi, First Edition, 2001, Page 47

Note : 1. P - Provisional.
2. Actual No. of UCBs for the year 1998, 1999, 2000 were 1811,1936 and 2050 respectively.
3. Figures in brackets show Annual Growth Rate in % .
4. W.C. - Working Capital.

Graph 1 : Indicating Performance of Urban Co-operative Banks in India From 1990-91 to 1999-2000

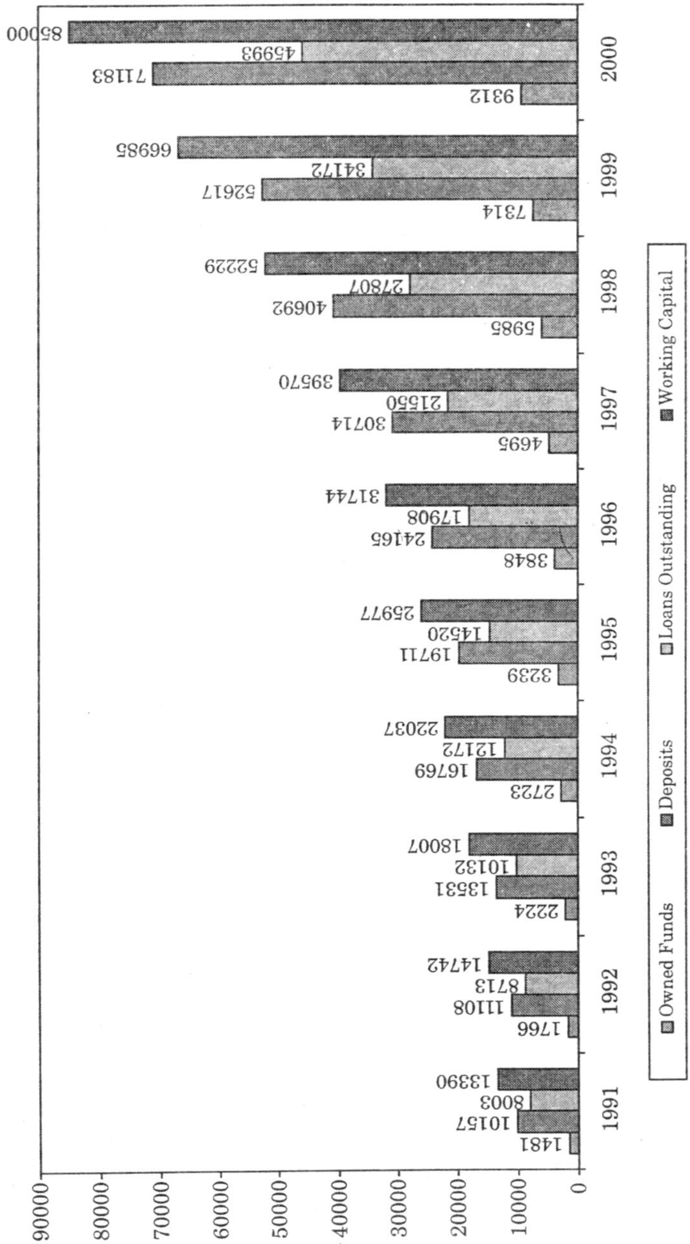

It showed the ability of UCBs to mobilize local resources and ability to sustain growing business.

An important feature of these banks during the last decade was that the credit-deposit ratio showed a continuous declining trend except in 1996. It has declined form 78.79% in 1991 to 64.61% in 2000 and now to 63.9% in 2003.

The growth of UCBs in India has been spectacular, but it is uneven.

Table 2 : Spread of UCBs - Statewise

No.	*State*	*1/3/66*	*28/6/91*	*31/3/03*
1.	Maharashtra	84 (27.43)	358 (27.43)	670 (31.84)
2.	Gujarat	62 (15.38)	288 (22.07)	362(17.21)
3.	Karnataka	64 (15.88)	201 (15.40)	324 (15.40)
4.	Tamil Nadu	87 (21.59)	128 (9.81)	136 (6.46)
5.	Andhra Pradesh	34 (8.44)	63 (4.82)	169(8.03)
6.	Other States	72 (17.87)	267 (20.47)	443 (21.06)
	Total	403 (100)	1305 (100)	2104 (100)

Note : Figures in brackets indicate percentage to total).
Source : RBI Bulletins.

From the above table, it indicates that out of 2104 UCBs in 29 states of the country as many as 1661 banks (79%) were located in five states, viz; Maharashtra, Gujarat, Karnataka, Andhra Pradesh and Tamil Nadu. The main reasons behind the regional disparities are lack of good leadership, lack of interest of state, co-op deptt. Appex bank and RBI and lack of proper environment. The percentage share of Maharashtra State in total UCBs in the country has been increasing and it stood first. Due to liberal licensing policy from 1993, the % share of other states except five leading states (regarding no. of UCBs), has raised from 17.87% in 1966 to 21% in 2003. At the same time the % share of Gujarat and Tamilnadu has declined, though actual no. of UCBs has raised.

The number of UCBs increased to 2,104 as at end - March 2003, which included 89 salary earner's banks and 133 Mahila Banks. Out of the total banks; 163 were under liquidation as at end of March 2003. Based on the new classification, 944 UCBs have classified under the Class I / II / III/ IV category as on 31/ 3/2003. 142 weak banks could not comply with CRAR norms. RBI has also prescribed asset-liability management norms to scheduled UCBs, effective from 1st July, 2002. These norms are to be extended to non-scheduled UCBs in due course, in phased manner. The period of advance for classifying as NPA has reduced from 180 days to 90 days, w.e.f. 31/3/2004. For this purpose, banks are instructed to charge interest at monthly rests w.e.f. 1/4/2002. UCBs have been going through difficult phase, since Madhavpura Mercantile Co-op Bank pay order scam (2001) at Ahamedabad, which brought to light the poor risk management system of UCBs in India.

With a view to examining their problems a committee was constituted under the chairmanship of Shri. Anant G. Geete, the them Minister of State for finance, GOI. Based on the recommendations of the committee, the RBI undertook several measures during 2002-2003. e.g. the norms of classifying UCBs as 'weak' and 'sick' were modified w.e.f. 31/3/2002 on the basis of CRAR, NPAs and record of losses etc. In the case of NPA norms, 'gold' loans and small loans upto Rs. One Lakh will continue to be covered by the 180 days norms. The non-scheduled banks have been allowed to place their surplus funds with strong scheduled UCBs. Following the recommendations of the Joint Parliamentary Committee and to prevent certain irregularities, a total ban has been imposed; on grant of loans and advances to directors of UCBs and their relatives and concerns in which they have interest w.e.f. 1/10/2003.

A CAMELS Model (Capital adequacy, Asset quality, Management, Earning Appraisal, liquidity and Systems and control) has been introduced to scheduled UCBs from 31/3/2003 and simplified rating system will be made applicable to non-scheduled UCBs w.e.f. 31/3/2004. With a view to enhancing transparency, the UCBs with deposits of Rs. 100 crore and above have been advised to give detailed information about CRAR, NPAs etc as "notes on account" to their balance sheets. Further, UCBs have to indicate the position of payment of DICGC premium in Directors' report attached to their annual reports.

Due to irregularities, the growth in deposits and loans outstanding of UCBs in India has declined.The growth rate which was 13.1% in 2001 in their deposits, reduced to 9% in 2003, whereas, growth rate of loans outstanding has declined from 18.2% in 2001 to 4.5% in 2003. On the same line, C:D ratio has reduced from 67.3% in 2001 to 63.9% in 2003. NPAs are the index of banking health. High levels of NPAs is an indication of poor credit management. The volume of NPA affects the yield on advances.

Table 3 : NPA position in UCBs in India

No.	*Year*	*No. of Reporting Banks*	*Gross NPAs Rs. in Crore*	*Gross NPAs as % to total advances*
1	1999	1474	3306	11.07
2	2000	1748	4534	12.24
3	2001	1942	9245	16.10
4	2002	1937	13706	21.90
5	2003	1941	13647	21.00

Source : RBI Bulletins.

It can be seen from the above table that gross NPAs of reporting UCBs in India has been increased (by 4.13 times) from Rs. 3306 crore in 1999 to Rs. 13647 crore in 2003. The percentage of Gross NPAs to total advances of UCBs in India, which was 11.07% in 1999, raised to 21.90% in 2002 and slightly reduced to 21% in 2003. It was found that the level of NPAs of UCBs had jumped during 2001-02 because of difficulties faced by a few banks in Gujarat.

Due to difficult financial position, RBI asked to initiate liquidation proceeding of 23 UCBs in India. In recent years the net profit of the UCBs in India has been reducing due to a larger provisioning made for NPAs. The operating profit of the UCBs is also showing a downward trend. This may be due to an increase in the cost of funds and non-profitable avenues for deployment. This problem of the UCBs is likely to intensify with increased competition and to survive and prosper, UCBs have to devise innovative schemes to attract members/customers and retain their loyalty. RBI is tightening its monitoring over UCBs solely to protect the interest of depositors by ensuring transparency in their working.

Problems Faced By Urban Co-operative Banks In India

Duel Control

Operations of Urban Co-operative banks come under the jurisdiction of RBI and the management aspects of these banks are being controlled by the State Government through Registrar of Co-operative Societies (RCS). The conflict due to the overlapping provisions of State Co-op Act and B.R. Act, has thus remained unsolved, which are coming in the way of development activities of UCBs. It has also become a real challenge for the UCBs to maintain the co-operative character and at the same time to do commercially viable banking business. So it is high time to put an end to dual control of UCBs.

Untrained Human Capital

UCBs generally recruit their staff on regional basis, through board of directors. Salary structure is low and work-load is more. Politicians interfere in day-to-day working of UCBs. Board of directors of UCBs seems to be working on the line of directors of private companies. They use their power and authority for vested interests, which in turn demoralizes the staff. In fact, the staff of the UCBs is not well trained. The amount and time spent on training of employees is very low. Training is treated as time-wasting business, though very few employees know new financial products, national and international banking operations, stock-exchange transactions and latest trends etc. Most of the Directors and employees are satisfactory with their daily routine and not willing to take more risk like investment in, GOI securities, innovative practices in banking etc.

Limited Area of Operation

UCBs are local area banks. They serve in their area of operation. But in the era of the information explosion, village has become a small unit of whole world. The concepts like home-banking, ATM, have emerged as a need of an hour. UCBs can not keep them aloof from the different changes occurred in the banking industry.

Lack of Marketing View

Marketing of banking services involve product, price, distribution, promotion, people, physical evidence and procedural development for customer satisfaction. Because of different operational restrictions and lack of training of personnel in UCBs, they have very limited banking products to serve for their members / customers.

Limited Resources

UCBs are self-reliant but they have limited area of operation. Due to their co-operative character, they are not entitled to enter into capital market and raise funds. Without fund, UCBs can not develop their infrastructure.

Lack of Proper Support form the Government

Government treats UCBs like normal society and creates all bureaucratic hurdles in their working which create operational problems for scheduled UCBs and also for non-scheduled UCBs. Due to support of GOI, NPAs of PSBs have reduced but UCBs need such financial support from GOI.

Problem of Recovery

Non-co-operative attitude of Govt. departments and non-availability of staff with co-operative department for setting up of co-operative courts leads to compiling of large number of cases and blockage of huge funds as NPA.

It is an open secret that the top management of UCBs has tendency to violate the time-tested norms of sound lending for their vested interests. Credit-Deposit ratio of UCBs has declined and the management is forced to lend. Lending without proper security, documentation, screening and lending to relatives of Board of Directors resulted in bad recovery position. Insider says that co-operative banks are making window - dressing in NPA to avoid criticism from RBI by issuing new loans without recovering dues.

Low Computerization

In most UCBs in India, computerization has developed at very slow rate. Though computers are installed, trained staff is not available. For the fully computerized activities, huge funds are needed.

Lack of Transparency

UCBs in India do not submit required reports and financial information in time to RBI. Data-base on all india basis is lacking. There is lack of transparency in the transaction of business of UCBs.

Incomplete Corporate Governance

HPC recommended to appoint at least two professionals in the board of directors of UCBs. But this is yet to be implemented in most of UCBs in India. Some Directors on the board of UCBs are not professionals or dedicated people but some of them are political figures, who use the banking machinery for their political interests.

Lack of Conceptual Awareness

Most of the directors and employees of UCBs are not aware of banking concepts and new products used in the banking industry.

Suggestions

1. Duel control on UCBs should be removed. Let there be only one regulatory authority.
2. Proper training to the staff of UCBs should be imparted. Management should focus on strategies on HRD, bench-marking, ethical education and Information Technology.
3. The real panacea to improve the working of UCBs is to avoid political interference and adopt Professional Management with co-operative value orientation.
4. There should be minimum educational qualification for a person to become a director of UCB. Directors' training should be encouraged.
5. UCBs should be allowed to issue debentures, and other debt instruments for raising funds.
6. UCBs should be allowed to offer different financial products, which commercial banks offer.
7. GOI should give financial support to weak UCBs.

8. Strict observance of sound lending policies and practices and proper recovery schedules will help to improve recovery position.
9. For proper corporate governance two directors with professional experience should be appointed. These directors may include minimum post-graduates in Commerce/ Management, Economics and also academicians, researchers in respective fields. Linkage between Universities, Colleges and UCBs will help to improve the operations of these banks.
10. They should undertake non-funded business like advisory services, electronic transfer of money, collecting light bills, telephone bills, Income-Tax (if GOI permits), consultancy and extension services, in order to improve their other income.
11. There should not be the political interference in the working of UCBs.
12. They have to ensure greater transparency in their overall working to rebuild the confidence of their members.

Conclusion

At present UCBs have nearly about 10% of the resources of the entire banking sector in India. They have Rs. 101546/- crore deposits, & 64,880- crore advances, Rs. 9830 crore owned funds and Rs. 111746/- crore working capital as at end - 2003. It is an important segment of banking industry. UCBs are the best vehicles of micro credit delivery system. They have provided more than 60% of their credit to priority sector. They are filling credit gap in their area of operation and winning the confidence of their customers. If UCBs plan and work properly, they have golden days in near future, provided they have to strive hard for excellence in providing services.

REFERENCES

RBI, (1999), The Report of High Power Committee on UCBs, Mumbai, pp. 18.

The Co-operator, Excerpts from FICCI Discussion Paper on the Occasion of Seminar on UCBs; Future Reforms 10/5/2000, New Delhi.

Report of Indian Central Banking Inquiry Committee, (1931), Majority Report, Published by GOI, New Delhi, p. 255.

Satyanaryana G.S. "Challenges before Scheduled and Large UCBs in the New Millennium" Urban Credit Vol. No. 21 (4), Dec. 1999, pp. 27-29.

Devadasan K, Dr. Resia Beegams, "Urban Banks in India - Is it Sheen or Wane". The Mah. Co-op. Society Vol. M. 84(1). July-Sept. 2000, pp. 59-61.

Report of HPC on UCBs, Urban Credit Vol.21 (4), Dec. 1999, p. 03.

Report on Trends and Progress of Banking in India, 1999-2000, Supplement to RBI Bulletin, Dec. 2000, p. 95.

RBI Cir. UBD No. P.T. PCB 45/09. 116/2000-01 dt. 25/4/01.

Sai Babu P.C. and Naidu M.R. "A Critical Review of Co-op. Urban Bank - A Case Study", Agricultural Banker, Vol.18 (1), Mar. 1995 pp. 16-20.

Tiruttani Munivelu, "Bank Balance Sheet Management" IBA. Bulletin, Vol. 22 (4 and 5), April - May, 2000, pp. 12-21.

Report on Trends and Progress of Banking in India 2002-2003, RBI, p. 95.

Raikar A.V. "Growth, Profitability and Cost Efficiency of UCBs in India. A Comparative Analysis", Indian Co-operative Review, Vol. 42(2) Oct. 2003, pp. 103-114.

21

Crave for Professionalisation in Urban Co-operative Banks

S.O. Junare

Introduction

Urban co-operative banks are popular in India and they are playing significant role in the non-agricultural credit sector, and in the Indian Banking System as a whole.

Gujarat State is the leading state in respect of Co-operative movement and recognized in the entire world due to AMUL. It is also recognized for its credit co-operative movement and particularly for the Urban Co-operative Banks. Today it has 367 urban co-operative banks working for the betterment of masses in the state. The Gujarat is the state of foundation of co-operative movement in India, where the co-operative movement was started through an Urban Co-operative Credit Society in 1889.

The urban co-operative banks in Gujarat state are familiar as ideal institutions to meet the credit and banking requirements of populace of small means, such as small entrepreneurs, traders, salaried people, artisans, small scale and cottage industries and professionals etc.

Out of the total urban co-operative banks in India (2084) Gujarat, Maharashtra and Karnataka accounts about 70 % of the banks in India. It has more than 1 Crore customers. The Maharashtra state is having 558 urban banks.

Although the urban co-operative banks operate under the purview of Banking Regulation Act, they are philosophically quite different from the Commercial Banks. They are smaller in size, their area of operation is limited, and they have limited but particular and committed clientele. The urban co-operative banks have less of "Walk-in" customers. The deposit base of them generally does not include corporate and large institutional funds. The urban co-operative banks being the co-operative institutions, they are abiding to follow the co-operative principles and values.

Considering the role, importance and responsibility of urban co-operative banks, they must be viable, productive and operationally efficient enough in performing their socio-economic responsibility in an effective manner. Due to the financial sector reforms in the banking sector, the urban co-operative banks are also feeling the heat of blistering pace set by the liberalized financial sector. Although in the first phase of the reform process the urban co-operative banks did not faced much problems like District Central Co-operative Banks and RRBs, but during the second phase, these banks are badly affected. These banks faced the challenges of deregulation i. e. income generation, existence in present business and acquiring of new business, competition with other banks/financial institutions, new services development, Human Resource Development and the major troubles now a days for them is to rebuild a trust of people with them. Despite their overwhelming importance in India's economy several urban co-operative banks in the state are in vary bad state of affairs. They suffer from various organizational, managerial, operational and financial problems. They continue to be stifled by the restraints imposed by the rigid co-operative law and undue interference, politicians, bureaucrats and other vested interests and they are grossly mismanaged. It is high time that the urban co-operative banks were liberated from various kinds of shackles, democratically governed and professionally managed.

This article identifies some of the issues in professionalisation of management which urban co-operative banks are facing now and will also face in the coming years and outlines strategies for coping with them. The author asserts that despite their overwhelming importance in the state's economy, most of the urban banks surer from a variety of internal and external problems including lack of professional management.

Meaning & Importance of Professional Management in Urban Co-operative Banks

The professional management is a process of planning, organizing, directing, coordinating, implementing, monitoring and controlling of the banking activities in effective and efficient manner to achieve the goal of the bank. In other words the professional management means performing the banking functions by professionally qualified and trained persons. In short, the professionalism means to employ the right person for right job.

Professionalisation does not applicable only to the personnel or employees of the banks, but those all who are responsible for the management of the banks including the board of directors. In reality, most of the board of directors of co-operative banks in our country does not posses the knowledge of banking business nor they are directly associated with banking business. It is expected that the directors and members of the co-operative banks after their association with the co-operative banks must try to understand the functioning of bank, its rules and procedure etc.

As the volume of banking business has grown with stiff competition and complex environment, the chairman, board of directors or the traditional manager alone cannot execute the functions of bank effectively. Considering the limitations of individual, there is a need of the personnel with knowledge, foresights, insights, management skills and ability, who perform the activities of the bank efficiently. The urban co-operative banks have grown in many fold and occupy the important position in the states economy, these banks also need to improve themselves by inducting professional management so that they can cope with the present competition and challenges.

Problems of Professionalism in Urban Co-operative Banks

The several urban co-operative banks, particularly in the big cities have employed professional managers. But still in most of the urban co-operative banks the management is being done by the traditional method. Some of the major obstacles for professionalsing the management of co-operative banks identified includes; the lack of professional manager having appropriate knowledge of co-operative principles, values and ethos & lack of appropriate training. It is found that in several urban banks the managers are recruited on the basis of relations and on not on the merits. These managers lack comprehensive and update knowledge of banking, law and current trends in banking and financial market at national and international level. Some times the managers are recruited from the nationalized banks after their retirement and they lack the knowledge of co-operative law and management system relating to co-operative banks. It is also experienced that several managers of the urban co-operative banks are forced to follow the instructions of some of the board members blindly without following the legal procedure.

Most of the urban co-operative banks have poor salary structure as compared to commercial banks and this is also one of the obstacle in attracting the professional managers. The traditional managers of urban co-operative banks are unable to manage the day to day managerial functions effectively. For examples the traditional managers do not believe in marketing activities of banking services. The manager of these banks doesn't approach the customers for knowing their needs, expectations from the banks so that the new services can be developed and business can be increased.

The traditional managers are unaware about the current trends and practices in banking sectors. These managers are not fully aware about the important asset liability management, liquidity management, risk management and investment portfolio, concept of costing of banks' funds, diversification of business etc. and therefore they are much behind the existing and new players i.e. private banks.

Apart from the above the managers are expected to perform the role of development agent of the bank but due to the lack professionalism they can not make strategic planning for the development of the bank. The traditional managers are lacking the professionalism and they are not able to cope with the transformation in the banking system. Some of the key issues are as under.

Key Issue in Urban Banks

- Strategic planning for Business Development
- Marketing of Banking Services
- Adoption of Latest Technology
- Effective use of Deregulated structure of Floating / Volatile rate of interest
- Profitable Investment in profitable securities
- Trading of Securities in the market.
- Maintenance of required Liquidity (SLR, CRR)
- Proper Asset Liability Management
- Accurate Risk Management
- Preservation of Capital to Risk Adequacy Ratio
- Transparency in Financial Statements
- Scientific appraisal and scrutiny of loan proposal
- Reading and Analysis of financial statements
- Awareness about notifications of Reserve Bank of India and Government
- Awareness of Co-operative, banking and other laws
- Effective Human Resource Management
- Effective Branch Management

Though, the Indian economy has been liberalized extensively, yet the banking is one of the most regulated Industries in our country. The dual control from the Government and RBI, political interference, and lack of good governance and leadership are also the causes for non-professionalisation in urban co-operative banks.

In the era of economic liberalization, the demand of more freedom, autonomy for urban co-operative banks is increasing. On the other hand, there is another view that the banks are the public institutions and acting as an agent of the depositors/public money. Hence there should be government intervention who can protect the interest of the general public. It is experienced that the rules and laws including co-operative societies act and banking regulation act and negotiable instrument act have some deficiencies and they need to be amended so as to enable the banks to protect the public interest. But on the other hand it is also experienced that there is no strict law or its implementation system in co-operative banking system, which can protect the interest of the depositors. Therefore, it is the need of the hour that there should be strict law and its effective implementation system in co-operative banks. It is a good sign that the Government of Gujarat and Policy makers are keen in this matter and the modified provisions are being included in the existing laws so that they can become more effective.

The Role of Board of Directors

Historically, person nominated for a director of co-operative bank would often agree to serve for the reputation that the position confers in the local community. Of course the banks also get benefits by associating them. But now the role of director has become a very complex than the previous time. They are given more responsibility of development of the bank as well as fulfillment of the needs of its members with protection of the interest of the depositors with honoring of the rules. A trait answer to the problem of splitting the duties between directors and managers is to say that the "board of directors is responsible for making policies and the managers for implementing it". The job of the director is to direct the manager for implementing the policy decision. It means the directors should manage the manager, not the day to day functions of the banks. There is urgent need of drawing clear line between the functions of the directors and the managers. When the urban co-operative banks recorded a phenomenal growth and also their financial transactions grew to such an extent as to affect the state and national economy, most of the eminent people in the society wish to associate them so as to contribute in the development of these banks. But some of people from the society had also become more anxious to get more personal benefits and control them.

The urban co-operative banks in few states are working better that the other states because the dedicated, sincere and honest board of directors manages the banks.

Measures for Professional Management in Urban Co-operative Banks

The professionalisation of management will definitely help the bank to overcome from the current troubles.

Now a day due to failure of series of urban co-operative banks in Gujarat, the public is loosing the faith in the co-operative banking. The problem of failure of banks is not that much serious than the loosing of trust of public in CO-OPERATIVE MOVEMENT as a whole. Till date more than 10 urban co-operative banks have closed their shutters and several are in the way. The policy makers, Government and co-operators have to play a role in rebuilding the faith of public at the earliest. The Government and Co-operators must study the situation and find out the reasons behind the failure of these banks. Only making a law alone cannot be a solution to this problem. Most of the banks have failed due to the liquidity problems created by the panic and these banks have good solvency. These banks and the future jeopardy can be survived if the proper awareness camps are organized by the banking associations, co-operators, governments and individual banks to educate the people about the banks health situation. The co-operative week is the best period for initializing the process of awaking the people about strength of co-operative movement in general and co-operative banks in particular.

Some of the changes can take place easily in the banks if the professional management is inducted. These are adoption of new technology, proper management of funds, human resource development, marketing and business development etc. But the following two factors are to be revitalized for inducting the professionalism in the urban co-operative banks.

Legislatory Measures

The urban bank are in urgent need of modification in the existing co-operative societies act or enactment of new co-operative legislation which give more freedom to the banks to perform their day-to-day activities and they need not to seek permission from the state government for a small things within the purview of the law. The law should prevent the banks from letting loose from unnecessary nurturing and protecting in several matters and law should have provisions of fixing of responsibility accountability and authority to disburse and recovery of loans. The enforcement of law also should take care of the retaining good leadership and management.

Training and Education

Training and Education is the foremost mechanism for improving knowledge, skill and attitude of the personnel working in an organization. Though the training and education is most important aspect of professionalisation, it is lacking in most of the urban co-operative banks. The employees and the board of directors associated with the urban co-operative banks lack the education and training facility for them. There are only four Formal training Institutes practically engaged in imparting training activities for the officials and non-officials of urban co-operative banks.

Considering the needs of the training and education of the workforce of Agricultural Credit Co-operatives, the many State Co-operative Banks have set up a modern training center (i.e. National Institute of co-operative Management, Gandhinagar), under the distinguished leadership of Shri Jairambhai Patel, which provides training & education to the officials and non-officials of Gujarat State Co-operative Bank, DCCBs and PACs. Recently, the National Institute of co-operative Management has also started to organize the need-based training programmes for officials and non-officials of the urban co-operative banks.

The State Co-operative Union are an organization engaged in imparting education and training to the officials and non-officials of co-operative societies at grass-root level. The State Co-operative Unions take care of providing Education and training to the employees and members of the primary co-operative societies at their doorsteps through its wide network of district co-operative unions and regional training Centres spread all over the State Co-operative Unions organize the training programmes for the clerical staff of urban co-operative banks on the operation aspects and the Leadership Development Programmes for the directors of urban co-operative banks.

In view of the numerous officials and non-officials associated with the urban co-operative banks the existing structure of training and education is inadequate and hence most of the urban co-operative banks could not be benefited through the training programmes. Though it is reality that the existing structure of training and education for the urban co-operative banks is not adequate to cope up the training needs of these banks but on the other hand it is also the truth that the most of the urban co-operative banks are unaware about need and importance of training and education and don't sponsor their personnel in the training programmes organized by these Institutes. Therefore, the facilities available with the existing training institute remain underutilized.

Therefore, there is an urgent need of developing appropriate training and education strategy to provide education and training to the officials and non-officials on various aspects of banking. The policy makers must design the policy and strategy for the same. The training institutes and policy makers must find out the gap between the required knowledge & skill of the officials and non-officials and design the appropriate need-based training programmes and curricula to fill up the existing gap as well as make them equipped for the future banking also.

It can be concluded that urban co-operative banks have a bright future in the banking sector as well if they are transformed into professionalism, member controlled autonomous organizations, managed professionally and literate from unnecessary legal and governmental control. Since, we know that the freedom without discipline cannot enjoyed properly, it is also become inevitable that there must be close supervised and monitored *(not controlled or managed)* by a government agency.

22

Information Technology For Co-operative Banks

Yashwant S. Patil

Introduction

In the last decade or so, the information technology has revolutionized the entire world affecting the every field. The personal, social and public life has made a significant impact on quality of life. The emerging changes in the information technology have made great impact on data and information represented in digital, text, image, graphics or voice media and with communication, storage and processing.

Information technology (IT) helps to optimize the use of scarce resources through intelligent information support for decision making, and helps further in its implementation by supporting coordination effort without wasteful delays. Decision making has become a very complex process due to competitive environment, scarce resources and compulsions to achieve goals. Information technology has made decisive inroads in all walks of life; in offices, factories, railway stations, airports, communications, entertainment, education, banking hotels, hospitals, transportation and shopping. It is being used extensively for decision making, ease of operations, communication, record keeping and for obtaining higher productivity from the system in which it is put to use. The private sector is leading in implementation of latest technology based solutions in their organizations.

The Government at both Central and State levels have already set up a separate cells to look into the implementations of information technology based solutions in various departments and sections to provide simple, moral, accountable, reliable and transparent services to the common citizens thereby reducing the service time and cost. The States like Andhra Pradesh, Maharshtra, Karanataka, Madhya Pradesh have already applied the information technology in their governance and are leading in implementation of e-governance forcing the other States in the country to give serious thought on applying the e-governance concept.

The present paper on *Information Technology for co-operative banks* covers the information technology implementation status and technology developments applicable to banking sector with focus on co-operative banks.

Information Technology Implementation In Co-operative Banks–An Overview

Information Technology based solutions for any business has become a common phenomenon in today's age of computers. The banking sector has emerged as one of the leading sector in computerisation and co-operative banks are no exception to this. Even for this matter the primary credit societies have also shown a remarkable progress in introducing computerisation for their various activities in some of the States like Kerala and Maharashtra. The co-operative banks in Maharashtra, Gujarat, Karnataka and Goa are leading in computerisation.The success of computerisation in Urban Co-operative banks in these is on the higher side than the State level and District level co-operative banks. Most of computerized Urban Co-operative banks have on-line branches and have succeeded in taking almost all the operational activities. But networking of these branches to head office and computerization of head office is still a distance dream. The co-operative banks have dual control of Reserve Bank of India/NABARD and Co-operative Department.

The Urban Co-operative banks are leading in Information technology implementation in co-operative sector. But State and District level co-operative banks are still lagging in computerization drive and are still in infancy stage in most of the States in the country. In view of this , the proceeding coverage focuses on Urban Co-operative banks. The Urban co-operative banks in Maharshtra have already entered in the information technology race and have moved from the traditional branch banking to bank banking by applying the information technology solution at par with the private and multinational banks. The Cosmos co-operative bank from Pune, and few other scheduled urban co-operative banks from Mumbai have entered into technology race by using core banking solution. Many other Urban co-operative banks in Maharsahtra have started their customer services through telebanking, inter branch transaction and providing 24 hour 365 days banking service through Automatic Teller Machines (ATM). All these facilities are possible due to the support of information technology.

Automation In Co-operative Banks

The banking sector has seen major changes in the recent past and this has resulted in large number of new foreign and private banks competing in the Indian market place with both the Public Sector banks and co-operative banks. The main difference between the co-operative banks and the these banks is Branch automation vs Bank automation. Banking technology the world over has concentrated on deployment of applications and services on their corporate network with the primary objective of providing state of the art customer services.

Computerisation and automation of Banks and financial institutions is a key focus area today and is receiving prime attention as it touches everybody's work in some way or the other and co-operative banks are no exception to this. Banks in India were operating in a protective environment till the eighties, characterised by administered interest rates, directed lending and high statutory requirements. Banking sector reforms were initiated in India in 1992 against the backdrop of challenges faced by Indian banks internally from within and externally worldwide. The aim of the reform processes, apart from improving productivity and efficiency of the financial system was to make it competitive internationally by introduction of standards accepted in developed financial markets. The major policy initiatives taken under the financial sector reform, among other things, included a planned reduction in the level of statutory reserve requirements and a gradual deregulation of interest rates.

In the competitive environment that these measures created, fast and correct information became necessary for a quicker response to market needs. Banks also looked at new avenues to improve operational efficiency-and provide better customer satisfaction. Technology enabled some of the co-operative banks to introduce innovative products to their customers in the form of ATM facility, tele-banking, and centralized banking, etc. While banks are striving to strengthen customer relationship and move towards 'relationship banking', customers are increasingly moving away from the confines of traditional branch banking and are seeking the convenience of remote electronic banking services.

Information technology and the communication networking systems have revolutionalised the functioning of banks and other financial institutions the world over. Banks play an important role in the payment and settlement system. The introduction of liberalisation measures in the banking sector and the emergence of new private sector and foreign banks equipped with latest technology, have posed stiff competition in banking sector.

Computerisation is increasingly being applied in day to day operations, but the pace at which it has moved so far, has been somewhat limited. At present about 50-60% of banking business has been computerized in co-operative banks. Further, a customer is restricted to a particular branch only. He is not a customer of the entire bank in the sense that he can carry out his transactions from only the branch where he has his account. Therefore, there is need for computerisation in a large number of areas of opera-tions of banks, with customer service as the main focus. On the lines of private banks the co-operative banks have to hasten the process of the computerisation with a view to improving competitiveness. Some of the Urban Co-operative banks in Maharashtra have already entered into technology driven bank-ing by applying core banking solution to satisfy their customer demands and to have on-line availability of business data of their branches centrally for timely decisions. The successful implementation of this solution will definitely built a higher degree of confidence in other Urban co-operative banks to enter into core banking solution.

Banks perform several important functions in the financial sector. First they act as intermediaries between the depositors and the borrowers. Second, they facilitate money transactions among various segments of the financial sector entities. Third, they are the financial sector arm through which the central bank regulates and controls the financial markets. For performing these functions efficiently banks have to cater to three main requirements namely

* Speed up the transaction processing time for better and more efficient service.
* Better communication links to enable greater and faster access to information.
* Better, faster and accurate MIS reports to assist the planning process.

Role of Information Technology

In all these above mentioned segments the information technology can be harnessed to great advantage. The rapid developments in communication and networking systems is set to change the operating environment of banks. Automating and networking of branches will ensure timely flow of information and aid decision making process. An efficient and faster Management Information System (MIS) can make a major impact on the pricing of deposits, loans and other services provided by banks. The Indian Financial Network (INFINET), a wide area satellite based network using V-SAT technology, set up by the Reserve Bank and Institute for Development and Research in Banking Technology (IDRBT) at Hyderabad will pave a way for furthering the use of networking.

It is possible to delineate the principal types of electronic banking services. These include Automated Teller Machines (ATMs), Shared ATM networks, Electronic Funds Transfer at Point of Sale (EFTPoS), Smart cards, Debit Cards, Stored Value Cards, phone banking and more recently, internet and intranet banking. These services are heavily dependent on information technology and the absence of physical bank branches to deliver services to the customers.

The Financial Benefits of Electronic Banking Services are

- Lowering transaction costs.
- Increased speed of response to customer requirements under electronic banking.

- The lower cost of operating branch network along with reduced staff costs.
- Enhances the possibility of improved quality and an enlarged range of services.

Many co-operative banks have constructed their own websites offering valuable information to their customers. While use of Internet is slowly but surely picking up in co-operative banks. Use of advanced technology for electronic banking is a relatively new phenomenon. In the past, technology has been able to adopt itself to the requirements of the field where applied and come up with variants suitable to the application. The benefits, for both the banks and customers, that computerisation promises are enormous. There is no doubt that electronic banking is set to drastically change the manner and the methods of banking business in the years to come. The information technology if used in a scientific manner, will help the banks.

- To offer new and innovative financial products in order to effectively build on its strength in relationship and goodwill, and take on the increasing competition.
- To get timely and accurate information which will help in effective decision making.
- To design a good MIS and Statutory reports.
- For Head Office Reconciliation.
- For improving customer service through the use of technology.

While Applying the Technology every Bank have to Consider that the Technology Addresses the Following Issues

- Inter-branch connectivity-the branch may in future require this hence the software should be able to support the same.
- RDBMS base which enhances the MIS, querying and analysis capability.
- High level security in banking transactions.

Enterprise Banking Solutions

The Intensified competition within the Banking industry, competition from global banking giants, threat of non-banking, and now non-financial companies, increasing customer demands and sweeping technology changes have changed the face of banking forever. To provide banks with the agility to compete in this scenario the solution be designed to encompass all the constituents of the banking space - the management of the bank, the employees of the bank and the customers of the bank that should offer a comprehensive business solution to a modern bank to fully leverage information technology in order to meet the challenges of the new banking age. The Solution should be architecture based on the following core business drivers in the Indian and global banking industry and should incorporate :

- Fully integrated on-line system that provides visibility across the banking enterprise.
- Provision for constant improvements in areas of use interface, ease of use, maintenance, etc.
- Support easy addition of new remote delivery channels and provide an integrated delivery channel framework.

The Advantages of this Solutions Architecture are :

- Single view of data to the bank.
- Single view to external systems and customers.
- Customer centric-provides the base for relationship management, customer profile and profitability analysis etc.
- Flexible, Modular & Scalable.
- Implementation configurability,
- Can be implemented in either Distributed, fully Centralized or Flexi-Centralized architecture depending upon the Bank's business objectives and maturity of the communication infrastructure.
- Web computing paradigm.
- Covers the entire banking enterprise.
- Can be implemented in a phase manner, to suit your business priorities and investment plans, with clear business benefits at every milestone.
- Investment protection. Protects the Bank's investment in software in the highly volatile global technology and business environment.

The Building Block of the Software Should be :

- RDBMS independence.
- Hardware Independence.
- Adaptability to Web Technology.
- Message based Architecture.

Benefits of Implementing the Solution

- Helps to launch and promote new financial products and services.
- Handles rapid growth, and resultant increase in complexity and volumes.
- Focus on improving customer service by introducing Single-window service, Customer centric relationship management and personalized services, Tiered Services.
- Effectively track and control on quality of advances and NPA's, by effective use of accurate and timely information
- Focus on broadening and increasing the fee based income of the bank, by charging the customers for services provided.
- Attract more low cost funds into the Bank.
- Tiered services.
- Better and more personalised services.
- Remote delivery channels like ATMs, Tele Banking etc.
- Increases the reach of the Bank by effective use of remote delivery channels like ATMs etc.

Following are the important areas that bank needs to ensure for its computerization with integrated approach.

Clearing (Inward and Outward)

- Savings Bank
- Current Account
- Fixed Deposits
- Term Deposit
- Cash Certificates
- Recurring Deposits

- Pigmy Deposit
- Overdraft
- Cash Credit
- Loans
- Lockers
- Remittances
- Inward Bills for Collection
- Outward Bills For Collection
- Bills Discounted/Purchased
- Advances
- Sub Day Book, Day Book, General Ledger

* *In addition to the above areas the non-banking activities like personnel management, customer relationship management etc.needs equal weightage in the Information Technology plan.*

Conclusion

Deployment of IT based solutions is essential now for survival of co-operative banks. In India many banking solution providers have emerged in the last decade and have come up with fairly sustainable solutions to take care of changing baking business requirements. The Relational Database Management System (RDBMS) is well accepted in many private banks for satisfying changing banking requirements. The key factor would be to have clearly defined business processes and goals, refined systems and procedures and a professional work culture to ensure that the benefits of IT reach the customers and that at the same time the employee productivity increases considerably. The co-operative banks therefore needs a *systematic approach and planning for IT implementation*.

REFERENCES

Information Technology in Cooperative Banks – Issues & Options – Dr.YS Patil, Land Bank Journal, June 2002,

Automation in banks & financial Institutions – AK Bhargava, PNB Monthly review, June 2000.

web site www.expresscomputeronline.com

23

Reasserting the Co-operative Movement in Maharashtra

D.S. Navadkar and D.V. Kasar

Rural development in the present context, can be defined as a process of improving the socio-economic conditions of the rural poor. The World Bank has observed that a national programme of rural development includes a mix of objectives, including projects to raise agricultural output, create new employment, improve health and education, expand communication and improving housing. The rural development is the most desirable process in a developing economy like ours where agriculture alone contributes 26 per cent of GDP. Despite the recent advances in industrial development, Indian economy is still dependent on agro-based activities. About 72 per cent of our population still live in rural areas and over 60 per cent are not able to make a decent living. Rural development has been given top priority in our national planning.

Co-operation has been accepted as an important medium for improvement of the socio-economic life in the developing country like India. Co-operatives serve a double purpose, firstly, by providing means to ameliorate the condition of the people living in the rural areas by giving them an opportunity to expose their talents through collective efforts and secondly, it eliminates concentration of wealth and power in the hands of few. The contribution of co-operatives in the process of development is well known through the measures of economies of scale, better bargaining, competitive marketing, processing and service orientation. The significance of co-operatives in national economy could be understood by following factual data given in Table 1.

Table 1 : Share of Co-operatives in National Economy

Sr.No.	*Activity*	*Percentage share in the total*
1.	Agricultural credit disbursed	49.3
2.	Fertilizers distributed	35.2
3.	Sugar production	62.4
4.	Spindleage	11
5.	Yarn production	16.4
6.	Cotton ginning and processing units	12
7.	Cotton yarn exported	11
8.	Handloom in coops	55.0
9.	Wheat procurement	30
10.	Jute procurement	21
11.	Fishermans in coops	21.0
12.	Powerloom in coops	5
13.	Rural fair price shops	21.0

Source : Indian Co-operative Movement – A profile, 2001, NCUI New Delhi.

It is, thus, clear that the co-operatives occupy an important place in the Indian economy, and as such these are essential for rural development of the country. The concept of rural development involves a multi-dimensional process to strengthen the economic condition of rural people. The rural development programme, on one hand refers to the development of agriculture, allied activities and social facilities and on the other hand it aims at rural upliftment, development of human resource, betterment of lifestyle of rural people, developing infrastructure, reducing unemployment. In this connection, the role of co-operatives in agricultural promotion and rural development is noteworthy.

Co-operative Movement In Maharashtra

The co-operative movement in Maharashtra has played a significant role in the social and economic development of the State, particularly in the rural areas. Initially, this movement was confined mainly to the field of agricultural credit. Later it rapidly spread to other fields like agro-processing, agro-marketing, rural industries, consumer stores, social services, etc. This has resulted in a considerable beneficial impact in raising the standards of the rural masses. In order to face the problems emerging out of the liberalisation, various possibilities need to be explored in order that the co-operatives compete with the new economic scenario and market trends. The progress of various types of co-operative societies since 1961 is given in Table 2.

Table 2 : Progress of Co-operative Movement in Maharashtra

Sr. No.	*Type of co-operative Societies*	*1961*	*2002*	*Percentage change over*
1.	Apex and central Agril. And non-agril. Credit institution	39	34	-12.82
2.	Primary agricultural credit societies	21400	20674	-3.39
3.	Non-agricultural credit societies	1630	23555	1345.09
4.	Marketing societies	344	1140	231.40
5.	Productive enterprises (Sugar factories,rice mills,etc)	4306	39521	817.81
6.	Social service and other co-operative societies.	3846	80865	2002.57
	Total societies	31565	165789	425.23

Source : Economic Survey of Maharashtra, 2002-03.

It is conspicuous that the non-agricultural credit societies rose by nearly 15 times. The marketing societies rose nearly 3 times during 36 years. There was also a significant increase in the case of marketing societies and productive enterprises like sugar factories, rice mills, etc. The highest magnitude of increase was worked out in the case of social service and other co-operative societies including consumer stores, housing etc. During the same period, some co-operatives such as agricultural credit and non-agricultural credit societies were merged in viable co-operatives, hence their numbers seems to decreased. Thus, the co-operative societies in the state rose from 31565 during 1961 to 165789 at the end of 2002, indicating more than five times increase over the base year.

Important Characteristics of Co-operative Societies

Some important characteristics of all types of co-operative societies taken together in the States for 1995-96 and 2001-02 are presented in Table 3.

Table 3 : Important Characteristics of Co-operative Societies in the State

Sr. No.	*Item*	*1996*	*2002*	*Percentage increase over 1996-97*
1.	Number of societies	139089	165789	19.2
2.	Number of members (Lakhs)	358	439	22.63
3.	Paid-up share capital	3783	7876	108.19
4.	Deposits	23915	801131	135.07
5.	Working capital	50439	141004	179.55
6.	Advances	14027	49181	250.62
7.	Number of societies in profit	72976	55898	-23.41
8.	Profit	701	1337	90.73
9.	Number of societies in loss	53821	42853	-20.38
10.	Loss	514	1036	101.56
11.	Number of societies with no profit or loss.	12292	9758	-20.62

Source : Economic survey of Maharashtara 2002-03.

The paid-up share capital of the societies as on 31st March, 2002 increased by 108.19 per cent to Rs. 7876 crore from Rs. 3783 crore as on 31st March, 1996. The State-Government's contribution in total paid-up share capital as on 31st March, 2002 was Rs. 1161 crore (14.7 %). Of the total societies , about 34 per cent societies were in profit, 26 per cent societies in loss and 6 per cent in no profit no loss position.

Rural Credit

The Indian farmers can not adopt improved technology in agriculture because of low level of income and savings. Besides, 75 per cent of our farmers belong less than 2 hectares of land and they are not able to raise credit from commercial banks due to lack of proper securities to pledge against loans. Thus, they are forced to go to the moneylenders to raise credit for cultivation who charge exorbitant rate of interest. To meet the basic requirement of farmers, co-operative credit societies were established to provide cheap credit in adequate quantity at the right time for agricultural development in the country. The Co-operative Societies Act 1904 provided for the formation of rural credit co-operative by cultivators to tackle the problem of rural indebtedness.

Co-operative is the major rural credit institution since it alone provides 43 per cent of the total credit provided for agriculture. There are several economic studies which clearly reveal that credit had enabled the farmers to make both short term and long term investments in agriculture resulting into improvements in productivity and thereby farm incomes. The impact of rural credit on farm economy is positive and encouraging. Credit has enabled the farmers to adopt improved farm productivity measures.

Co-operative Marketing

Exploitation of the producers in its most virulent form continued for many decades till the starting of co-operative movement. The role of marketing co-operatives is a crucial with assured market for the produce of the member farmers. The basic objective of the co-operative marketing is to prevent exploitation of the agriculturists by traders and to enable the cultivators to have better returns of their produce by making arrangements for purchase and sale of their produce and also to benefit consumers to avail quality goods at reasonable prices. With these objectives in view, financial assistance in the form of share capital and loan is provided by the State Government to co-operative marketing societies. In the recent years co-operative marketing of agricultural produce has registered an impressive growth. The Government has taken decision to purchase cotton through Maharashtra State Co-operative Cotton Growers' Marketing Federation in four grades viz. FAQ (Fair Average Quality), Fair, Fadtar and Kawadi for each variety of cotton during 2002-2003 season as in the earlier season. The varietywise and gradewise per quintal purchase price (Guaranteed Price) of raw cotton as declared by the State Government for the season 2002-2003 ranged from Rs. 1,560 to 1,975 for *F.A.Q. grade,* Rs. 1,360 to 1,775 for *Fair grade,* Rs. 1,005 to 1,210 for *Fadtar grade* and Rs. 650 for Kawadi grade. For the season 2002-2003 the procurement of 'kapas' was done in the main cotton producing track viz.Vidarbha, Marathwada and Khandesh. For the season 2002-2003, the procurement of cotton upto 31 January, 2003 was 23.23 lakh quintals which valued at Rs. 383.28 crore.

Productive Co-operative Enterprises

There were 36,521 co-operative societies engaged in productive activities as on 31st March, 2002, of which 849 were independent processing societies. Of these 849 societies, 201 societies (23.67 %) were sugar factories; of which 135 were in production. The details of independent co-operative societies engaged in productive activities are given in following table 4.

Table 4 : Independent Processing Co-operative Societies

Sr. No	*Type of society*	*Total no of societies*		*No. of societies in production*		*Quantity processed ('000' tonnes)*	
		1995-96	*2001-02*	*1995-96*	*2001-02*	*1995-96*	*2001-02*
1.	Sugar factories	155	201	104	135	50181	48397
2.	Cotton ginning / processing	232	281	217	263	253	606
3.	Rice mills	88	90	83	88	50	109
4.	Oil mills	7	21	4	18	15	27
5.	Other	206	256	149	220	35	53
	Total	688	849	557	724	—	—

Source : Economic Survey of Maharashtra.

Employment and Income Generation Through Co-operatives

The co-operatives have played an important role of employment generation in Maharashtra. According to 1991 census, there was 339.10 lakh total working population. Out of these, the employment generation through public / private and co-operative sectors was 11.1 and 6.96 per cent, respectively.

Table 5 : Employment Generation Through Co-operatives in Maharashtra

(No. in lakhs)

Sr. No.	*Particulars*	*Number*
1.	Total working population (1991)	339.10
2.	Total employment in public and private sectors	37.66
3.	Percentage of total employment in public and private sectors to the total working population.	11.10
4.	Total employment generated in co-operative sector	2.62
5.	Percentage of employment in co-cperative sector to total employment	6.96

Agriculture is the main thrust of rural development in India. View of the changed scenario in the world, the research in rural development has to be diversified to strengthen data base in the areas of production and resource economics, agricultural marketing and prices, natural and human resource development, agri-business management, farm finance and development economics. The reorientation of research and education with multi - disciplinary approach, inter institutional interaction and collaboration becomes imperative for directing the process of rural development.

If the rural development has to be achieved to the maximum extent possible, pumping of credit alone cannot make possible. The most important point to be observed for its success is that the machinery involved in the implementation of the rural development programmes either directly or through government, co-operative or other agencies should be commitment for the cause of rural development. In order to make co-operative to play a vital and still better role, the immediate step to be taken is to revitalise the weak and non-viable co-operatives. The co-operatives should be given adequate autonomy, freedom in order to make them to be more democratic organizations. Since the rural development is the vital issue, Government alone cannot shoulder the responsibility and therefore it has to be supplemented by other organizations under co-operative, public and private sector and more particularly NGO's. So let us hope that atleast in the current millenium the Rural India will witness the 'Suvarna Yuga' (Golden Period) and 'Sarvajano Sukhinobhavantu'.

24

Co-operatives in Agro-processing in Maharashtra : A temporal Status Analysis

Pagire, B.V., Shinde,H.R and D.S. Navadkar

Introduction

The co-operative sector has been playing an important role in the economy of the country. The co-operative movement has become and is being recognized as an integral part of economy not of the nation but also of many states in the country. The sectors like sugar, dairy, textile, fishery, distribution of agricultural inputs such as fertilizers, seed etc are prominent examples. The co-operative sector is also on the forefront in making the agricultural credit available to the millions of farmers in the country. The activities or functions like storage and marketing of the agricultural products are also been taken up by the co-operative sector in many of states in the country.

In India, the state of Maharashtra is being looked upon as an ushering state in case of co-operation and the co-operative movement. Right from the existence of the state, the co-operative movement thrived its roots in many aspects viz., credit, processing of agricultural produce, dairy, textile and marketing of agricultural products etc. The co-operative sector covering these different fields contributed Rs.263 crore in the state economy during VIIIth Plan, which was just Rs.8.36 crore in IInd

Plan. This clearly points out its role in the state economy and progress of the state.

In the present exercise, an attempt has been made to analyze the status of the co-operative sector in the field agro-processing in Maharashtra.

Materials and Methods

For examining the role of co-operative sector in the agricultural produce processing, agri-business, etc. the various State and Central Governments Statistical Reports, published time series data, information relating to co-operative sector have been used. The data, information thus gathered were compiled and analyzed with simple statistical tools.

Results

Progress of Co-operative Sugar Factories

The co-operative sugar factories in production which was numbered 67 in1981 increased to 102 in 1997 showing an increase of 52.24 per cent over the period (Table 1). The share capital reached to Rs. 26,672 lakh in 1997 which was just Rs.9, 443 lakh in 1981 thus, indicated a rise of 182.45 per cent over the period of 17 years. The co-operative sugar factories were having Rs.26004 lakh as their own funds in 1981 increased to a high of Rs.2,44,843 lakh in 1997 i.e an increase of more than 800 times over the period. The sugarcane crushed during the year 1981 was 16,953 thousand tonnes whereas in 1997, the quantity of it was 30,228 thousand tones indicating the increase by 66.53 per cent. Thus, the sugar industry in the state in the co-operative sector made a spectacular progress and helped the thousands of farmers, rural economy and other social factors to a great extent.

Cotton Ginning and Pressing Co-operative Societies

The number of cotton ginning and pressing societies in the state in 1971 was 69 which increased to 249 in 1998, i.e. a rise of more than 260 per cent was noticed (Table 2).These societies were having membership just 61,400 in the year 1971 which increased to 2,42,100 in 1998 indicating a rise of 294.30 per cent over the period. The quantity of raw cotton ginned which was

Table 1 : Progress of Sugar Factories in the State

Sr. No.	*Particulars*	*1981*	*1991*	*% Change**	*1995*	*% Change**	*1997*	*% Change**
1.	Factories Registered	78	138	76.92	135	73.08	165	111.54
2.	Factories in Production	67	93	38.81	104	55.22	102	52.24
3.	Membership ('00')	4376	9140	108.87	14362	228.20	16362	273.90
4.	Share Capital (Rs. Lakh)	9443	28885	205.89	70362	645.12	26672	182.45
5.	Deposits (Rs. Lakh)	14129	64000	352.97	104763	641.47	115983	720.89
6.	Owned Funds (Rs. Lakh)	26004	99000	280.71	172816	564.57	244843	841.56
7.	Working Capital (Rs.Lakh)	66843	288552	331.69	672844	906.60	903285	1251.35
8.	Sugarcane Crushed (000' tonnes)	16953	37231	101.63	45994	145.55	30228	66.53
9.	Sugar Produced (000' tonnes)	1872	4010	114.21	4793	156.04	3150	68.27

'*' indicates percentage change over the year 1981.

Table 2 : Progress of Cotton Ginning and Pressing Societies

Sr. No.	Particulars	1971	1981	% Change*	1991	% Change*	1998	% Change*
1.	No.of Societies	69	110	59.42	213	208.70	249	260.87
2.	Societies in Production	59	103	74.58	201	240.68	229	288.14
3.	Membership ('00')	614	1055	71.82	2177	254.56	2421	294.30
4.	Share Capital (Rs. Lakh)	120	208	73.33	658	448.33	667	455.83
5.	Owned Funds (Rs. Lakh)	173	666	284.97	1943	1023.12	2283	1219.65
6.	Working Capital (Rs. Lakh)	355	947	166.76	4115	1059.15	5414	1425.07
7.	Raw otton Ginned (in '000' tonnes)	57	608	966.67	386	577.19	468	721.05
8.	Bales Pressed ('000') bales of 170 kg. Each	106	333	214.15	358	237.74	NA	

'*' indicates percentage change over the year 1971.

57 thousand tonnes in 1971 increased to 468 thousand tonnes showing the increase of 721 per cent. The progress of these societies also observed to be very remarkable in the State.

Primary Handloom Co-operative Societies

The number of such societies operating in the state was 586 in the year 1971, increased to 842 in 1991 and remained 740 in 1998 (Table 3). Their membership was 48,000 in the year 1971 increased to 96,600 in 1991 and then stabled at 89,000 during the year 1998 indicating a rise of 85.42 per cent. Their own funds increased from Rs.149 lakh in 1972 to Rs.2054 lakh in the year 1998 exhibiting a rise of more than 12 times over the period. The number of profit earning societies also increased by more than 38 per cent over the period. The progress of these societies, thus noticed to be a remarkable one in the State.

Primary Power-loom Co-operative Societies

These type of societies which were 159 in number in the year 1971 increased to 806 in 1991 and 798 remained in operation in 1998 showing an overall rise of 401.59 per cent (Table 4). Their membership also observed increasing in each decade in general, and the number was 38,500 in 1998 expressing an increase by 89.66 per cent over the year 1971. These societies were possessing their own funds amounting to Rs.71 lakh in 1971 and this increased to a high of Rs.1719 lakh in 1998 expressing a very tremendous increase over the period. The sale value of these societies increased to Rs.2454 lakh in 1998 from Rs.736 lakh in 1971. The number of profit earning societies in 1971 were just 65 which increased to 282 in 1998. These societies too, shown a good progress in the state.

Co-operative Rice Mills

The co-operative rice mills operating in the state in 1971 were 112, however, their number decreased to 102 in 1981, 86 in 1991 and 1998 (Table 5).

Though their number decreased over the period, their owned funds and working capital increased by 228.71 and 134.70 per cent, respectively. The number of profit earning societies declined by 26.25 per cent over the period.

Table 3 : Primary Handloom Co-operative Societies

Sr. No.	*Particulars*	*1971*	*1981*	*% Change**	*1991*	*% Change**	*1998*	*% Change**
1.	No.of Societies	586	670	14.33	842	43.69	740	26.28
2.	Membership ('00')	480	717	49.38	966	101.25	890	85.42
3.	Share Capital (Rs. Lakh)	108	605	460.19	1051	873.15	1613	1393.52
4.	Owned Funds (Rs. Lakh)	149	729	389.26	1090	631.54	2054	1278.52
5.	Working Capital (Rs. Lakh)	501	1500	199.40	3756	649.70	14542	2802.59
6.	Total Handlooms ('00')	614	483	-21.34	463	-24.59	518	-15.64
7.	Production Value (Rs.Lakh)	1381	2676	93.77	4668	238.02	8561	519.91
8.	Sale Value (Rs.Lakh)	1942	2685	38.26	4032	107.62	7400	281.05
9.	Societies in Profits	352	380	7.95	514	46.02	487	38.35

'*' indicates percentage change over the year 1971.

Table 4 : Primary Power-loom Co-operative Societies

Sr. No.	*Particulars*	*1971*	*1981*	*% Change**	*1991*	*% Change**	*1998*	*% Change**
1.	No.of Societies	159	297	86.79	806	406.92	798	401.89
2.	Membership ('00')	203	346	70.44	331	63.05	385	89.66
3.	Share Capital (Rs. Lakh)	54	283	424.07	619	1046.30	1659	2972.22
4.	Owned Funds (Rs. Lakh)	71	501	605.63	701	887.32	1719	2321.13
5.	Working Capital (Rs. Lakh)	487	1532	214.58	1935	297.33	3987	718.69
6.	Total Power-looms ('00')	187	213	13.90	473	152.94	420	124.60
7.	Production Value (Rs.Lakh)	532	1008	89.47	1381	159.59	2897	444.55
8.	Sale Value (Rs.Lakh)	736	1239	68.34	1420	92.93	2454	233.42
9.	Societies in Profits	65	99	52.31	202	210.77	282	333.85

'*' indicates percentage change over the year 1971.

Table 5 : Co-operative Rice Mills

Sr. No.	*Particulars*	*1971*	*1981*	*% Change**	*1991*	*% Change**	*1998*	*% Change**
1.	No.of Societies	112	102	-8.93	86	-23.21	86	-23.21
2.	Societies in Production	94	89	-5.32	83	-11.70	82	-12.77
3.	Membership ('00')	502	547	8.96	531	5.78	491	-2.19
4.	Share Capital (Rs. Lakh)	53	50	-5.66	47	-11.32	46	-13.21
5.	Owned Funds (Rs. Lakh)	101	172	70.30	221	118.81	332	228.71
6.	Working Capital (Rs. Lakh)	268	391	45.90	384	43.28	629	134.70
7.	Quantity Processed ('000' tones)	122	83	-31.97	141	15.57	108	-11.48
8.	Sale Value (Rs.Lakh)	416	60	-85.58	26	-93.75	20	-95.19
9.	Societies in Profits	80	62	-22.50	57	-28.75	59	-26.25

'*' indicates percentage change over the year 1971.

Progress of Fruit, Vegetables and Other Co-operative Societies

The number of societies which were 70 in number in the year 1971, showed a rise of 152.86 per cent over the period of 28 years (i.e. 177 in 1998) (Table 6). Of the total societies registered in 1971, only 16 were in operation/working but over the period their number increased to 173, i.e. more than 9 times increase. The membership of these societies was 8,100 in 1971, increased to 1,25,500 i.e. more than 14 times rise was noticed. Similarly, their owned funds and working capital also shown a very high rise/increase over the period. The quantity processed however, decreased from 12000 tonnes in 1971 to 5000 tonnes in 1998. The number of profit earning societies increased very remarkably i.e. from 9 in 1971 to 54 in 1998. Thus, the progress of these societies in the state observed very remarkable and helped the thousands of farmers and other related agencies.

Dairy Co-operative and Fisheries Societies

There were 21,535 primary co-operative dairy societies and 65 dairy unions with membership of 16.18 lakh and 2.45 lakh, respectively in 1997-98. These dairy societies and dairy unions had working capital of Rs.161 crore and Rs.285 crore, respectively. In 1997-98, the total value of sale of milk and milk products together of the dairy societies was Rs.964 crore and that of dairy unions was Rs.1986 crore. In 1997-98, there were 2242 primary fisheries societies, 31 fisheries unions and one fisheries federation. All these societies have membership of 2.42 lakh and working capital of Rs.296 crore.

The Present Scenario

The present position of major processing co-operatives is presented in Table 7.

The total number of sugar factories in the state were 143 in the year 2000-01 of which 137 were in operation and processed 57.64 lakh tonnes of sugarcane. The quantity of cotton (*Kapas*) processed 260 cotton ginning and pressing societies in the year 2000-01 was 5.01 lakh tones. The quantity of paddy processed by 87 rice mills was 1.12 lakh tonnes. The quantity of oil seeds processed by 12 oil mills was 24000 tonnes during the year 2000-01.

Table 6 : Fruit Vegetables and other Co-operative Societies

Sr. No.	*Particulars*	*1971*	*1981*	*% Change**	*1991*	*% Change**	*1998*	*% Change**
1.	No.of Societies	70	59	-15.71	169	141.43	177	152.86
2.	Societies in Production	16	26	62.50	125	681.25	173	981.25
3.	Membership ('00')	81	117	44.44	947	1069.14	1255	1449.38
4.	Share Capital (Rs. Lakh)	62	73	17.74	462	645.16	1572	2435.48
5.	Owned Funds (Rs. Lakh)	74	94	27.03	772	943.24	1830	2372.97
6.	Working Capital (Rs. Lakh)	158	276	74.68	2995	1795.57	9402	5850.63
7.	Quantity Processed ('000' tonnes)	12	17	41.67	24	100.00	5	-58.33
8.	Sale Value (Rs. Lakh)	11	50	354.55	758	6790.91	315	2763.64
9.	Societies in Profits	9	14	55.56	51	466.67	54	500.00

'*' indicates percentage change over the year 1971.

Table 7 : Present Status of Agro-processing Co-operatives in Maharashtra

Sr. No.	Type of Society	Total No. of societies		No. of in societies production		Quantity processed (in thousand tones)	
		1999-2K	2000-01	1999-2K	2000-01	1999-2K	2000-01
1.	Sugar Factories	133	143	123	137	55700	57641
2.	Cotton ginning and pressing societies	279	289	248	260	470	501
3.	Rice Mills	93	91	88	87	110	112
4.	Oil Mills	23	22	12	12	22	24
5.	Others	231	252	182	188	62	68

Source : Economic Survey of Maharashtra, 2001-02.

Co-operative Department and State Plans

In the IInd Five Year Plan, the expenditure of the state was Rs.266.30 crore of which the share of co-operation department was Rs.8.36 crore exhibiting a share of 3.14 per cent (Table 8). In IIIrd Five Year Plan, the share increased to 5.84 per cent. From the Vth F ive Year Plan onward, the share of the co-operation department however, declined to 2.42 and 1.42 per cent in V[th] and VIth Plan respectively. The share remained the same in the VIIIth Plan. In general, the co-operation department was having good and due share in the State Plans indicating the efforts and attention of the state Governments towards this section in the state continuously.

Table 8 : Share of Co-operation Department in the State Plan Scheme

Sr. No.	Five Year Plan Period	Expenditure (Rs. Crore)		Percentage
		Maharashtra State	Co-operative Department	
1.	IInd Five Year Plan	266.3	8.36	3.14
2.	IIIrd Five Year Plan	434.73	24.4	5.84
3.	V[th] Five Year Plan	2660.13	64.5	2.42
4.	VIIth Five Year Plan	10454.9	148.89	1.42
5.	VIIIth Five Year Plan	18520	263	1.42

Conclusions

From the foregoing discussion, the following conclusions could be drawn.

(i) In the state of Maharashtra, the co-operative movement has been found very strong,

(ii) The co-operative sector has made very remarkable progress in the fields viz., sugar, cotton, milk, and fruit and vegetable processing and marketing,

(iii) These co-operative societies also made well progress in their own business and contributed to a large extent in the state progress,

(iv) The co-operation department was also given due share and attention in the State Five Year Plans in general.

In the changed scenario of agricultural business and liberalized economic domain, the co-operative sector if nurtured and given proper attention, it can play a very prominent role in the agriculture produce processing, marketing and distributions. Therefore, this sector has to receive prime importance thereafter for the welfare of the farming community.

25

Crave of Strengthening the Consumer Co-operatives

M.M. Tapkir

The consumer movement in India is as old as trade and commerce itself. Even in Kautilya's *Arthshastra*, there are references to the concept of protection of consumers against the exploitation by trade and industry, short weighment and measurements, adulteration along with the punishment for these offences. There was, however, no organized and systematic movement actually safeguarding the interests of the consumers.

Though there were several consumer stores working on the co-operatives basis in informal way, the first certified co-operative consumer store in India, the Triplicane Urban Co-operative Society, in Madras, was started in 1904. And afterwards several co-operative consumers stores were set up in different parts of our country. But the real growth of consumer co-operative movement in Indian has geared up only after Second World War and that too after Independence. During the second world war, scarcity conditions were prevalent all over the country, and therefore Indian Government also encouraged consumer to orgainse their own co-operative societies for ensuring steady supply of scarce commodities. The successive five years plans of government of India specified a distinct role for the consumer co-operatives as an institutional vehicle for socio-economic activities particularly in the rural areas. The consumer co-operatives thereafter emerged a very strong organization in the distributive trade. A number of co-operative consumer stores were set up at district, taluka, urban and rural places. This resulted in the growth of a large number of consumer stores.

Prior to Independence, consumer interests were considered mainly under laws like the Indian Penal Code, Agricultural Production Grading and Marketing Act 1937, and Drugs and Cosmetics Act, 1940. Even though different parts of India had varying degrees of awareness, in general the level of awareness was low.

It is generally believed that the consumer movement in India as of today is quite strong when it is compared with other developing countries in Asia, Africa and Latin America. India is a vast country with a very large population of which a sizeable percentage lives below the poverty line. Because of economic inequality, low level of literacy and ignorance, particularly amongst women, the level of consumer awareness is not too high and , therefore, the consumers are not able to assert and protect themselves. They easily get exploited by trade and industry and service providers. With the liberalization process which started in 1991 the entire economic scenario is undergoing a complete change from a government-driven economy to a market-driven economy. Protecting the interests of consumers has, therefore, become one of the paramount concerns of the Government than ever before.

Structure of Indian Consumer Co-operatives

India's consumer co-operatives have 4-tier structure. At the grass roots level, there are about 28560 primary co-operative consumers' stores. They have about 9500 branches, retail outlets and 75 departmental stores. At the district level there are 730 wholesale/central stores. They have about 5600 branches and about 900 departmental stores. At the state level there are 29 State Co-operative Consumers Federations and state co-operative marketing-cum-consumer coop Federations, with 194 branches. At the apex is the National Co-operative Consumers' Federation of India.

In addition to the primary stores at the grass-root level, about 55000 village level Primary Agriculture Co-operative Credit Societies (PACs and LAMPs) in addition to their other activities undertake sales and distribution of consumer goods and essential commodities. There are more than 4300 Students Consumer Co-operative Stores, which supply the books and other educational materials to the students of various collages / Universities and educational institutes at reasonable rates. Under the Public Distribution System scheme of Government of India, over 125000 Fair Prices Shops in co-operative sector are handling distribution of selected essential commodities of daily use.

Membership

The consumer co-operatives have a total membership of about 17 millions in our country. The primary consumer co-operative societies have a membership of more than 7 million, and the wholesale stores 2.50 million. Membership of the State Federations and National Apex is mainly institutional. State Federations have a membership of about 5000 consumer co-operatives and another 0.20 million individuals. The national federation of consumer co-operative federation (NCCF) has in all membership of about 150. The membership of almost all the co-operative consumers societies right from primary level to national level either is decreasing or stagnant.

Share Capital

The total share capital contribution of the State Federations is about Rs. 410 million. 80% of the share capital has been contributed by the Government. The wholesale stores have a share capital contribution of Rs.550 million. About 70 % of this share capital has been contributed by the Government. The primary consumer co-operative stores have a total share capital of Rs.470 million. In their case the government contribution is about 25 %. The rural co-operatives that deal in the distribution of consumer goods and essential commodities have also received government financial assistance of about Rs.300 million through NCDC sponsored programmes. The state level federations have mustered an average working capital of about Rs.300 million, the wholesale stores Rs.2200 million and the primaries Rs.1900 million during the previous year. It revealed through various studies, that most of the consumers co-operatives are not in a position to increase funds through share capital.

Functions of Consumer Co-operatives

While the national and state federations are almost exclusively handling wholesale distribution of consumer goods, essential commodities and consumer durables, the wholesale store at the central level, the primary stores at the grass roots level and the village societies, by and large, carry out retailing. There are about 325 large-sized departmental stores set up by the wholesale and primary stores engaged in large scale retailing of consumer goods. The consumer co-operatives at the national and state level do not generally do much of import business. Neither is the consumer credit business being carried out by the consumer co-operatives in India on a large-scale; a few of the department store though have made arrangements with the banks for credit sales for consumer durables but these schemes have yet to gain any significant popularity. Also, consumer credit is extended in the rural sectors in a limited scale. The total sales of the Indian consumer co-operative movement accounts for more than 110 billions in 2002-03, which is around 2.5 % of the total retail sales of the consumers goods in the country. Though the quantum of sales is not very significant but the area coverage and presence in the market, particularly in the semi-urban and rural area have created a positive impact in the national economy. There are several names who have known and recognized as big consumers stores in co-operative sectors. For example - various Kendriya Bhandars, Apna Bazars, Grahak Bhandars, Grahak Peth, Sahakari Bhandars, Sahakari Vikri Kendra, Shetkari Sangha, Warna Bazar etc.

Most of the renowned and big consumer co-operatives carry out consumer education programme through day to day sales activity. In our country, the consumer has come to develop trust and confidence in the merchandise and services offered by the consumer co-operatives. The consumer education programme as such is generally carried out by the state co-operative unions, consumer protection agencies and the state and central governments.

Apart from the co-operative consumers, the central government and state governments through various schemes undertake consumer education programmes and protect the interest of consumers. One of the most important milestones in the consumer movement in our country is the enactment of the

Consumer Protection Act, 1986 to better protect the interest of the consumers. This has revolutionized consumer rights. This Act applies to all goods and services and covers all sectors, whether private, public or co-operative. The Consumer Protection Act was amended in 1991 mainly to incorporate provisions for the quorum of District Forum, appointing persons to preside over State Commission/District Forum in case of absence of the President to enable the court function uninterruptedly. In 1993 and in 2001 the Act was once again amended exhaustively to make it more effective and purposeful. These amendments in CPA has resulted in the quick disposal of complaints, widening the scope of the Act, strengthening the Consumer Courts, streamlining the procedure and a proposal to strengthen the consumer movement.

Under various programmes, the Central and State Governments and the consumer co-operatives are engaged in strengthening the distributive co-operative structure both in the urban and rural areas. The objective is to ensure efficient public distribution system specially in the remote rural areas and for the weaker sections in the urban areas. The focus is better consumer services through the co-operative structure at all level.

Problems of Co-operative Consumer Stores

In spite of playing a vital role in the distributive trade over a century, the consumer co-operatives could not achieve its goal to ensure the availability of quality of consumer goods to the common man at affordable price. The following factors have affected the growth of consumers' co-operatives:

1. *Poor Resource Mobilization :* Any Individual can become a member of a primary co-operative consumers societies by paying mere Rs.10 and as against this the cost of handling and servicing of a member is more than the individual contribution. Most of the co-operative consumers societies are facing a problem of funds.
2. *Mushroom Growth :* The co-operative consumers societies can be set up by group of some persons and the other factors like viability and marketability are not taken in to consideration and therefore, most of the co-operative consumers societies are unviable and sick units.

3. *Management and Democratic Control :* As per the study conducted by Government of India on professionalisation of co-operative organizations, revealed that most of the co-operative organsatios including co-operative consumers societies are not fully professional and they are lacking in increasing members' participation and involvement as well as democratic control.
4. *Competition :* There is a cut-throat competition between private traders, public enterprises and also co-operative consumers societies and most of the co-operative consumers societies are not in a position to sustain in the market.
5. *Sales Policy and Pricing Policy :* The pricing policy of the co-operative consumers societies has by and large, been competitive. The retail consumer stores keep a keen eye on the open market and try to sell merchandise at competitive rates. There are certain controls on essential commodities that leave fixed selling prices and margins of profit. In the pricing mechanism for a number of commodities handled by co-operatives, however, the margin-spread at time is rather wide. This allows a limited surplus to the co-operative consumers societies.
6. *Business Policies and Practices :* The co-operative consumers societies are to operate in the limited and restricted legal, market and economic conditions, where as the private traders are free to adopt and change their policies and procedures. For example, restriction on selling on certain items, the purchase and sale policies, pricing policies, restrictions on purchase/sales on credit, transaction with non-members, providing discount etc.. All the business policies and procedures of co-operative consumers societies are more or less inelastic, even in case of market demand and opportunities these can not be altered.
7. *Absence of Co-operation and Coordination* among the co-operatives particularly amongst the 4 tiers of co-operative consumer movement. The National Level Co-operative Consumer Federation, State Level Consumer Federations, District Consumer Federation/Kendriya Bhandars and Primary co-operative consumers societies are not having active coordination and co-operation and therefore, all the

tiers of co-operative consumer units are suffering.

8. *Shortage of Professional and trained manpower.*
9. *Involvement of Government* in managing the affairs of the co-operative consumers societies also affect the democratic character of consumer co-operatives.
10. The co-operative consumers' societies do not enjoy any special tax concessions or benefits in India.

Strategies for the Development of Consumers' Co-operatives

1. Strengthening of Financial Positions of Consumers Co-operatives by increasing membership and revising rate of minimum share capital per individual.
2. To survive in the era of stiff competition the co-operative consumers societies must reduct their cost and increase their operational efficiency and productivity, efficient inventory management and also offer attractive intensive schemes to the customer, so as to achieve the sustainable growth in business.
3. As the consumer co-operatives operate with nominal surplus margin so that the consumers get maximum price advantages. Therefore, the consumers co-operatives are not in a position to earn considerable surplus. However, they have to pay a major part of their income by way of Income Tax or sale tax and they can not build their own funds. Therefore, the Government of India may allow special concessions in Income tax and sale tax for primary level consumers' co-operatives atleast for one decade.
4. The NCCF and state level federations must become active and help all the consumer co-operatives at all level by way of active coordination and co-operation.
5. Setting up of Consultancy and Promotional Cell at NCCF level and at the level of State Federations to meet the consultancy needs and demands of the consumers co-operatives.
6. Setting up of new student consumers co-operatives and strengthening of existing students consumers co-operatives.

7. Encouraging NCCF, State Federations and leading consumer co-operatives to undertake processing activities and also to go in for production of certain consumer goods requires for sale by consumer co-operatives.
8. Strengthening Central Consumer Co-operative Stores in urban areas for setting up of departmental stores and retail outlets.
9. Encouraging "on the job training' facilities in consumer co-operatives and building up a trained cadre for managerial and supervisory positions to improve operational and business efficiency of consumer co-operatives.
10. The infrastructure of the consumer co-operative should be utilized by the government as a mater of policy for PDS.
11. The government of India may formulate a national policy for development and promotion of consumer co-operatives.
12. The small and unviable consumer co-operative stores should either be merged with other nearest successful co-operatives or they may be liquidated.

The co-operative consumers' movement can play a vital role in the public distribution system and trading and supply system for the betterment of the masses, if the consumer co-operative movement is strengthened. But the real success of the co-operative consumer movement mainly depends upon the level of consumer awareness around the country. The Government can only be playing the role of a facilitator or catalyst. The growth of co-operative consumer movement is a voluntary effort involving the participation of one and all. Only alert consumers can protect themselves and the society.

List of Contributors

P.R. Dubhashi, IAS, (Rtd.), Director Administrative Staff Academy (Rtd.) Deharadoon, presently in Pune.

R. S. Pundir, Faculty, Institute of Rural Management, Anand.

Vishwa Ballabh, RBI Chair Professor, Institute of Rural Management, Anand.

V.B. Kakade, Reader, Department of Economics, Shivaji University, Kolhapur.

S.T. Bhide, Organizer Agriculture and Co-operative Forum, Yashawantrao Chavhan Foundation, Mumbai.

R.D. Biradar, Reader, School of Commerce and Management Science, Swamy Ramanandteerth, Marathwada University, Nanded.

P.A. Koli, Professor, Department of Economics, Shivaji University, Kolhapur.

D.J. Edwinraj, Lecturer in Co-operation, T.B.M.L. College, Porayar, T.N.

Sangram Chavan, Lecturer, Walchand College of Arts and Science, Solapur.

V.B. Jugale, Professor, Department of Economics, Shivaji University, Kolhapur.

V. Kulandaiswamy, Reader & Head, Department of Co-operation, Ramkrishna Mission Vedyalaya's College of Arts & Science, Coimbatore.

P. Murugesan, Lecturer in Co-operation, S.R.M. Vidyalaya's College of Arts & Science, Coimbatore.

Y.S. P. Thorat, Managing Director, NABARD, Mumbai.

M. Pradeep, RBI, Mumbai.

P. Das, RBI, New Delhi.

K. Ravichandran, Senior Lecturer, Department of Co-operation, Ghandhigram Rural Deemed University, Gandhigram.

M.R. Bala, Research Scholar, Department of Co-operation, Ghandhigram Rural Deemed University, Gandhigram.

A.P. Kansal, Former Professor, VAMNICOM, Pune.

G.V. Madiwal, HOD, Govt. College of Arts & Commerce, Pernem, Goa.

Y.V. Reddy, Reader & Head, Department of Commerce, Goa University, Goa.

P.K. Deshmukh, Reader, Department of Business Economics, Y.C. Warana Mahavidyalaya, Kolhapur.

P.N. Gavade, Sl. Gr. Lecturer, Department of Economics, Shivaji University, Kolhapur.

B. Tamilmani, Reader, Department of Co-operation, Gandhigram Rural Deemed University, Ghandhigram.

Samwel Lopoyetum, Senior Post Doctoral Research Fellow Dept.of Co-operation, Gandhigram Rural Deemed University, Ghandhigram.

A.S. Joshi, Reader, Department of Economics, Vyankatesh Mahavidyalaya, Ichalkaraji.

M.R. Patil, Reader in Commerce, DMS College of Commerce, Arts, & Science, Mhapusa, Goa.

R.B. Teli, Shivraj College, Gadhinglaj, Tal. Gadhinglaj, Dist. Kolhapur.

S.O. Junare, Director, CMD, National Institute of Co-operative Management, Ghandhinagar, Gujrat.

Y.S. Patil, Assit. Professor, Vaikunth Mehta, National Institute of Co-operative Management, Pune.

D.S. Navadkar, Asstt. Statistician, Department of Agricultural Economics. Mahatma Phul Krishi Vidyapeeth, Rahuri.

D.V. Kasar, Head, Department of Agricultural Economics, Mahatma Phule Krishi Vidyapeeth, Rahuri.

B.V. Pagire, Assitt. Professor, Department of Agricultural Economics, Mahatma Phule Krishi Vidyapeeth, Rahuri.

H.R. Shinde, Jr. Research Assitt, Department of Agricultural Economics, Mahatma Phule Krishi Vidyapeeth, Rahuri.

M.M. Tapkir, T. J. College, Khadki, Pune